The Migrant's Table

Meals and Memories in
Bengali-American Households

Krishnendu Ray

The Migrant's ✧ Table ✧

Meals and Memories in
Bengali-American Households

Temple University Press

Philadelphia

Temple University Press
1601 North Broad Street
Philadelphia PA 19122
www.temple.edu/tempress

Text design by Kate Nichols

⊗ The paper used in this publication meets the requirements of the
American National Standard for Information Sciences—Permanence of Paper for
Printed Library Materials, ANSI Z39.48-1992

Library of Congress Cataloging-in-Publication Data
Ray, Krishnendu.
The migrant's table : meals and memories in Bengali-American households /
Krishnendu Ray.
p.   cm.
Includes bibliographical references (p.) and index.
ISBN 1-59213-095-X (alk. paper) — ISBN 1-59213-096-8 (pbk. : alk. paper)
1. Food habits—United States.   2. Food habits—India—Bengal.
3. Bengali Americans—Food.   4. Bengali Americans—Social life and customs.
I. Title.
GT2853.U5R39 2004
394.1'2'0899144073–dc22   2004046004

2   4   6   8   9   7   5   3   1

To Babai, Ma, and Babul for keeping faith

in spite of much bad behavior

Contents

Acknowledgments

I must begin by acknowledging the great debt of gratitude I owe to my adviser, Professor Mark Selden, for his untiring effort, encouragement, and guidance through many years. Thanks to my other fabulous teachers: Giovanni Arrighi, Terence Hopkins, Caglar Keyder, Dale Tomich, and Immanuel Wallerstein. Thanks are also due to Barbara Kirshenblatt-Gimblett for her astute comments on early drafts and for pointing me in the right direction through the minefield of cultural studies. I also extend my gratitude to Amy Bentley, James Geshwender, Anthony D. King, members of my dissertation committee, for their helpful comments and willingness to review this text on short notice.

Long conversations and many disagreements with my friends Abye Assefa, Florence Molke, Khaldoun Samman, and Steven Sherman sharpened my perspective and egged me on. I owe much to my wife, Shari Schultz, whose critique of my intolerably long sentences was crucial in developing a more readable style, and to my stepchildren Joey and Stasia for their patience and understanding through all the years when I could not be available for many a fatherly duty. My newborn son, Rudra, in keeping me away from the manuscript, helped me in the task of editing by generating creative distance from the text.

Finally, I am indebted to numerous anonymous reviewers and to Janet Francendese, William Regier, and Andrew Smith, whose encouragement and critiques have improved the final product. Sidney Mintz's appraisal of what was the introduction in the manuscript, a vastly different chapter on ethnicity, and on the concluding chapter enabled me to see my folly and sharpen my perspective while focusing my story. I owe him a deep debt of gratitude. Thanks to Pauline Adema for the last-minute editorial work. Most importantly, I could not have written this book without the patience, participation, and encouragement of numerous Bengali-American respondents and hosts. This is really their work, which I have merely narrated and been credited with. I hope I have not disappointed them.

Credits

A preliminary version of some sections of Chapter 3 was published as "Meals, Migration and Modernity: Domestic Cooking and Bengali Indian Ethnicity in the United States," *Amerasia* 24, no. 1 (1998): 105–27.

A section of Chapter 4 was published as "Why Isn't Irish Food Hip? A Review Essay," *Newsletter of the Association for the Study of Food and Society,* March 2002.

Sections of Chapter 6 were published as "The Nation Betrayed: Or About Those Who Left," *Economic and Political Weekly* 38, no. 26 (June 28, 2003): 2722–29.

The map on Indian vegetarianism (p. 33) is reproduced from K. T. Achaya, *Indian Food: A Historical Companion* (1994), by permission of Oxford University Press India, New Delhi.

The Migrant's Table

Meals and Memories in
Bengali-American Households

CHAPTER 1

Introduction

"Home" has become such a scattered, damaged, various, concept in our present travails.
SALMAN RUSHDIE, EAST, WEST: STORIES (1995: 93)

The government has observed that next to rice and water, stories are the most-demanded stuff in daily life. . . . Every moment someone or other is always asking for a story.
R. K. NARAYAN, A WRITER'S NIGHTMARE (1988: 69)

This is a story about "rice and water" and the violations of geography by history. Galvanized by voluntary exile, it is an attempt to read the grain for the encounter between cultures buried in the depth of hearth and home, not simply between East and West but also within ourselves—the colonized and decolonized fragments of our minds and the complicit and resistant practices of cooking and eating. "Immigration often involves dislocation and social demotion," writes Bharati Mukherjee, a Bengali-American author. "Immigrants carry the bruises, and often the scars, from missed signals and misread signs. They've traded their certain place (sometimes humble, sometimes exalted) in a fixed society for a crazy chance at something elusive called personal happiness. I don't say they'll find it; it's enough that they try" (Mukherjee 2003: A8).

Cuisine, like religion, is one of the sites where the migrant turns away hesitatingly from the embrace of the metropole. In the case of most of my respondents, the migrant has come to the metropole at her husband's bidding to partake of its fabled riches, raise Bengali children, maintain the home, and cook Bengali food. It is a difficult task that must be fulfilled with a certain finesse that balances the needs of maintaining particularity while participating in the universalizing project of capitalist modernity.

Of course, taste evokes, often in a disjointed way, a whole structure of feeling, which Marcel Proust has immortalized. On a cold, wet, wintry day, the narrator's mother in *Swann's Way* offered him tea and "one of those short, plump little cakes called 'petites madeleines'" (Proust 1970: 34). Soon enough, his childhood memories of Combray burst forth in an inadvertent torrent, triggered by that "inseparable paramour, the taste of cake soaked in tea" (Proust 1934: 35):

> And suddenly the memory returns. . . . [W]hen from a long-distant past nothing subsists, after the people are dead, after the things are broken and scattered, still, alone, more fragile, but with more vitality, more unsubstantial, more persistent, more faithful, the smell and taste of things remain poised a long time, like souls, ready to remind us, waiting and hoping for their moment, amid the ruins of all the rest; and bear unfaltering, in the tiny and almost impalpable drop of their essence, the vast structure of recollection. (Proust 1934: 36)

Recently, Chitra Divakaruni, reflecting on the specificity of Asian American poetry, wrote: "I think the aim of poetry in general is to recreate in the reader the powerful emotions the writer experienced while in a certain place or situation. . . . One of the things Asian American poetry draws on to achieve this is the writers' rich heritages—the home cultures that are always inside our heads and hearts" (Divakaruni 1994: 35). This book is in that sense a prose poem.

I inhabit three lands: the United States, where I now reside; India, which is in my being and memory; and the kitchen, the desk, and the classroom, which are my active everyday lands. Out of these lands I have fashioned a story. It is peopled with lost and newly discovered tastes, friends, and enemies, too, that I have acquired in my travels through these lands.

Traveling, of course, entails infidelity. It is undertaken with the sly hope of interrupting domesticity. But the search for home reasserts itself like a riptide, drawing us toward the hearth as if it were an elemental force, particularly when we have left it behind, as James Baldwin (1956: 116) knew:

"Why, you will go home and then you will find that home is not home anymore. Then you will really be in trouble. As long as you stay here, you can always think: One day I will go home." . . .

"Beautiful logic," I said. "You mean I have a home to go to as long as I don't go there?"

Giovanni laughed. "Well, isn't it true? You don't have a home until you leave it and then, when you have left it, you never can go back."

Yet behind the dread of homelessness is a desire for it, because the familiar world of our homes can be suffocatingly small. Perhaps it is impossible to know our authentic selves. We are forever mired in polarities of dread and desire for home and homelessness.

This story is in another sense a struggle to come home while fleeing from it. It is a return from Marxist utopia to the magic, myth, and tedium of cooking. It is the whittling down of big dreams into smaller ones. Two decades ago as I was becoming an intellectual, I also became a Marxist. As a Marxist I sought big questions, and in particular as a Third World Marxist I was compelled by the developmentalist promise of the Soviet experiment. After years of activism, I was confronted with martial law in Poland and the Soviet invasion of Afghanistan. (That feels so long ago now!) That is when my Marxism began to falter, which eventually took me on a route that led to this place—a retreat from the public drama into the private universe.

Nevertheless, big Marxist questions continued to fashion my intellectual interests. I went to graduate school at the State University of New York at Binghamton so I could work with some of the stalwarts of the intellectual New Left, such as Giovanni Arrighi, James Petras, Mark Selden, and Immanuel Wallerstein. I began work on the rise and the fall of the Soviet Union from the perspective of long-term, large-scale social change. But by 1994, I had exhausted my interest in the socialist experiment and was intellectually tired of big questions and the quest for ponderous answers. In part, the shift of interest was a product of changing taste and political climate: I hungered for the concrete detail so valorized by the antipoliticians of the Velvet Revolutions of 1989. I began the recoil toward the quotidian, the small questions of everyday life. I was intrigued by the way people craft much of their identities around the minutiae of everyday existence. That is what drew me to food. Fernand Braudel was the bridge for me between large-scale long-term change and the details of material culture as elaborated in *Structures of Everyday Life* (1981).

This book attempts to get out from under the structural flows of long-term, large-scale social change. Instead, it looks at how some people try to come to terms with social processes such as migration, modernity, and globalization. It is a view of social change as a lived everyday experience. The scale is intimate rather than monumental, yet it belongs to the same spiritual world.

In part, my story has haltingly poured itself into an inadequate container. In part, like the quotidian, it has been carried by sheer inertia. There is no epiphany, no singular revelation, no moment of truth, rather the steady accumulation of a thousand anecdotes and observations. I am after small truths rather than lumbering ones. Or, as Ralph Waldo Emerson would have said, "I am a fragment, and this is a fragment of me." I have tried to remain true to that process in the following pages. At the end of large, apparently empiricist tracts I have sought to give meaning—to read a symbol and give it significance. In some sense, this is my groping for meaning in the quotidian.

I have sought plausible readings of sociological facts without self-destructing my story in a frenzy of interpretation and overinterpretation. Further, I have tried neither to resolve all contradictions accepted by my respondents nor, at the other extreme, to read a mundane fact necessarily as a conundrum. Whether I have strayed into the limits of empiricism or into those of unconstrained interpretation is left to the reader to decide.

Central Questions

What are the changes wrought by immigration in the deep structures of everyday life, especially in the realm of food practices? What do these transformations tell us about the processes of globalization and modernization? These are the two questions that animate this work.

My attempt is to make cuisine speak to the experiences of migration and show the resultant transformations of taste. What can the eating and cooking habits of migrants tell us about assimilation and accommodation? How does food relate the native to the migrant, and the ethnic to the universal? In the end, we arrive at theory, which takes as its central theme the problem of what to eat.

Through much of the twentieth century, anthropology—especially cultural anthropology—stood almost by itself among the social sciences, seeking to think systematically about the "blinding fetish" that is food (Douglas 1977: 7). Nevertheless, anthropological studies of food remain rooted in a place, a locale, usually the "original" site of a cultural system in isolation from any other place. In keeping with these anthropological impulses, researchers of South Asian food practices have ignored the diaspora. Ravindra S. Khare, the preeminent anthropologist of South Asian cuisine, concentrates almost exclusively on the Kanya-Kubja Brahmins of the Rae Bareli region of India, drawing an exquisitely detailed portrait of a "traditional" culinary culture. Khare (1976b: 7) has warned that, "if the orthodox culinary pattern is not studied now, one may lose an opportunity to record a vanishing segment of culinary culture, and to examine its systematic significance." But the more interesting question for me is: What are these orthodox practices vanishing into and why? In trying to answer that question, Arjun Appadurai has initiated work on the practices of the urban middle classes that are beginning to overwhelm what Khare calls the "orthodoxy" (Appadurai 1988). Appadurai expands the scope of his inquiry to include the *intra*-national diaspora within India. I follow his lead in taking one more step to include the culinary practices of the *inter*-national diaspora.

My work deals with food as a place-making practice. Nobody has written more presciently on space and place than Michel Foucault, who contended in a 1967 lecture that "the great obsession of the nineteenth century was, as we know, history; with its themes of development of the ever-accumulating past, with great preponderance of dead men and the menacing glaciation of the world. . . . The present epoch will perhaps be above all the epoch of space" (Foucault 1986: 22).

After describing various kinds of spaces, such as places of temporary relaxation (cafés, cinemas, beaches) and sites of rest (the house, the bedroom, and the bed), Foucault settles on an analysis of sites "that have the curious property of being in relation with all other sites, but in such a way as to suspect, neutralize, or invert the set of relations that they happen to designate, mirror, or reflect. These spaces . . . are of two main types" (Foucault 1986: 24). They are "unreal spaces" such as utopias, which are often inverted analogies of the real space of society, and heterotopias, which are real spaces but counter-sites that, among other things, "juxtapose in a single real space several spaces that are in themselves incompatible" (Foucault 1986: 25). In my case, one place, such as a suburb of Chicago, can be many places: Bengal, America, India—and, of course, a suburb of Chicago, too. Migrant cuisine has a heterotopic effect insofar as the practices of a local peripheral people, such as Bengalis who were made global through British imperialism, are then relocalized in an American suburb. What I mean is that the local and provincial (in my case, Bengali food practices) penetrates the global (America) and reconstitutes the latter. It brings the Orient home and in the process disorients the Occident (cf. Hall 1997). It is not a very assertive reorientation yet, but a slow, seeping corruption of Anglo-Saxon conceptions of the world.

In some senses, such practices are destabilizing because these particular "Orientals" come with all of the meritocratic qualifications of the Occidental world. The Bengali Americans under discussion are mostly doctors, engineers, and academics. In another sense, these particular "Orientals" are much less a threat to bourgeois conceptions of the world because they come fully socialized into global middle-class values and prejudices. Hence, they easily become model minorities who are counterposed to domestic classes and races that will not assimilate into middle-class oblivion. In that sense, this local protagonist (the Bengali middle class) is complicit in the global imperial claims of the metropole. It is globalization with a brown face. The protagonist is Nietzsche's "state nomads without home"—a new kind of man, arrogant and servile, corrupt and resilient at the same time.

Underpinning much of the discussion of globalization is the assumption that such a process is primarily a matter of Americanization of the world—the thesis of increasing homogenization of the globe under the hegemony of American icons such as Coca-Cola, McDonald's, and Levi's jeans. Over the past few decades, however, in the work of Appadurai, Stuart Hall, and Ulf Hannerz, a sophisticated counter-argument has developed (Appadurai 1996; Featherstone et al. 1995; Hall et al. 1996; King 1997). It has been shown that even apparently homogeneous and transparent commodities such as hamburgers and Coke acquire complicated local resonance. For instance, what is "fast food" in the United States is often considered elaborated cuisine in Beijing (Watson 1997). So the meanings are not homogeneous, even if there is a certain vector of globalization leading from the West to the East. Sometimes the hypervalorized commodities are themselves materially transformed, as McDonald's hamburgers in New Delhi are bereft of any beef. Nevertheless, both the theorists of cultural homogenization (such as W. W. Rostow and Samuel Huntington) and their critics have concentrated on empirical work that looks at the dispersal of

Western culture and commodities, even if they concede that the transmission complicates the process.

What if we imagine other trajectories of globalization, such as globalization in the old-fashioned way when peripheral peoples migrated to the metropole? The issue is further complicated when these peripheral peoples are not the working classes of yore but belong to the affluent middle class. West Bengali migrants in the United States provide a particularly interesting window of opportunity for inquiry, because almost all West Bengali immigrants belong to this class. I am particularly interested in this class because it is often a protagonist of globalization; in addition, its members are under tremendous assimilative pressure and yet have the most resources to resist it if they choose to do so. To keep my analysis focused on the middle class, I have excluded Bangladeshi migrants, who are Bengali but also mostly working class. Furthermore, Bangladeshi migrants are predominantly Muslims and bring a sensibility quite distinct from that of the middle-class Hindu protagonists in my story. Eventually, I hope to compare the two across lines of class and religion, but that is not my project here.

It is my focus on the intimate world of middle-class migrants that makes my work distinctive and, I suggest, interesting. Even the most sophisticated discussions of globalization, as in the case of Appadurai, have concentrated on the public sphere, such as restaurants, electronic media, movies, and sporting events (Appadurai 1996; Breckenridge 1995). In contrast, I look at the private sphere of the middle class of these global flows. These social actors are not of the metropolitan core; they were produced by earlier phases of globalization. Today they are the agents of globalization at the most mundane level. I am interested not in their performance in the marketplace of commodities and ideas but in their private worlds. My interest is not in the role of global financiers or state makers or peripheral peasants outside the reach of the market. I focus, rather, on middle managers in their mundane, nonpublic lives—the domestic lives of the unromantic bourgeoisie of global capitalism. My project problematizes the role of professionals as globalizers who nevertheless have to face a personal consequence of that process—disinterring the deep structures of their everyday lives. What do these paragons of globalization do when their deepest routines of redundant habits become inadequate? Perhaps he only likes to build it, and does not want to live in it, as Dostoevsky's Underground Man suggests about the Faustian deal between modern man and modernity in *Notes from Underground* (1990 [1864]).

An aspect of this work that is relatively new is the attention to the South Asian diaspora. South Asia has a population base of more than 1 billion people, but it has contributed only about 20 million people to overseas migration. Overseas Chinese, in contrast, number three times as many (Clarke et al. 1990: 1). The lack of attention to the lives of South Asian migrants may have something to do with this paucity of numbers and the migrants' great dispersal. But as a largely professional and highly skilled migrant community in the United States, South Asians have a far greater weight and visibility than their numerical strength of about 2 million may justify.

With Indian migrants counted separately only since the 1980 census, Indian-American studies is in its infancy, still concentrating largely on providing aggregate data about numbers, age, family structure, and income. Ethnographic studies continue to be a rarity. Without ethnographies, we cannot begin to get a sense of the lifestyles of Indian Americans. As a consequence, very little has been written about Indian-American culinary practices (especially non-commodified, domestic ones) and their importance in imagining, affirming, and undermining a sense of community. There is no book-length treatment of the subject, and what exists is overwhelmed by the rhetorical devices of postmodernism, through which we learn very little about what migrants do and much too much about the writer's anxieties about what she or he thinks migrants are trying to imply in doing what they appear to be doing. This work seeks to bring sociology and anthropology to the international South Asian diaspora.

Some of the originality of this work also resides in its multidisciplinarity. It draws on concepts and traditions in cultural studies (especially studies of globalization), sociology of taste, anthropology of food, and immigration history. It is marked by an awareness that sometimes we can study a community only by ignoring national boundaries, especially in a world that is an integrated yet differentiated global economy, geopolitical system, and geocultural order.

Method and Technique

This work mines four kinds of data for meaning. One line of inquiry is based on a sociological survey of food practices completed by 126 Bengali-American respondents representing households with 436 individuals. This line of inquiry includes a perusal of the ethnic press, cookbooks, and food-related websites. The second line of inquiry is an ethnography produced by directly observing the daily food practices of three Bengali-American households through three summers over a three-year period. The third vector is a synthesis of the secondary literature in anthropology and sociology. Finally, my own experience as an Indian immigrant in the United States undergirds the whole project.

In the historical section, I tell the story of Bengali culinary culture. Indian historians of food are the main source. What is original here is the comparative view of Bengali and American cooking. The distinctive perspective of this work is that of a researcher who brings his own cultural and biographical history to point out differences and similarities between the two traditions. Thus, the book is in some senses not only a history but also a mythography of what is "American" food and what is "Bengali" food.

As stated earlier, this work draws on the responses of Bengali-American respondents to a detailed questionnaire, their names drawn randomly from the *Directory of Bengalis of North America* (1994). The questionnaire had two sections (see Appendix 1). The general section asked for information about year of immigration, income, family structure, educational level, caste, and so on. The second section dealt with specific questions about cooking and eating that ranged from who does the cooking, the previous week's menu, and the size of the grocery bill to the serving of beef and alcohol. These surveys enabled me to do two things: (1) construct a profile of food practices of Bengali Americans, including commonalities and idiosyncrasies; and (2) frame the next line of inquiry—the ethnography.

The ethnography is a product of direct observation of the culinary practices of three Bengali households in the United States over a three-year period. I use the term "ethnography" in the generic sense of participant observation, which allowed me to look at things that are often unstated or misread because they are too obvious and hence would not be identified by the sociological survey. Participant observation is a feat of immersion and a product of some experiential distance. Empathetic immersion enables one to catch the nuances and the allusions, and distance makes visible what is often too obvious to be noticed by the insider. Distance also makes a comparative perspective possible (Gans 1968; Geertz 1983: 70).

Of the two—immersion and distance—perhaps the greater danger in my case remains that of being an insider. That is, it is possible that I will not see what would be visible from the outside. It remains to be seen whether I can transcend these limits. I am an insider as a middle-class Bengali-Oriya migrant to the United States, and an outsider in the sense that I am not an active member of the Bengali community and my milieu is largely one of First World intellectuals. Am I an ethnographer or a native informant? I am probably a "stranger" in Simmel's sense—an element of the group but not fully part of it. By virtue of this partial involvement in group affairs, I am called on to play a role that others cannot: that of objective confidante (Simmel 1950: 402–8).

There is an additional danger. The closer I get in intensity and depth, the farther I recede on the possibilities of generalizing because of the tension between the general and the particular that social science has to live with. I attempted to overcome this problem in part by using the questionnaires. The questionnaires, then, are a foil to the deep ethnography.

Since this work is one of transcultural interpretation, my position as both an insider and an outsider enables me to reveal nondiscursive knowledge that makes it possible for Bengalis to live in America. Following Pierre Bourdieu, I pay close attention to the practices of ordinary living: the little routines that people enact, again and again, in working, eating, sleeping, and relaxing, as well as the little scenarios of etiquette they play out in social interaction, underpinned by notions of temporal, spatial, and social ordering. Ethnography allows the study of people in their own time and space—that is, it allows me to get closer to the hermeneutic dimension of the social sciences, the dimension of understanding that is constitutive of constructing a plausible explanation for things. Furthermore, as an immigrant I attempt to connect my personal troubles to the public issues of social structure, as suggested by C. Wright Mills (1959: 6), who wrote, "The sociological imagination enables us to grasp history and biography and the relations between the two within society" (see also Laslett 1991).

I began this book not with a hypothesis but with a number of empirical questions. In seeking answers to these questions, I developed theories about certain relationships. As the project matured, I moved from asking basic empirical questions about what are Bengali-American food practices and the mentalities associated with them to viewing these practices through theories of three kinds of overlapping relationships: the traditional and the modern; the ethnic and the universal; and the local and the global. In the process, I came to see food as a place-making practice and feeding as one of the processes by which we structure time and space. I also learned much about the symbolic ingenuity of people in the consumption of things and in the making of their communities through the process of consumption.

At the most general level, my thesis is that globalization is neither the Americanization of the world nor the Westernization of people. I show, by looking at the food practices of Bengali-American migrants, that there is no one-directional change toward *Homo occidentalis*. Migrant food practices illuminate the ambivalence of modern actors toward locality, community, and authenticity and toward the home and the world.

Organization of the Text

In Chapter 2, "West Bengali Food Norms," I draw the pre-immigration baseline to prepare the ground for the post-immigration comparison. I begin with an outline of the geographical characteristics of West Bengal and their resultant influences on food choices. Next, I use a 1970 study of food habits in Calcutta conducted by the U.S. Agency of International Development (USAID 1972) to identify the dietary norms of typical urban, middle-class Bengalis in terms of calorie intake, food budget, and daily and weekly cycles of meals. Then I describe the foundational principles of Bengali cuisine, such as the Core–Fringe–Legume Pattern, the spice repertoire, and cooking techniques. Finally, I discuss some of the binary oppositions that Bengalis identify with their cuisine, such as vegetarianism and non-vegetarianism and modern versus traditional foods. I conclude with some sociological generalizations on Bengali food.

In Chapter 3, "Bengali-American Food Consumption," I identify the daily, weekly, and seasonal cycles of consumption. In the process, I highlight some of the more intriguing changes and seek to explain why they have come about and how Bengali Americans explain them. This and the following two chapters contain the most detailed empirical descriptions in the book and attempt to draw larger conclusions and connect them to the themes introduced in this chapter.

In Chapter 4, "Gastroethnicity: Reorienting Ethnic Studies," I grapple directly with the problems of identity and cuisine. I address the question: What makes a food Bengali—or, for that matter, what makes something "authentic" to a culture? Much of what is considered authentic is defined in opposition to "others." Bengali Americans construct their cuisine in opposition to the "American." Then, with the help of ten acutely liminal respondents, I generate a contrast between insider and outsider constructions of culinary group identity.

In the last empirical chapter, "Food Work: Labor of Love?" I identify the distribution of labor in Bengali-American households and compare it with the pattern in Anglo-American households. The chapter begins with such simple questions as: Who works? How much? I then move on to discussions of why this is so, how it can be explained, and what it says about the distribution of power within Bengali-American households. As in the chapter on consumption, I highlight interesting and counterintuitive patterns, such as the impact of migration on the re-gendering of labor. Chapter 5 ends by raising questions about our conceptions of power within the household.

In the concluding chapter, "Meals, Migration, and Modernity," I draw heavily on the fictional and nonfictional work of the Bengali Nobel laureate Rabindranath Tagore and diasporic Indian literary figures such as Anita Desai, Jhumpa Lahiri, V. S. Naipaul, and Salman Rushdie to elaborate on the structure of feeling of a migrant and his attempt to create a place for himself in an alien world. The problem is in some ways a quintessentially modern one of finding one's place—spatially, socially, and temporally. We do that by hanging on to a myth of stability in a world that is perpetually changing. Food, and especially nostalgia about home cooking, plays a crucial role in anchoring us in a world that refuses to stay still.

Finally, a note on transliteration: Because the Bengali alphabet has more letters than the Roman alphabet, it is necessary to approximate additional sounds within the limits of English by adding certain diacritical marks. After much thought, I have decided to forgo the scholarly notation system for two reasons: (1) ease of reading for a nonacademic audience, which is substantial for a book on food, and (2) many of my quotations are from cookbooks and other popular texts that do not use the scholarly notation system, hence using it would create unnecessary confusion between my text and the various quotations.

In most cases I use "a" for the inherent vowel o (a short o as in g°rom = hot) *and* for the long vowel ā in Romanized names such as Satyajit Ray, the famous Bengali filmmaker, although the three "a"s in his name are pronounced o, a, and ā, respectively. There is one exception: I identify the long vowel ā in *chāna* for farmer cheese to distinguish it from *chana,* which is chickpea.

There is a further source of confusion because the o sound can be produced either by the inherent vowel ° or the full vowel o. Thus, the word
for hot is pronounced "g°rom," where the vowel between g and r is an
inherent vowel (a short o), and the vowel between r and m is a full o. In
most places, I have rendered the full vowel as an o and the inherent vowel
as an a, which is standard in Romanized Bengali. Yet words such as garam
masala (and halvah) that have entered the English lexicon are used in the
familiar form. To avoid confusion, I have kept the number of Bengali words
to a minimum. I apologize to those who may have preferred a firmer grasp
of the pronunciation of the few Bengali words that I do use.

CHAPTER 2

West Bengali Food Norms

Geography, Economy, and Culture

Having performed austerity, he understood that
Brahma is food. For truly indeed, beings here
Are born from food, when born they live by food, on deceasing they
    enter into food;
Mankind is food for death; he is nourished and nourishes;
I, who am food, eat the eater of food!
I have overcome the world!

TAITTIRIYA UPANISHAD (CA. 700–600 B.C.)

My intention in this chapter is to provide the pre-immigration baseline for the discussion of Bengali-American foodways in the subsequent chapters. What matters for my purposes are the practices of middle-class Bengalis from Calcutta.[1] I address only the practices of the middle class, because that is the demographic characteristic of West Bengali migrants, and I present data for 1970–80, the period when most of my respondents left India. I consider earlier foodways only when they have a bearing on later generations.

I begin with the ecological factors that continue to shape Bengali food habits, such as the preferences for rice, fish, and tea, and provide a quick sketch of the economic foundations that shape the typical Calcuttan's food budget. I ask a series of questions about Calcuttans' food consumption and patterns of eating. Then I point to what I think is the distinctive style of cooking that can be called Bengali and draw attention to cultural norms such as vegetarianism, life-cycle rituals, and notions of "modern" and "traditional" eating.

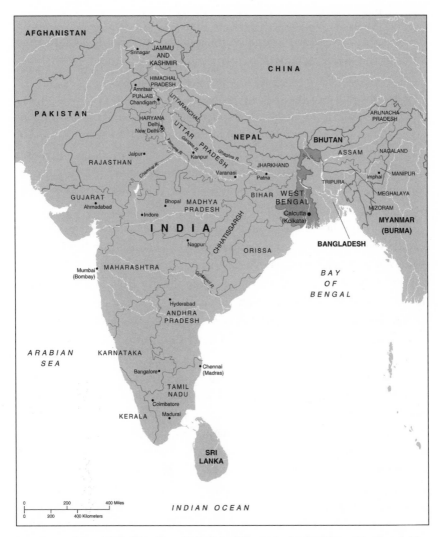

FIGURE 1. *Map of India. West Bengal (highlighted) lies in the flat floodplain of the Bengal delta.*

Geographical Limits

The Bengal delta, the largest deltaic landform in the world, is a relatively flat, horseshoe-shaped floodplain that opens into the Bay of Bengal to the south. Surrounding its rim is the Chottanagpur plateau to the west, the Himalayas to the north, and disconnected hill systems to the east (Figure 1).

The Bengali linguistic region is divided into two political units. Bangladesh, with about 140 million inhabitants, occupies the eastern two-thirds of the gently sloping delta formed by the Ganges and the Brahmaputra rivers; and West Bengal, with about 80 million people, occupies the western one-third of the delta (population figures from raw 2001 census data). In this study, "Bengali" refers only to people who trace their origins to the Indian state of West Bengal. According to the 1991 Census of India, 72 percent of the population of West Bengal lives in rural areas in about 40,000 villages. The remainder of the Bengali population is urban, mostly concentrated in cities such as Calcutta (about 12 million), Asansol, Burdwan, Durgapur, and Kharagpur.

West Bengal lies in east-central India, between 21 and 27 degrees north latitude and 85 and 89 degrees east longitude. The rampart of the Himalayas that bounds the state to the north blocks polar air, and the sea to the south further moderates temperature ranges. Even the northern extremity of the state is only about 300 miles from the sea.

Temperature and precipitation patterns divide West Bengal into four main climatic regions. The extreme Himalayan north, around Darjeeling, is wet and has the widest variations in temperature. The northern end of the plain, around Jalpaiguri, is wet and moderate. Asansol, on the Chottanagpur plateau at the western end of the state, is relatively dry and warm. Finally, the deltaic south around Calcutta, which is home to most of my respondents, is wet and hot. The main climatic differences within West Bengal are determined by precipitation, and the monsoon rhythm is the dominating characteristic in the state (as it is elsewhere in India). Most of West Bengal, other than the dry western Chottanagpur plateau, receives average annual rainfall of 59–158 inches, with most of the precipitation falling from June to October. Irrigation is available on only about a quarter of the cropped land; agriculture is thus dependent on the monsoon rains.

Major transformations in food production have come to West Bengal in the past two decades, partly as a consequence of policies of the Left Front government—an alliance led by the various communist parties of India—and partly because of the autonomous mobilization of rural classes (Harriss 1993). The Left Front wagered that agricultural productivity would rise if land were returned by absentee landlords to cultivators (Bandyopadhyay 2000). Over the past twenty-five years, almost 1 million acres of land has been redistributed among landless peasants and sharecroppers. Agricultural production has burgeoned.

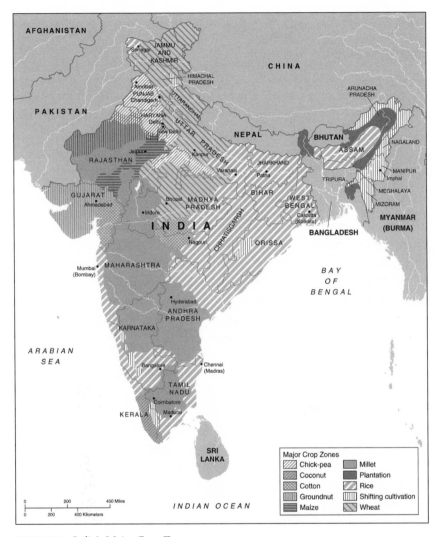

FIGURE 2. *India's Major Crop Zones.*

Rice and wheat are the main food crops produced today in West Bengal.[2] According to the Indian Department of Agriculture and Cooperation (DAC 2000), West Bengal is India's top producer of rice, which occupies 75–85 percent of the cropped area. Legumes such as beans and pulses (*masur, khesari,* and *maskalai*) occupy about 8 percent of West Bengal's cropped area (Figure 2). Nevertheless, West Bengal's production of pulses in 1998–99 fell far short of consumption rates. Rice and *masur* dal are staples of the Bengali diet.[3] But unlike rice, pulses are not an ecological fit with the wet deltaic conditions.

After pulses come oilseeds in order of culinary importance. The main oilseeds produced in Bengal are mustard, sesame, and linseed.[4] Mustard is the chief source of cooking oil today, although competition from heavily subsidized soy oil from the United States is posing a serious economic challenge throughout West Bengal's mustard and peanut belt (Shiva 2002).

West Bengal is the second-largest potato-growing state in India, contributing a third of the national yield. The other major vegetables produced in the state are eggplant, cabbage, cauliflower, okra, and tomatoes (DAC 2000).

About 87 percent of West Bengal's agricultural acreage is dedicated to food crops. However, substantial arable land is also devoted to the two most important cash crops: tea and jute. Tea—particularly high-quality Darjeeling tea—is grown on the terraces of the lower Himalayas, in northern Bengal.[5]

Given the agricultural foundations of West Bengal, it is no wonder that most Bengalis are rice eaters. Potatoes are the most important "vegetable" in the Bengali diet, followed by cauliflower, tomatoes, okra, cabbage, and eggplant. "After the Irish," Chitrita Banerji (1997: 139) notes, "Bengalis are probably the greatest potato eaters in the world, and yet this is such a relative upstart in the hierarchy of our food. With rice [and, I might add, dal], it is the inevitable daily ingredient in the diet of vegetarians and non-vegetarians alike." A 1970 survey identified the potato as the second most common item in the Calcuttan grocery basket, after salt (USAID 1972: 108; see Table 1, Appendix 2, for a listing of the top 83 items). The fat base of the cuisine is mustard oil, which is the fifth most common item in a Calcuttan's grocery basket (Table 1). Field greens and fish play a tertiary role, their importance increasing with rising income.[6]

Thus, much of what is typical to Bengali cuisine is a product of the local ecology. But West Bengal is not an isolated economic region. Some of what is consumed on a daily basis is not produced in the state, pulses being one of the most important examples. Urbanite Bengalis, such as my respondents, are particularly dependent on the market both for income and to supply their pantry.

Although most of the economy of West Bengal depends on agriculture, there are three major industrial pockets. One is around Calcutta, where engineering, petrochemicals, textiles, and food processing predominate. The state government and numerous colleges are also located there; thus, the service sector is a major employer. Another industrial region is around Durgapur and Asansol, where mining is pre-eminent. A third region, although much less important, is the Midnapur district around Kharagpur, which concentrates on industries that play an ancillary role to the railroads. West Bengal's population is only about 7 percent of the Indian national total, but its industrial output is about 20 percent of the total.

Most Bengali migrants to the United States are from families working in the service sector, most often employed by local, state, and central governments. Government agencies and the railroads have been the two greatest employers of the Bengali *bhadralok* (gentlemen) who are the subjects of this study. West Bengali migrants to the United States are highly educated. Almost all of my survey respondents held a bachelor's degree, compared with only 14 percent of Calcuttan men in 1980. Among women, only 6 percent of Calcuttans had a college education in 1980, in contrast to 94 percent of my female Bengali-American respondents.

Baseline in Food Consumption

In 1972, the U.S. Agency for International Development (USAID) released the findings of a remarkable survey titled *A Study of Food Habits in Calcutta*. Conducted over a one-year period in 1969–70, the study covered a random sample of 2,386 households in Calcutta. Since most (West) Bengalis in the United States are from Calcutta (146 of the 222 adult respondents), having left sometime between 1965 and 1985, the study offers an appropriate surrogate for establishing pre-immigration dietary norms.

Food Budget

In 1970, the Calcutta Municipal Corporation area had a resident population of 3.1 million, comprising 500,000 households, with just over six persons per household. The average household spent about 300 rupees (about US$38 in 1970 dollars)[7] per month on food, or more than 50 percent of its monthly budget (USAID 1972: 2). For the (economically) top 19 percent of the population, food consumed 40 percent of total household expenditures; in contrast, the bottom 10 percent spent two-thirds of their budget on food.

The average Calcuttan spent 1.58 rupees per day on food in 1970 (USAID 1972: 16). The most important components of the daily expenditure were cereals, animal protein (fish, meat, and eggs), fruit and vegetables, and milk. These items together accounted for 68 percent of the food budget. The budget of the poorest households differed radically from that of the elite, however. The difference was most dramatic in patterns of consumption of fish, meat, eggs, milk, and fruit. Table 2 (Appendix 2) provides a comparative overview of the daily food budget of the poorest and the most affluent households.

While Table 2 shows each item as a percentage of the food budget, Table 3 (Appendix 2) compares the items by weight, which is more relevant in terms of nutrition. Overall, a Calcuttan in 1970 consumed an average of 909 grams of different foods per day, with individuals in high-expenditure households consuming 1,126 grams and those in low-expenditure households consuming 752 grams. By weight, more than one-third of the average Calcuttan's diet in 1970 was composed of cereals, and the amount of cereal consumed was more or less the same for affluent and poor households. As a proportion of the total daily intake, however, almost one-half of food consumed by poor households took the form of cereals. In contrast, a little less than a quarter was composed of vegetables, with high-expenditure families consuming substantially more vegetables than low-expenditure households. Milk, constituting an average 12 percent of the daily diet, was the most class-segregated item in the Calcuttan's diet, with affluent households consuming twice the amount consumed by poor households. After milk came fish, meat, and eggs, with high-expenditure households consuming twice the amount consumed by low-expenditure households. In contrast, affluent households consumed only about 30 percent more legumes than poor households. This is relevant because after immigration we will see an escalation in the consumption of milk, fruit juices, fish, and other high-value, high-status items.

Daily Cycle of Meals

The average individual in Calcutta consumed two principal and two supplementary meals a day from the household kitchen. The principal evening meal (dinner) was usually eaten between 8 P.M. and 10 P.M., while during the day the wage earner ate breakfast at home between 8 A.M. and 10 A.M., and the homemaker ate lunch between 1 P.M. and 2 P.M. (see Table 4, Appendix 2).

In general, the principal meals of the day—lunch and dinner—included rice; *rooti* (wheat flat bread); dal; sauteed or boiled vegetables; meat, fish, or egg curry; *chāna* (farmer cheese); and plain yogurt. Supplementary meals included a wider variety of foods, such as tea, coffee, crackers, bread, puffed rice, *loochi* (deep-fried wheat-dough bread) or *paratha* (pan-fried wheat-dough flat bread), sweetened snacks such as halvah and *chāna,* fruit, milk, and various carbonated drinks.

An overwhelming majority of Calcutta households in 1970 ate rice at lunch and *rooti* at dinner. Even those who could afford to buy rice at a higher price, it appears, preferred *rooti* at dinner. That is surprising. From family histories of middle-class Calcuttans it would appear that rice was central to both of the principal meals, not just lunch, but the aggregate data do not show such a preference. This discrepancy is important for the post-immigration discussion.

If we focus our attention only on those items that were consumed by a substantial number of households—that is, at least a quarter of the surveyed families—we can reach a number of conclusions. First, rice was strongly associated with the principal meals. Almost all households served rice on any given day: 85 percent at lunch, 34 percent at brunch, and 31 percent at dinner. Rice (boiled, not puffed) was hardly ever served as a late-afternoon supplemental meal. In contrast, *rooti* was served at breakfast (48 percent), as a late-afternoon snack (30 percent), or dinner (77 percent). *Rooti* replaced rice in many households as the staple at dinner.

Rooti was one of the few items that broke the association as an exclusively principal or supplementary item. Milk also was categorized as supplemental by 19 percent of households and served at breakfast, while 22 percent served it with dinner. In contrast, lentil soup (dal) was an exclusively principal item, as were curried vegetables, fish, and meat. Boiled eggs were exclusively supplemental, while curried eggs were exclusively principal. Sliced loaf bread was exclusively supplemental, while flat breads were served at both principal and supplemental meals. Tea was served exclusively with the supplemental meal in the early morning or the late afternoon; it was never consumed at lunch or dinner. As Chapter 3 will show, after immigration certain dishes identified as exclusively principal items would become more important at dinner than others.

Further, an inverse relationship seems to exist between certain items, such as puffed rice and sliced bread. Those who reported eating puffed rice do not eat sliced bread. Moreover, sliced bread replaces puffed rice with rising income. Once again, this points to the data in Chapter 3 showing that after immigration, certain cereals, such as cornflakes, are preferred over the low-status puffed rice, while consumption of toast persists.

Weekly Cycle of Meals

Generally, there was not much variation in the consumption of food dishes over different days of the week. One component that could be differentiated by weekday was goat meat. Only 7 percent of households in Calcutta in 1970 served meat on Thursdays, and 16 percent served it on Sundays. On most other days of the week, about 11 percent of households served meat (USAID 1972: apps., 24). We will see that the difference between weekday and weekend meals develops dramatically after migration.

Life Cycle, Gender, and Meals

Some food items were strongly associated with certain age groups. Consumption of milk was high among children, for example, the volume increasing until the second year, then slowly falling until the child reached five to six years of age. Then consumption of milk dramatically fell off while consumption of rice climbed. Milk became important once again in old age, climbing to infant levels, with consumption of rice falling in conjunction.

Interestingly, older men's consumption of high-status items such as fish and sliced bread (along with milk) continued to increase hand in hand with a sustained decrease in the consumption of all other items. Older women's consumption of all food items other than milk fell.

Most Calcuttan girls and women were getting fewer calories than the recommended daily allowance (which in all probability is too high). But so were boys and men. The surprising thing is that the only nutrient showing substantial difference in consumption between the genders was iron, with young girls (age 12–16) getting much less than the recommended daily allowance. Nevertheless, as girls grew up they got more than the daily recommended allowance of iron—even more than men—perhaps because of their greater consumption of low-status and less masculine items such as leafy green vegetables.

The survey further showed that the man in the house consumed a little more of everything than any other member. Nevertheless, these figures appear surprisingly gender-neutral, with one exception: Older women appeared to bear the brunt of gender and age discrimination, losing access to high-status items such as sliced bread, milk, fish, and meat. Hinduism, especially Vaishnavism, provides convenient ideological justification for older women's reduced access to most animal products and Westernized items such as sliced bread, viewing them as either polluting or producing excessive "heat," or sexual energy. Predictably, older women compensated by consuming more low-status items, such as puffed rice and leafy vegetables.

Economic Means and Food

In 1970, consumption of every item increased with rising per capita expenditure, which I will use in place of income. Consumption of rice, the fundamental staple, increased until the upper 40 percent of the population was reached; consumption of wheat flour, the other staple, increased until the upper 60 percent of households. Only the top 50 percent of households got enough pulses. The consumption of most items, including potatoes, vegetables, milk, butter, animal protein, and bread, continued to increase with rising income, suggesting unfulfilled need even at the highest expenditure levels.

Beef, *chhattu* (roasted chickpea flour), and puffed rice had the clearest inverse relationship to rising income. Beef consumption was the highest for the poorest 10 percent of households; that fell by half for the middle classes and again by half for the richest 19 percent of households. Beef is taboo; hence, its consumption is highest among lower-caste (or lower-class) Hindus. Affluent (typically upper-caste) households disdain beef. *Chhattu* is popular among day laborers in Calcutta, many of whom migrated from the neighboring state of Bihar. Puffed rice is the staple of rural Bengalis; it is unpopular among urban elites.

Eating Out

The USAID survey concluded that eating out was rare. On any given day, researchers found, only 10 percent of Calcuttans were eating meals not prepared in the home, and 90 percent of those who ate out did so for only one meal. The majority of those eating out (80 percent) were men in the working-age group of 17–56 (USAID 1972: 13). Unfortunately, we know very little about commercial eateries and their clientele in Calcutta.

Bengali Cooking Patterns

Rice and dal makes a Bengali.
BENGALI SAYING

Three features define Bengali cooking: (1) the Core–Fringe–Legume Pattern, (2) the repertoire of spices, and (3) the primary cooking processes. I will elaborate on each.

Core–Fringe–Legume Pattern

One way to define a meal is to build it around the binary opposition elaborated in Audrey Richards's description of the dietary practices of the Southern Bantu people called the Bemba. For them, a preferred starch provided the nutritive anchor of the entire culture: "To the Bemba each meal, to be satisfactory, must be composed of two constituents: a thick porridge (*ubwali*) made of millet and the relish (*umunani*) of vegetables, meat or fish, which is eaten with it" (Richards 1939: 46). The anthropologist Sidney Mintz (2001) has refined and elaborated on Richards's binary scheme, calling it the Core–Fringe–Legume Pattern (CFLP). According to Mintz, most people in the world maintain a diet that can be identified by its CFLP. The core is usually a complex carbohydrate such as rice, wheat, or maize, which provides 70–80 percent of the calories. The fringe is usually a spiced mixed vegetable, meat, or fish, often complemented by a third element—the legume (see Table 5, Appendix 2, for examples).

In the past 200 years, industrialization, urbanization, and rising standards of living in Western Europe and its white settler colonies (such as the United States) have led to the deterioration of the original CFLP. In contrast, rice or wheat continues to be the core of the meal for most Bengalis. Vegetables and animal protein are important but remain fringe items in terms of the caloric contribution they make to the whole meal. Bengali meals usually consist of a stir-fry or curry of vegetables and a small piece of fish or a few bite-size portions of meat in a curried sauce. The complex-carbohydrate core and the vegetable and animal-protein fringe are paired with the third defining element: a legume soup, or dal.

Bengalis, like most rice eaters, complement their core carbohydrate with a vegetable or fish fringe. Bengalis rarely eat meat, and when they do, they consume it in small amounts. The reason is at least partly ecological.

Wet rice cultivation in floodplains provides easy access to freshwater fish but does not provide a suitable environment for cattle raising. (Wheat and maize cultivation, by contrast, depend on the rotation of main crops with nitrogen-fixing plants such as alfalfa and soybeans, which make good cattle feed.)

Although they avoid meat, Bengalis, unlike most rice eaters, consume large quantities of milk. Their valorization of milk is partly borrowed from Vedic Northern Indians. The rice–milk complex makes Bengali cuisine unique in global terms. Although Bengalis raise cattle for milk, the animals are rarely slaughtered for meat. Pig raising also has never been an important occupation in Bengal; the reasons may be partly ecological and partly influenced by ritual notions of clean and unclean animals. When meat is eaten by Bengalis, especially Hindus, it is usually chicken or goat. Goat meat ranked forty-fifth in the Calcuttan's grocery basket (Table 1).

If we confine the analysis to the items that were most commonly consumed by Calcuttan households, the typical grocery basket included forty-two items. Among them, the main categories of food were:

Cereals—parboiled rice, wheat flour, puffed rice, loaf bread
Vegetables—potato (so defined by Bengalis), eggplant, pumpkin,
    potol (pointed gourd), okra, bittergourd, ridgegourd, green
    papaya, and leafy greens
Legumes—lentil, green gram, red gram
Fish—*rohu*
Dairy—cow's milk and plain yogurt (made at home from bought
    milk)
Oils/fats—mustard oil, ghee, *vanaspati* (hydrogenated vegetable
    oil)
Seasonings—salt, sugar, jaggery
Spices and herbs—turmeric, dried red chili, cumin seed, fresh
    green chili, coriander powder or seed, ginger, small and large
    onion, garlic, lime, mustard seed, black pepper
Fruit—guava
Snacks—crackers, tea (dust and leaf)
Other—betel leaf and areca nut

The rice–fish–legume pattern held for the principal meals. The major combinations for supplemental meals were:

Breakfast—puffed or parched rice with milk, sugar, and a banana
   or mango
Late-afternoon snacks—deep-fried, lentil-battered vegetables;
   potato turnover or *singara* (called *samosa* in northern India);
   tossed spicy mix of puffed rice, fried lentils, and herbs;
   omelets.

Dry and Wet Spices

In *Ethnic Cuisine* (1992), Elisabeth Rozin identifies the flavor principles of
the major cuisines of the world, underlining what she considers the distinctive flavoring ingredient in each region's cuisine. Flavoring a dish with
soy sauce, for instance, immediately marks it as East Asian:

> Soy sauce is so ubiquitously used in Oriental cooking, imparting its
> own unique and characteristic flavor to food, that it acquires some
> sort of intense symbolic value as a culinary marker. Orientals use soy
> sauce in their foods and other ethnic groups do not; to put soy sauce
> into food is to say that the food is in some sense Oriental and is *not*
> Russian or French or Algerian. (Rozin 1992: xiv)

Next, she breaks down the somewhat general soy sauce-equals-East Asian
equation into smaller and more discrete subunits, such as soy sauce plus
black bean and garlic equals Cantonese cuisine, or soy sauce plus sake and
sugar equals Japanese cuisine. If I were to specify the flavors that identify
Bengali cooking, the equation might look like this:

Bengali cooking equals turmeric
   plus *panch phoron* and dried red chili (with fish and vege-
      tables);
   plus *kalonji* (onion seed) and green chili (with fish and
      vegetables);
   plus the "dry" trinity of cumin, coriander seed, and mustard
      seed (with fish and vegetables);
   plus cumin and freshly ground black mustard paste (with fish
      and vegetables);
   plus the "wet" trinity of onion, ginger, and garlic paste
      (with meat).

Bengali cuisine's use of the five-spice combination called *panch phoron* distinguishes it from that of the rest of India. *Panch phoron* includes fennel, *methi* (fenugreek), *kalonji,* cumin, and *randhuni* (or mustard seed). Wide use of mustard and mustard oil brings Bengali food close to the North Indian paradigm. Also in common with North India, Bengali cooking makes extensive use of an array of spices and seasonings, including coriander seed, clove, cardamom, turmeric, bay leaf, mace, mint, nutmeg, poppy seed, saffron, sesame seed, dried red chilies, green chilies, *ajwain,* asafetida, dried mango, and various nuts. With southern peninsular India Bengali cooking shares coconut and cilantro (coriander leaf, as distinct from coriander seed). Typical Bengali wet spices include onion, ginger, garlic, tamarind, and yogurt (usually used in marinades for meat). Clarified butter (ghee) is also important.

As does every cuisine, Bengali cuisine follows certain rules and principles for combining ingredients, as is evident in the Bengali saying, "*Panch phoron* with dried red chili and *kalonji* seeds with green chili" (Kirchner 1992; Raychaudhuri 1981). Note also that spices are used with vegetables and fish interchangeably but not with meat. On top of it all, it is fish that provides a dish's flavor, as far as a Bengali—especially a middle-class Bengali—is concerned. This is evident in the number of proverbs relating to fish in the Bengali language. "To hide a fish with greens" means to conceal superficially; "a shallow water fish" refers to an insignificant person, whereas "a deep-water fish" is a noble man; "He does not know how to turn a fried fish" means someone who is pretending to be innocent; "Even the bones of a large fish are tasty" means that even the small deeds of a person of admirable character are valuable; and finally, "to fry a fish in its own oil" is to get something for nothing (see Morton 1987). These proverbs are derived from the material fact that the fish catch in West Bengal is the largest among all Indian states, and most of it is consumed within the state (DAC 2000).

Cuisine of Impregnation

Bengali concepts for the domestic craft of cooking (*ranna*) and the "science" of alchemy (*rasayanvigyan*) are both derived from the Sanskrit root *rasa-,* whose variety of associations includes juices, flavors, moods, and their magical combinations. Alchemy, a "science" that makes no distinction between matter and belief, is a felicitous image with which to initiate the discussion of a cuisine that routinely conflates cosmology with taste and health. Further, alchemy asserts the possibility of the transmutation of substance. Bengali cooking transmutes vegetable matter and fish into food (*anna*) through the mediation of moist heat, spices, and prayer. The beauty of Bengali food derives from its boundary-breaking aesthetic of aromas presented in otherwise mundane yellows and browns rather than the visual aesthetic of, say, al dente carrots, green beans, and red meat.

Part of the contrasting aesthetic of color and aroma derives from constraints of class-based cooking techniques. Claude Lévi-Strauss (1978: 484) identified boiling with plebian and roasting with aristocratic origins. With a few notable exceptions, such as the preparation of sweets, Bengali cuisine is still very close to its peasant origins. For Bengalis, dry-heat cooking (baking, grilling, and frying) is the exception, confined to the entrée in the classical sense (as the beginning), consisting usually of a stir-fry of greens, or to street food (*pokora* and *singara*). On festive occasions, dry-heat dishes are an important part of banquets that include red meat curried "au sec" with a range of "rich" spices, such as cloves, cardamom, and saffron. Such dishes have a strong Mughlai flavor—a nod toward the North Indian-centered court culture of modern India. For a Bengali, *pullao-mangsa* (pilaf and meat curry) is a metaphor for fine dining. Everyday meals are mostly stewed or braised.

In claiming the superiority of French over English food, lovers of French food from the "great master" Jean-Anthelme Brillat-Savarin on have argued that theirs is a cuisine of intermingling while English food is the product of mixture (Revel 1982). If we concede that to the French, then Bengali food is the result of an even deeper interpenetration where the original substance loses its distinctive identity, as in a stew. An ideal Bengali meal consists of a *bhaja* (saute of vegetables), a dal, and fish cooked in a sauce called *jhol* or *jhaal* with steamed rice. Dal poured over rice is eaten with the vegetables, and the *jhol* poured over rice is eaten with the fish. This "messed up" food is slurped down using the fingers of the right hand.

"Food," writes the Nobel laureate Octavio Paz (1997: 85), "is a reliable way to approach a people and its culture." Having spent about a decade as Mexico's ambassador to India, Paz is in a particularly privileged position to comment on comparative culinary styles.

> In European cooking, the order of the dishes is quite precise. It is a
> diachronic cuisine. . . . A radical difference: in India, the various dishes
> come together on a single large plate. Neither a succession nor a parade,

but a conglomeration and superimposition of things and tastes: a syn-
chronic cuisine. A fusion of flavors, a fusion of times. (Paz 1997: 85–86)

The Bengali table has no silverware and very few utensils, only a plate (*thala*)
and a bowl (*bati*). Bengali sauces—*bhape, checki, chochori, dalna, dom, ghonto,
jhaal, jhol, kalia, korma,* and *tok*—are all products of a cuisine of impregna-
tion produced by moist heat.

Dry-heat cooking processes are most amenable to keeping ingredients
distinct and are marginal to Bengali cuisine. Deep-frying with a chickpea
batter is usually confined to "teatime" snacks and street foods; it does not
constitute a "meal." Baking of raised bread and cakes, though increasingly
popular with the Bengali middle classes, is a recent development and still
not adopted widely. Grilling of tandoori chicken and kabobs came to Bengal with the court cuisines of the Afghans, Turks, and Mughals in the sev-
enteenth and eighteenth centuries. Underlining their marginality is the fact
that the products of all three of these techniques are usually bought at shops
or in restaurants rather than prepared at home. The Bengali home is the
realm exclusively of stovetop moist-heat cooking.

Breads—some of the best of which are made in the tandoor in India—
never acquired the ritual significance of rice in Vedic Hinduism. Even
among Bengali Muslims, who view the Afghan and Mughal heritage with
pride, rice remains the cultural super-food (Lindenbaum 1986). Even on
festive occasions, the Bengali culinary repertoire stays close to its domestic paradigm. For a typical Bengali *bou-bhat* (marriage banquet), the number of dishes multiplies, spices are more generously used, and sweets become
important, but the same *dom, jhaal, jhol,* or *kalia* is reproduced, and the visual
aesthetic continues to be subordinate to the senses of smell and taste.

Having broken Bengali food down into its constituent ingredients, flavor principles, and cooking processes, I will now put the cuisine back
together by providing what in my view is a "typical" middle-class, urban,
Bengali menu (see Table 6, Appendix 2).[8] A few things about the menu in
Table 6 are worth noting: It is relatively repetitive (as most everyday menus
are); no desserts are present (although Bengalis are known for their sweet
tooth, desserts are not served on an everyday basis); and, as stated earlier,
the food is not served in courses but simultaneously, with the rice and the
saute of vegetable served on the same plate, accompanied by the dal and
the fish in separate bowls. The dal and the sauce of the fish curry are typically poured over rice and eaten with the fingers of the right hand.

Bengali Cultural Norms

Vegetarian–Nonvegetarian

So far, I have talked about how access to particular food items depends on the ecological niche occupied by the Bengalis and on market factors such as income and employment opportunities. I have also elaborated on the distinctive combination of ingredients that makes a cuisine—a set of cultural choices made within ecological and economic limits. But what are the important non-economic cultural assumptions that shape Bengali cuisine? It is to these cultural categories that we now turn.

Unlike Brahmins from other parts of India, Bengali Brahmins are not vegetarians. It is important to know that even among non-Bengali Brahmins, vegetarianism developed slowly. K. T. Achaya (1994) has shown that, contrary to widespread misconceptions, meat eating was prevalent in early Vedic times. No fewer than 250 animals are referred to in the Vedas, and 50 of these were deemed fit for sacrifice and, by inference, for eating (also see Auboyer 1965; Ghurye 1979; Iyengar 1912; Jha 2002; Kosambi 1975).

Nevertheless, abstaining from meat eating was considered a Brahmin virtue even in early Vedic times. Achaya cites a hymn to nutrition (*pilu*) in the *Rigveda* where only vegetable foods are listed, and it carries two verses in praise of "the cow, *Aditi*, the sinless." In the later Dharma literature, starting with the *Dharma Sutras,* various prohibitions begin to appear. In the *Satapatha Brahmana,* the eating of beef is declared a sin. The *Manu Smriti*—one of the *Dharma Sutras* attributed to Manu, the first man, and codified by the second century A.D.—forbids a long list of meats in no fewer than fifty-four verses, including all carnivorous birds, birds that strike with their beaks or scratch with their toes, web-footed birds, birds that dive, and birds that live on fish. The village cock and the village pig are disallowed, yet nowhere is beef expressly prohibited (Achaya 1994: 55).

The battle over vegetarianism was eventually won by heterodox cults such as the Buddhists and the Jains between 600 B.C. and A.D. 800, which in the course of their expansion generated pressure for the elimination of Vedic sacrifices among the Brahmins, thereby creating a peculiar social formation (in global comparative terms) where the upper castes abstained from meat and fish eating. In other parts of the world, vegetarianism is generally a child of necessity, practiced mostly by subaltern classes.

From being simply one virtue of a priest, these powerful heterodox cults pushed the concept of *ahimsa* (nonviolence or non-killing) and its corollary of a vegetarian diet into common consciousness (Rocher 1978). As these vegetarian cults took hold of the imperial center, they put emulative pressure on the courtiers. Under emulative pressure, the Vedic schools thrust ritual sacrifice aside. Vegetable substitutes were found, such as the round pumpkin or the coconut smeared with vermilion powder to replace the bloody head of the sacrificial animal (Achaya 1994: 56). Renouncing—a major source of symbolic power within Hinduism—slowly came to include giving up meat eating.

W. Norman Brown lists at least two other factors in the veneration of cattle: the role of the cow, its products, and milk in Vedic sacrificial ritual; and the ties of the mother-goddess cult with the cow (Norman Brown 1957: 28; Simoons 1994). Whatever the reasons, beef eating slowly became taboo for upper-caste Hindus between 600 B.C. and A.D. 800.

Al-Biruni, the Arab traveler who spent thirteen years in India in the middle of the eleventh century, records the widespread popularity of vegetarianism among the courtly elite and city dwellers (Sachau 1910). By this time, India's first important pre-Islamic haute cuisine had been elaborated that included distinctive rules of vegetarianism, balance between hot and cold elements, detailed rules of commensality, and valorization of rice and milk. Al-Biruni also provides the first rationalist argument about Indic vegetarianism:

> As for the economic reason, we must keep in mind that the cow is the animal which serves man in traveling by carrying his load, in agriculture in the work of ploughing and sowing, and in the household by the milk and the products made from it. Further man makes use of its dung, and even of its breath. Therefore it was forbidden to eat cow's meat. (as quoted in Sachau 1910: 151)

The same argument was elaborated almost a millennium later by the "materialist" anthropologist Marvin Harris in *Cows, Pigs, Wars and Witches: The Riddles of Culture* (1974: 6–27).

In spite of Brahmanic reservations about meat eating, Bengali Brahmins eat fish. Thus, Bengal's tropical deltaic location has contributed more to its cuisine than the centrality of rice. Bengal's location on the coast and on the fringe of *aryavarta* (the Hindu heartland) may explain why Brahmanic and Buddhist vegetarianism never took hold here. Or it could be argued that in Bengal geography trumped Brahmanic precepts.

The USAID survey found Hindu households making up 86 percent of the population in Calcutta and Muslim households accounting for 10 percent. The survey identified 91 percent of Calcutta households as non-vegetarian. The number of nonvegetarian households was marginally higher among the poorer sections of the population; vegetarian households were more often encountered among the upper classes. Table 7 (Appendix 2) provides some details about vegetarians and nonvegetarians in Calcutta.

Current census reports reveal that, while 25–30 percent of the Indian population (mostly upper castes) is vegetarian, very few Bengalis abstain from eating meat. The states with high proportions of vegetarians are either in the Brahmanic heartland, such as Punjab, Haryana, Uttar Pradesh, and Madhya Pradesh (where about one-half of the population is vegetarian), or from the bordering regions where Buddhism and Jainism were successful, such as Gujarat and Rajasthan. There, vegetarians account for more than 60 percent of the population. The regions with the lowest instance of vegetarianism are those farthest from this heartland, such as Kerala, Orissa, and West Bengal (all less than 10 percent). These three states are on the coast and distant from the Brahmanic heartland. Anywhere from 6 to 9 percent of West Bengal's population has been estimated to be vegetarian by different surveys. As Figure 3 shows, Andhra Pradesh, Assam, and Tamil Nadu also show low rates of vegetarianism, as do the intermediate states (that is, intermediate between the heartland and the margin), such as Karnataka, Maharashtra, and Bihar (Achaya 1994: 57).

Renunciation of meat is associated with the acquisition of spiritual power, which is part of the complex relationship within Vedic Hinduism between the renouncer and the householder (Dumont 1960; Heesterman 1964; Thapar 1978). Defensive against Buddhist pressures to renounce, the Brahmins of Bengal justified their eating of fish by referring to the authority of the early Vedic literature, which deals with meat eating with equanimity. The twelfth-century scholar Bhatta Bhavadeva says: "All this prohibition is meant for the prohibited days like Chaturdasi and others . . . so it is understood that there is no crime (*dosha*) in eating fish and meat" (Majumdar 1943: 611). The *Brhaddharma Purana* recommends the *rohita, shakula, saphara,* and other fish, which are white and have no scales. Srinathacharya also allowed Bengali Brahmins the consumption of fish and meat except on some *parva* days, and the *hilsa* was particularly popular. Only

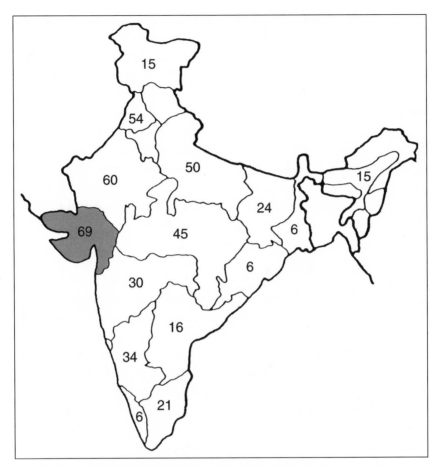

FIGURE 3. *Distribution of Vegetarianism in India. Numbers on the map represent percentages of vegetarians in particular states. The pattern of vegetarianism reflects geography, history, and religion. For example, coastal states, with ready accessibility of fish, tend to be less vegetarian than states in the heartland. In Gujarat (shaded), however, culture triumphs over geography to produce a high rate of vegetarianism.*

raw and dried meat was not allowed to Brahmins, as were onions, garlic, and mushrooms because of their heat-producing qualities.

Achaya (1994: 128) quotes the great Shakta spiritual leader Shri Ramakrishna Paramahansha as saying in 1822:"I love to eat fish in any form." Swami Vivekananda, Shri Ramakrishna's disciple and a very popular figure among Bengali Hindus, is said to have enjoyed a meal that included rice, *shukto, macher jhol,* sour fish curry, sweet yogurt, and *sandesh* (Gupta

1984). In contrast, the Vaishnavites of Bengal were converted to vegetarianism by the evangelical enthusiasm of Shri Chaitanya (A.D. 1486–1533). The Vaishnavites abstain not only from fish and meat but also from such hot foods as onions and *masur* dal. Until about 1900, they eschewed new foods such as potatoes and tomatoes in favor of the traditional *arvi* (colocasia) (Achaya 1994: 128–29).

According to the 1970 survey, rice, wheat flour, non-leafy vegetables, milk, ghee, edible oil, puffed rice, and sliced bread are the items consumed in different amounts in Calcutta's vegetarian and nonvegetarian households. Nonvegetarians appear to consume significantly more rice, puffed rice, and sliced bread than vegetarians, who appear to consume more wheat flour, *chhattu,* pulses, non-leafy vegetables, ghee, and oil.

Life-Cycle Rituals and Seasons

Every major Vedic ritual, from which contemporary Hindu custom is at least partially derived, is a sacrifice that includes cooked food offerings. At the heart of every rite, as Charles Malamoud (1996) contends, is a matter of cooking the world. Every sacrificial operation employs a derivative of "one of the roots signifying 'cook': *PAC* or *SRA* (or one of their partial synonyms, such as *US, GHR, TAP,* or *DAH*)" (Malamoud 1996: 36–37). Agni, the fire god who is also considered the god of the priests and the priest of the gods, presumably stated: "You should not offer by pouring into me that which is raw" (Malamoud 1996: 39).

In cremation, the body is "cooked" for the gods. The sixteen sacraments (or ten, depending on the source) leading up to cremation render the body perfect as an offering to the gods. As shown by Jonathan Parry (1985), a recurrent symbol in Indian mortuary rites is the eating not only on behalf of the deceased by family members and Brahmins, but also some aspect of the deceased by way of *pindas* (balls of rice, barley flour, or *khoa,* a thick paste of reduced milk). On death, the domestic hearth of the bereaved household is extinguished. On the day after cremation, *dudh-bhat* (literally, "milk rice") is shared by the closest agnates of the bereaved family. *Dudh-bhat* is sometimes described as the deceased's first *anna-prasanna* (first taking of rice). This is a recapitulation of a child's first eating of solid food, which also consists of milk and rice. A "food sentence" takes a lifetime to complete, argued Mary Douglas (1977), pointing to the inadequacy of linguistic analysis (Lévi-Strauss notwithstanding), while a sentence can be said in a minute.

Other than mortuary rites and *anna-prasanna*, perhaps the most important rituals are those associated with marriage. In *The Gift of a Virgin* (1994), Lina Fruzzetti provides detailed descriptions of marriage rituals in Bengal (especially rural Bengal). At the heart of the marriage ritual is the chanting of *slokas* in Sanskrit by the officiating Brahmin priest who both feeds the fire with ghee and transforms the bride and groom into contingent deities, calling on family members and ancestors to witness the tying of the knot. The bride and groom fast through the day-long ceremonies after an early-morning meal of *chira* (flattened parboiled rice) and yogurt.

Married women perform numerous rituals at the bride's house that dramatically appropriate food as a symbol. Among others things, the *stri achara* (or women's rites) include blessing of the rice-husking foot paddle, roasting of rice that is fed to the fire god during the Brahmanic ritual, blessing of the hearth, smearing of turmeric on the bride and groom, and presentation of a whole fish to the bride. Fish are potent fertility symbols among both tribal and caste Hindu Indians in eastern India. Matsya, the fish, is an avatar of Vishnu, one of the major deities. It is also one of the eight iconographic symbols of good luck among Hindus. Similarly, an earthenware pot full of unhulled rice with mango leaves and a coconut on top is an explicit wish for prosperity and fertility (Archer 1985: 8–10). When the bride enters her new home, milk kept boiling on the fire is allowed to boil over, symbolizing the wealth of the house; only then is she shown the kitchen and the room of worship. In the last ritual of marriage, *bou-bhat* (literally, "wife rice"), the new wife cooks a meal to which friends and family are invited, marking her acceptance among new kin.

The wedding banquet itself is a sumptuous affair. Into the 1960s and 1970s, Calcuttan banquets were invariably served on banana leaves spread in front of each guest. In all probability, as Chitrita Banerji notes, there would first be *loochi,* to be eaten with sauteed vegetables such as *potol* and eggplant. Next there would be a vegetable stew cooked with the entrails and heads of fish, eaten either with *loochi* or with rice. Then a dal and the fish *kalia* would be served, often with a pilaf of basmati rice cooked in ghee, yellow split peas, and a bouquet garni of garam masala, nutmeg, mace, saffron, and cumin. In wealthy households, the *kalia* and pilaf might be followed by prawn curried in a coconut sauce or *hilsa* in mustard oil. The fish would be followed by various chutneys of tomatoes and green mangoes served with crisp, fried lentil wafers called *papor.* The final course would be *mishti doi* (sweet yogurt) and a variety of cheese-based sweets. A sweet-spiced betel-leaf packet called *paan* brought the curtain down on the banquet.

In the 1970s and 1980s, it became fashionable to serve a goat-meat curry after the fish course. In many households, the sauteed greens and the *chhachra* (stewed vegetable and fish entrails) were dropped from the menu, due partly to changing taste and partly to streamlining by catering companies. The banana-leaf plates have been replaced by china. The pilaf preparation has also become less elaborate. This transformation probably follows concerns about saturated-fat intake, price of expensive spices such as saffron, and matters of convenience. But not all recipes are created equal; thus, the streamlining of the menu is constrained by certain conceptions of appropriate food for the appropriate occasion, as Ronald Inden and Ralph Nicholas (1977: 18–19) show:

> A sharp contrast is drawn in Bengali culture between ordinary cooked
> food . . . on the one hand, and a variety of special foods (e.g., *ghi-bhat,*
> *pakvanna, payas, paramanna*) on the other. Ordinary cooked food—
> boiled rice, lentils, vegetables—is felt to provide for full nourishment
> of a person's body for one day. Persons of a family who live together
> and eat ordinary food on a daily basis are thus thought to obtain full
> and proper nourishment, enabling them to carry out their daily activities. Special cooked food, which is "richer" and lasts longer, is fed to
> *kutumbas* [in-laws]. . . . When gift-giving relatives visit each other,
> they are fed not ordinary cooked food, but special cooked food. Ordinary cooked food, the food of the family, is quickly digested and
> hence suitable only for providing nourishment on a daily basis. Special cooked foods, such as rice prepared with clarified butter (*ghi-bhat,*
> *pakvanna*) or rice cooked with milk and sugar (*payas, paramanna*), are
> thought to be digested slowly and hence to nourish the body over a
> sustained period of time, as between visits.

Life-cycle rituals punctuate our lives from birth through tonsure and marriage to death. There are also seasonal folk customs, with associated foods, that are a mnemonic for the passage of time. The folk calendar is a product of an interweaving of (1) the agricultural cycle, with its rhythms of sowing, weeding, ripening, and harvesting; (2) the Brahmanic tradition of high Hindu holy days; and (3) the various little traditions of saints, *sanyasis,* and goddesses. The Bengali calendar is divided into six seasons: *basanta* (spring); *grishma* (summer); *barsha* (monsoon); *sharat* and *hemanta* (early and late autumn); and *sheet* (winter). No one has written as eloquently on Bengali food and seasonality as Banerji (1997), and I can do no better than paraphrase her here.

The year begins with the month of Baishak in mid-April. This is the time for making spicy pickles, which can be sun-dried through the summer. In Jaishtha, from mid-May to mid-June, the hottest month in the Bengali calendar, Hindus turn to worship their sons-in-law, and "tradition demand[s] a whole head of rui fish for each son-in-law" (Banerji 1997: 67). Every Tuesday in Jaishtha, women fast on a *phalahar* diet of mangoes, bananas, and sweetened yogurt or milk mixed with flattened rice soaked in water to appease the goddess Mangalachandi. "All fish, meat, onions and garlic were forbidden" (Banerji 1997: 62).

The monsoon months of Asharh and Shraban are greeted with *khichuri* (rice and dal cooked with a few spices and vegetables). It is also during the monsoon that the land proliferates with the leafy greens that Bengalis eat in abundance. Some of these greens are cooked with fish, or they are cooked with a rich mix of bay leaves, cumin, chili, turmeric, and coconut to provide a more elaborate alternative. The blossom (*mocha*) and the pith of the banana plant (*thor*) are also eaten.

These are the times par excellence for fish, especially *ilish,* or *hilsa.* The *hilsa* is like salmon: Starting its life in the sea and reaching into the estuarine waters of the Bay of Bengal to spawn, it continues upstream into northern India. *Hilsa* netted during the monsoon are heavy with roe, which is considered an extraordinary delicacy by Bengalis. In season, an affluent Bengali household can develop a whole meal around the *hilsa,* beginning with rice and *daga* (steaks) fried with salt and turmeric (often eaten with bites of fresh green chilies), and finishing off with a *hilsa peti* (fatty stomach portion) in mustard sauce.

Bhadra is the last month of monsoon (mid-August to mid-September), when, "To relieve the aches and pains of monsoon flu, and prevent the monsoon sniffles, many . . . swear by a concoction made with *kalo jeera* or onion seeds" (Banerji 1997: 102–103). Bhadra is also the month in which Lord Krishna's birth is celebrated with particular devotion among the Vaishnavs. For believers, it is a day of complete fasting. In compensation, many sweets

are made on the next day. Banerji mentions one in particular—a creamy
kheer of milk, ripe palm, and grated coconut. The last Hindu festival of
Bhadra is *sankranti,* when Vishwakarma (literally, the maker of the world),
the patron deity of artisans, is worshiped by shutting down business and
extinguishing the hearth. All of the festive foods are prepared the day
before, including sweets and the *hilsa* fish.

After Bhadra come the autumnal seasons of *sharat* and *hemanta,* when
the harvest is ready and Bengalis prepare to welcome the goddess Durga
as a daughter into their homes. Among all the seasons, it is the autumnal
festivals associated with the goddesses Durga, Lakshmi, and Kali that are
the most important for Calcuttan Bengalis. In Banerji's evocative words:

> The hour of the goddesses is now at hand and Bengal awaits them
> expectantly. Stepping daintily on rose-tinted feet, they come, one, by
> one, by one, to be worshipped in a blaze of light and sound and
> colour.
>
> Ashtami, the second day of Durga's visit, is the most important
> day of the festival. In the morning everyone is supposed to fast, bathe
> and go over to the nearest place of worship where the priest chants
> special prayers to the goddess. . . .
>
> Even those who are lax during the year tend to obey the vege-
> tarian restrictions of Ashtami, although these do not mean austerity.
> (Banerji 1997: 107–8)

For lunch, *loochi* is typically served with *alur dam*—a steamed potato curry
lightly flavored with asafetida—and a dal of yellow split peas with bits of
coconut. The Ashtami dinner concludes with *kheer.* "Navami, the last day
of Durga's stay, is gastronomically the opposite of Ashtami; meat-eating is
the order of the day" (Banerji 1997: 112). The meat is cooked in a sauce
of onion and garlic, spiced up with turmeric, yogurt, and garam masala.
The last day of the three-day *puja* is brought up by Bijoya Dashami, the
tenth of the new moon, when the goddess is bid a tearful farewell:

> As the evening deepens, relatives, friends and neighbours drop in to
> convey their Bijoya greetings. They must be offered sweets, which can-
> not be refused. . . . And so the visits go on until the day of the full
> moon, the visitors bringing along more sweets to add to the house-
> hold stock. (Banerji 1997: 116–17)

This autumnal worship of the goddess is one among a multitude of seasonal festivals, but none is more elaborate than this. The autumnal festival comes as a climax to smaller rituals throughout the year.

Durga Puja is quickly followed by Lakshmi Puja and Kali Puja. Durga's daughter Lakshmi is the goddess of wealth. She is associated with Bengali rice pudding called *payas,* which is cooked in milk (a sign of bounty) (Banerji 1997: 120). Two weeks later, Kali is worshiped. Kali Puja leads into the late-autumn months of Kartik and Agrahayan. Agrahayan is the month of harvest of the most important rice crop—*Aman.* In these autumn months, the waters bristle with fish—"small fish like punti, mourala, tangra and bele, the round-bellied pomphret, the pankal, baan and gule of the eel family, shinghi and magur of the catfish family, estuarine delectables like parse, bhetki, bhangar and, of course, the earliest specimens of king prawn, the galda chingri" (Banerji 1997: 127).

In tropical Bengal, the early-winter month of Poush brings in a riot of tender greens and other vegetables, such as *lalshak,* various gourds, eggplant, cauliflower, carrots, tomatoes, beets, cucumbers, spring onions, and cilantro. Poush also brings a folk festival dedicated to the connoisseurship of various kinds of rice-based pancakes called *pithaparban* (literally, the festival of pancakes).

Spring returns with Saraswati Puja—the worship of the other daughter of Durga, the serene, white-draped double of the red and golden Lakshmi. Saraswati is the muse of learning and music. On Saraswati Puja,

> from early morning the house was a bustle of activity as we all got and took turns to bathe and put on fresh clothes. My grandmother, mother and aunts would sit at several *bontis* [a special cutting blade] and slice a huge mound of fruit such as apples, *shakulas, safedas,* which together with bits of sugar-cane, bananas, dates and *kul* (a kind of plum) would be offered to the goddess. (Banerji 1997: 173–74)

The day after Saraswati Puja, a dish called *gotasheddho* is a must. It literally means "boiled whole," and it is a lightly spiced dish of new potatoes in their jackets, green peas in pods, tiny eggplants, and spinach boiled in salted water with green chilies. It is finished by drizzling spoonfuls of pungent mustard oil.

This brings to an end the cycle of seasons and rituals associated with them. There is another important cultural factor that shapes middle-class

Bengali food habits. That is the Bengali notion of "modern" and "traditional" foods and their uses in crafting their identity. It is to that discussion I now turn.

The Modern and the Traditional: The Political Uses of Food

Since the Bengal Renaissance in the beginning of the nineteenth century, food has been an important symbol in the contest between Westernizers and Traditionalists. Many Bengalis have a fond place in their hearts for the iconoclasts of the Young Bengal Movement, such as Henry Vivian Derozio, who, in the early decades of the nineteenth century, relished beef and downed innumerable "pegs" of whiskey and rum in public, to the great consternation of orthodox Hindus (Ghosh 1961; Raychaudhuri 1988). As Tapan Raychaudhuri (1988: 27) notes, "Open defiance of Hindu social convention in matters of food and drink was then considered almost *de rigeur* by the *avant garde* students of the College. To be reckoned a civilized person, one had to eat beef and consume alcohol." Other Bengalis, such as Bhudev Mukhopadhyay, were deeply offended by the exaggerated Anglophilia of the students orbiting around the same mercurial professor at Hindu College, who in response vowed to his father never to eat or drink anything his father disapproved. Bhudev found it nauseating that his college friends ate beef kebabs from Muslim shops and chased it down with whiskey (Raychaudhuri 1988: 30). He blamed the Bengali *babu* for the British stereotype of an educated Bengali as one too eager for an invitation to an Englishman's table. According to his son, Bhudev had the courage to tell his English friends, "If I now eat [with you] in violation of [our] social practice, I shall fall very low in my own eyes for the rest of my life" (cited in Raychaudhuri 1988: 49).

Although the task of closely reading the various nationalist contestations around food awaits its historian, here I intend to provide a flavor of that dispute.[9] The Bengal Renaissance, born in the 1820s, was a complex reaction to the modernist seduction of Westernization and the simultaneous revulsion against the racist assumptions of British imperialism. The Renaissance began as an embrace of British Orientalism, which until the 1870s was sympathetic to Indian "traditions" and engaged in academic research geared toward rediscovering the "glorious" Hindu past. British Orientalists and Calcutta intellectuals such as Raja Rammohun Roy viewed themselves as syncretic modernizers of the Hindu tradition, often attempting to create a monotheistic Hinduism. Nevertheless, by the 1870s British attitudes had shifted to a wholesale condemnation of Hinduism—as shown by the vitriolic pamphlet by the Scottish missionary Reverend William Hastie titled *English Enlightenment and Hindoo Idolatry* (1883). It is only then that the Bengal Renaissance, as represented in figures such as Rajnarayan Basu, took a distinctively nationalist turn. The process was remarkably tortuous, especially for individuals such as Keshub Chandra Sen, who never could abandon his universalism and become a nationalist (Kopf 1969, 1979).

The trajectory from the initial embrace of the West to the eventual distancing from it may be a universal pattern in the contact between the West and the non-West. Samuel Huntington (1996: 76) has argued:

> In the early phases of change, Westernization thus promotes modernization. In the later phases, modernization promotes de-Westernization and the resurgence of indigenous culture in two ways. At the societal level, modernization enhances the economic, military and political power of the society as a whole and encourages the people of that society to have confidence in their culture and to become culturally assertive. At the individual level, modernization generates feelings of alienation and anomie as traditional bonds and social relations are broken and leads to crises of identity to which religion provides an answer.[10]

Withdrawal and reaffirmation of local habits and customs have always been among the elemental reactions to novelties that threaten established verities and routines of life, especially when the contact with the West takes the form of colonization and predatory racism.

Other scholars such as Partha Chatterjee have inverted the sequence, however, and elaborated on the same process in terms that are less self-congratulatory than Huntington's. Chatterjee (1993: 6) contends that

> anticolonial nationalism creates its own domain of sovereignty within colonial society well before it begins its political battle with the imperial power. It does this by dividing the world of social institutions and practices into two domains—the material and the spiritual. The

material is the domain of the "outside," of the economy and of state-craft, of science and technology, a domain where the West had proved its superiority and the East had succumbed. In this domain, then, Western superiority had to be acknowledged and its accomplishments carefully studied and replicated. The spiritual, on the other hand, is an "inner" domain bearing the "essential" marks of cultural identity. The greater one's success in imitating Western skills in the material domain, therefore, the greater the need to preserve the distinctness of one's spiritual culture. This formula is, I think, a fundamental feature of anticolonial nationalisms in Asia and Africa.

According to Chatterjee's reading, everyday practices of food production and consumption were usually considered a part of the "inner"—that is, the spiritual and private domain. In his reading, the private sphere was nationalized *before* the nationalist movement was born in the public sphere.

The process, in fact, is more complicated. Even within the "inner" domain, efforts were made by urban and elite minorities to borrow foreign ideas and adapt them to local use, to the great consternation of conservative critics such as Bhudev Mukhopadhyay (1827–94) and Bankimchandra Chattopadhyay (1938–94). Intellectuals of the Bengal Renaissance, as elites whose imaginations spanned both civilizations, sought creatively to appropriate modernization and established an organization to further that agenda—the Brahmo Samaj.

In its various incarnations, the Brahmo Samaj was the pre-eminent organization of the Bengal Renaissance within whose folds the most important debates of reform and cultural resistance were elaborated through much of the nineteenth century. David Kopf has convincingly argued that modern Bengali *bhadralok* culture was shaped largely in the image of the Brahmo Samaj (Kopf 1979: 313). Since Bengali migrants of the *bhadrasamaj* in the United States continue to draw on the various themes adumbrated by the Bengal Renaissance, I will elaborate a little on their troubled contentions about food.

Members of the Brahmo Samaj were buffeted between the Derozians of Young Bengal, who argued for wholesale Westernization in education, clothing, and diet, and members of the Dharma Sabha (to name just one organization), who sought to retain the influence of Brahmanic Hinduism among Bengali intellectuals. Conservatives such as Aghorechandra Kavyatirtha expressed anxiety with Westernization in the following way:

See the course of *Kaliyuga, dharma* has declined/Vedic ritual and customs have vanished, men and women become the same. . . . [T]he
Shudra will place his foot on the Brahman's head. . . . [T]he son will
disobey the father/the mother will be the servant of her daughter-
in-law. . . . [S]o many factories, impossible to list. (as quoted in Sarkar
1998: 186–87)

At the risk of oversimplification, one could argue that there were at
least three sides to the debate. On one side were post-Orientalist Christian missionaries who belittled Indic traditions and everyday practices,
including Bengali food habits, and were aided in their endeavors, perhaps
inadvertently, by the Derozians of Young Bengal. On the second side were
newly reconstituted "traditionalists" who rejected any criticism of Brahmanic Hinduism, including upper-caste vegetarianism. On the third side
were the Brahmo Samajists, who sought to mediate between what they perceived to be the two extremes—that of Anglophilic meat eating and alcohol consumption on one hand and xenophobic vegetarianism on the other
hand. They represented what Partha Chatterjee has called the hegemonic
"middleness" of the Calcutta middle class who came to construct "new
forms of public discourse, laid down new criteria of social respectability,
[and] set new aesthetic and moral standards of judgment" (Chatterjee 1992).

Intellectuals of the Bengal Renaissance were struggling to create a
paradigmatic dietary model for a modernizing Bengali between these two
extremes. In an internal polemic, the Sadharan Brahmos—a fragment of
the Brahmo Samaj—editorialized against the charge of blindly aping the
West brought on by the "traditionalists": "No doubt that our girls dine [at]
tables and use spoons and forks but it is because they find it convenient
and decent to do so" (as quoted in Kopf 1979: 40). The vital concern about
meat was brought up in the same editorial and defended not as a food that
would de-nationalize the women but as one that "makes them healthy and
civilized members of society."

Nevertheless, the habits of Sadharan Brahmos, who creatively appropriated non-indigenous food practices within the paradigm of Bengali traditions, contrasted radically with the practice of figures such as Ishwar
Chandra Vidyasagar, a leading intellectual of the Bengal Renaissance, who
was a rationalist social reformer and atheist and yet dressed, ate, and acted
according to orthodox Hindu norms. Bengali intellectuals developed a
whole range of strategies to solve the problem of what to eat. Some, such

as the Sadharan Brahmos, appropriated English etiquette while consuming Bengali food. Others, such as Vidyasagar, rejected everyday customs of the English while appropriating atheism, and Keshub Chandra Sen practiced a sophisticated dualism, eating in Bengali style in the quiet of his home and following English etiquette in the presence of Europeans and Americans.

Bankimchandra Chattopadhyay, the first and arguably best novelist of nineteenth-century Bengal, struggled with his dietary norm. He would eventually convert to vegetarianism (in 1885) and become the most eloquent defender of the Brahmanic tradition in theory, but in practice his life was a mixed bag. In the early part of his adult life not only did he appropriate the knife and fork into his repertoire of etiquette; he also looked down on the Bengali way of eating with "one's fingers as an uncivilized practice" (Raychaudhuri 1988: 123). It is reported that he finally gave up the pretense when faced with a particularly intractable *koi* fish and his wife's mockery (Ray 1979: 35, 38, 178; Raychaudhuri 1988: 123). Nevertheless, this theorist of ascetic Hindu virtues (in his exemplary work *Dharmatatva*), remained a moderate drinker all his life in spite of his wholehearted appropriation of Victorian Puritanism (once complaining about the "erotic venom" that the Tagores had introduced into Bengali literature).

Debendranath Tagore, another prominent figure of the Bengal Renaissance, rebelled against his own Anglicized background and gave up meat, wine, and most of the "luxurious tastes" acquired from his father. He went so far as to purify himself by bathing in the Ganges after dining with Europeans on the occasion of Durga Puja. In 1905, another Brahmo, Brahmobandhab Bhawani Charan, allegedly reconverted to Hinduism by eating cow dung, publicly declaring that "we must preserve the integrity and distinctiveness of Hindu society at any cost" (as quoted in Kopf 1979: 213). Yet when Bijoy Krishna Goswami, one of the most successful Brahmo missionaries in the *mofussil* (provincial) towns of eastern and northern Bengal, was disturbed about eating meat and fish, Debendranath Tagore consoled him that if he could "kill bedbugs and mosquitoes, why not eat meat and fish?" (as quoted in Kopf 1979: 220).

Among proto-nationalist reformers a consensus emerged that political exclusion could not be countered without reconstructing the Hindu home. The author of a tract on "domestic science" around 1869 wrote that "food soaked in ghee or oil, sweets and unripe fruit are all like poison to the child" and that a great nation cannot be erected on the bodies of weak children who are effectively being poisoned by their "uneducated" mothers (Bandyopadhyay 1869, as cited in Chakrabarty 1997: 378). A number of such tracts by both men and women called for the improvement of Bengali women so that the Bengali home could stand up to the comparison with the "scientific" British home and its daily norms. As Dipesh Chakrabarty (1997: 377) has concluded from a study of numerous essays on the Bengali home at this time:

> The internal "discipline" of "the European home" was now seen as a key to European prosperity and political power. Bengali books on "domestic science" extolled the "attractive" qualities of "the house of any civilized European," which was now compared to the "abode of the gods." It was a place where *srinkhala* (discipline) reigned, things were clean, attractive, and placed in order. The Bengali/Indian home ... suffered badly in comparison. It was said to be like hell—dirty, smelly, disorderly, unclean, and unhealthy.

There were many who regretted the decline of traditional Hindu domestic routine. Once again "modern" Bengali women—that is, the women of the 1870s—were blamed for their attention to education at the cost of the household. Some, such as Bhudev, however, put the blame on the non-Aryan element in the Bengali, which allegedly made him particularly vulnerable to mimicry, especially in the pursuit of immediate pleasures of the palate. It is nevertheless important to note that Bhudev and other so-called conservatives, such as Bankim, were far more trenchant and clear-eyed than Brahmos in their critique of English racism and imperial arrogance. In a fascinating lesson on comparative imperialisms with some relevance to our subject matter, for instance, Bhudev astutely noted that Latin imperialists—the Portuguese, Spanish, and French—were more cruel than the English (because they were less constrained by the rule of law) yet allowed the possibility that other "races," if they converted to their religion, dress, diet, and customs, could become like the colonizers. In contrast, the Englishman's attitude was: "You are not English. If you want to copy my religion, my codes, manners, language, dress, etc. go ahead and do so. But you can never be an equal, for it is I who am English; you are not" (Mukhopadhyay 1904: 99, as quoted in Raychaudhuri 1988: 70). Hence, Bhudev could not understand why any Bengali would mimic the everyday aspects of the English lifestyle and deeply regretted the decline of traditional patterns of behavior even among intelligent Bengalis, such as

Michael Madhusudhan Dutt, Bengal's best known epic poet and a contemporary figure in the Bengal Renaissance.

In the regret for the demise of the old order there appeared a consistent concern about changing meal times. In 1823, Bhabanicharan Bandyopadhyay, a prominent journalist and social commentator in early colonial Calcutta, wrote *Kalikata Kamalalaya* in the form of a dialogue between a Calcuttan and a newcomer from the country. Referring to the newly emergent practice of eating breakfast, the unnamed newcomer asks, "Is it true that Calcuttans eat too early and leave home early to work in British firms, spend the entire day working, return home late and retire immediately after the evening meal?" He continues:

> They have abandoned the dhoti and have taken to wearing tunic, pants, and black leather boots that come in all different shapes ... complete with shoelaces. . . . They would employ any stranger that came along and claimed to be of the Brahmin race. . . . Their speech is a mixture of their own language and those of foreign races. (as quoted in Chakrabarty 1997: 388)

In his 1874 essay *Se kal ar e kal,* Rajnarayan Basu repeats the complaint about the rushed morning meal, which, he says, is "not at all suited to this country" (as quoted in Chakrabarty 1997: 395). Basu's contemporary Bhudev elaborates in *Achar prabandha,* an essay on Hindu domesticity:

> It is the first half of the third part of the day, i.e. from 9 to 10:30 [A.M.] that is the time [assigned in the scriptures] for work related to the earning of one's livelihood. How different our circumstances are now from those of the ancients! One and a half hours' work was [once] sufficient to enable one to earn money. Nowadays even twenty-four hours do not seem enough. . . . These days the salaried people are forced to have their [midday] meal between 9 and 10:30 so that they can be at work on time. Many of them, therefore, have to complete their afternoon and evening prayers in the morning. (as quoted in Chakrabarty 1997: 395)

Worse sins would lie ahead, as we shall see. For Bengali migrants, the dietary issues they confront today were addressed in energetic disputations in the lives of the intellectuals of the Bengal Renaissance. The issues were never really resolved, and American Bengalis can and do draw on the great debate between Bengali modernizers and traditionalists of the nineteenth century to justify their conflicting choices between the traditional dinner and the modern breakfast and, especially, their consumption of taboo items such as beef and alcohol.

C ooking is where culture meets nature. Bengalis have shaped their cuisine within the ecological limits of their land, which they have transformed in turn to yield what they seek from it. In the process, they have crafted a pattern of eating that, through repetition, they have turned into a norm, and its distinctive ingredients, methods of cooking, spices, and signature dishes have come to embody Bengaliness. They have developed skills to replicate the norm and invent new ways to feed their hunger. Cooking is never just about nutrition. Bengalis have loaded the process of cooking and eating with meanings about "meals," kinship, family, and communion. All human practices change, and every human community thus defines what is traditional and what is modern. It is these norms, skills, and aspirations that Bengalis bring to the problem of eating in the context of the New World.

CHAPTER 3

Bengali-American
Food Consumption

Memory is Hunger.
ERNEST HEMINGWAY, *A MOVEABLE FEAST* (1996: 57)

*When from a long-distant past nothing subsists, after the people are
dead, after the things are broken and scattered, still, alone, more fragile,
but with more vitality, more unsubstantial, more persistent, more faith-
ful, the smell and taste of things remain poised a long time, like souls,
ready to remind us, waiting and hoping for their moment, amid the
ruins of all the rest; and bear unfaltering, in the tiny and almost im-
palpable drop of their essence, the vast structure of recollection.*
MARCEL PROUST, *SWANN'S WAY* (1934: 36)

B reakfast for almost every Bengali-American interlocutor is milk and
dry cereal or toast. Lunch consumed at or near the workplace is a
slice of pizza, sometimes a sandwich. In contrast, dinner remains
the realm of "tradition," where there is still a literal truth to the question
asked by a Bengali: "Have you had rice?" when she means "Have you eaten?"

Although changes in breakfast and lunch are moving in the same direction, these meals have different stories to tell. Breakfast is eaten at home,
lunch at work; one meal is taken in the privacy of the home, the other
in the public sphere; one begins the day, the other bisects it. Both reflect
global trends that are making the world the same place. Then there is dinner, which stems these homogenizing tides of change. Dinner puts us back
in our places by dropping the curtain on the workday, that most modern
fragment of our daily lives.

In this chapter, I will catalogue the answers to a few empirical questions, such as: What do Bengali Americans eat? How is that different from the Calcuttan meal cycle? And how does that compare with typical "American" patterns? Only after answering these questions can we move to the more complicated questions of why.

Breakfast: Toast and Cereal

On weekdays, four out of five Bengali-American households eat breakfast between 7 and 8 A.M.; the rest eat between 6 and 7 A.M. This is early by traditional Calcuttan middle-class standards. Nineteenth-century Bengali reformers pointed to the abnormal tendency of having an early breakfast and explained it by way of what they thought was the ridiculous "modern" necessity of working through the whole day, when a decent Bengali gentleman "in the past" could have easily supported his family by a few hours of work in a day. Migration has only accentuated what was considered quite "bad" almost 200 years ago. Higher consumption expectations, greater efficiency, and longer commutes have made a bad situation worse and moved breakfast even earlier for many.

In Bengali households in the United States, the typical weekday breakfast of toast or dry cereal with milk gives way on weekends to homemade or frozen flat breads (*rooti*) with vegetable curry or eggs, pancakes, and toast. Such distinctions between the workweek and the weekend are one aspect of the relentless march of modernity, when "natural" rhythms are replaced by the unforgiving toll of modern work schedules. In response, human societies have excavated an old relic—the sabbath—and invested it with new meaning. So have Bengalis in the United States.

More than one-half of the Bengali-American households surveyed said that breakfast has changed substantially since migration. The reasons listed were convenience, pressures of time, and changing taste. In Calcutta in 1970, about 50 percent of all households ate different kinds of homemade flat bread with a vegetable curry for breakfast. Hardly any Bengali-American families have the time or inclination for such an elaborate breakfast on a weekday. However, 31 percent of all households in Calcutta in 1970 consumed sliced raised bread, eaten as toast, as a typical breakfast. That figure has increased to 50 percent among Bengalis in America.[1]

Toast is a metonym for the modern and the Western. The trend lines to modernity appear to have been hastened a little for Bengalis in this most modern of the modern world—the United States. Yet it can be argued that they have remained the same if we include the food habits of only upper-class Bengalis.

What else has changed? About 15 percent of upper-middle-class households in Calcutta in 1970 consumed a cereal for breakfast—*moori* (puffed rice) or *chira* (flattened parboiled rice) with milk and bananas (or mangoes in summer). This figure has jumped to almost 50 percent since emigration. The transition to industrialized cereal is eased by the habit of consuming cereals before emigration. Nevertheless, very few Bengalis appear to choose the cereal closest to the Calcuttan favorite—Rice Crispies. Instead, cornflakes are the most popular cereal among Bengali Americans. An element of prestige and association with modernity comes with the alien corn and its industrially extruded flakes.

Evidently, not everything in the breakfast has changed in the same direction. Tea continues to be the drink of choice for those who consume a hot beverage with breakfast in three out of five Bengali-American households. Like the British, Bengalis drink their tea with cream and sugar. Is this a colonial's reprise of the imperial gesture in a tiny cup: Tea from China and sugar from the New World, anchored by that Northern European comfort food, milk? Perhaps.

Only one in five has taken to the new beverage, coffee—*the* drink of bourgeois modernity, and surely *American* modernity (Schivelbusch 1993).[2] In 1970, there was hardly any consumption of coffee in Calcutta. Some exceptional elite households did serve instant coffee, but more as a late-afternoon beverage than as an early-morning stimulant. Coffee in Calcutta has an aristocratic and languorous association, with none of the hurried bourgeois affiliations it has acquired in the United States. You drink coffee in Calcutta to mark a special moment, an occasion, a get-together, not to get a hurried fix for a working day's distracting appetite.

Bengali-American children are served neither tea nor coffee, which are considered strictly adult drinks, much as they are in Calcutta. Fruit juices are the most popular children's early-morning drinks. Almost 50 percent of Bengali-American households consume a piece of fruit or a glass of juice daily, in contrast to only about 22 percent of upper-class Calcuttan households.

Milk is the other major constituent of upper-class Calcuttan meals, with 69 percent of households consuming some milk daily, although only 39 percent of upper-class households consumed milk at breakfast. The proportion of households consuming milk for breakfast has doubled between the Calcuttan elite and their expatriate brethren. It is in affluence, convenience (with refrigeration), and the Vedic valorization of milk that we must seek the reasons for that transformation. Fruit and milk are expensive items associated with status, and as the capacity to pay for them increases, so does consumption. Nevertheless, breakfast figures have more to do with convenience and the changing nature of breakfasts everywhere in the world than anything else. Upper-class Calcuttans in 1970 consumed an average of 109 grams of milk per capita daily (about half of that with breakfast, and the other half with dinner); Bengali Americans consumed almost three times as much milk daily, mostly at breakfast. But if we consider elite vegetarians in Calcutta (435 out of 2,392 affluent people in a sample size of 13,570), we see that they consume about the same amount of milk as nonvegetarian Bengali Americans.

About 50 percent of the respondents stated that their breakfast did not change subsequent to migration. They correctly pointed to toast and cereal as the primary exemplars of continuity (Table 8, Appendix 2).

Lunch and Dinner: Rice and Fish

About 90 percent of the respondents claimed that lunch has changed radically, especially for those who work outside the home. For them, lunch is often a slice of pizza or a sandwich, maybe a burrito or a hamburger. Very few take packed lunches to work, but those who do usually carry leftovers or typical cold-cut-and-cheese sandwiches, often with an eclectic twist of chopped green chilies or onions.

For those who identified themselves as full-time "housewives" (one-third of the female respondents), lunch usually consisted of rice-based leftovers from dinner or soup and a sandwich.[3] Most of these women belonged to a group (10 percent of the respondents) who claimed that lunch has not changed since emigration. On rare occasions, some of them said, they eat a salad—quite a dramatic change, because most Bengali Americans (three out of five) do not find salads filling or satisfying as a meal.

For most of the respondents it appears, as it does to Arun in Anita Desai's novel *Fasting, Feasting,* that "slices of tomatoes and leaves of lettuce—in his time in America he has developed a hearty abhorrence for the raw foods everyone here thinks the natural diet of a vegetarian" (Desai 2000: 167, 184–85).

Eventually, people assimilate. Preference for salads increases over generations. Nevertheless, for the first generation, salads are not food. In some ways, the Bengali attitude toward salad is not very different from that of Jewish immigrants almost 100 years ago. The protagonist in Anzia Yezierska's novel *Bread Givers* (1927), identifies "spinach and salad" as quintessential American eating.[4] Americans themselves, however, often identified these items as "French."

The most common lunch in Calcutta among the upper middle class in 1970 was rice, dal, vegetable curry, and fish. That is not the lunch that most Bengali Americans eat. But, as we shall see, they eat along similar lines at dinner.

Dinner has become the most important and valorized meal for Bengali Americans, although that was not the case for Calcuttans. Eighty-five percent of Bengali-American respondents claimed that dinner is the most important meal of the day, mostly because it is the only meal that all members of the household eat together. Many claimed that dinner is important because it is the only *Bengali* meal of rice and fish, and some underlined its importance as the most "relaxed meal."

This is the other side of the decay of breakfast and lunch as commensal meals. As modern work schedules have made breakfast and lunch less important, dinner has moved to the center of the re-enactment of ethnicity and "culture." Thus, it is not surprising that two out of three respondents claimed that dinner has not changed since migration.

Most Bengali Americans eat dinner an hour or two later than middle-class Americans and an hour or two earlier than their Calcuttan cousins. Recall the early nineteenth-century commentator who prescribed a midnight meal for a decent Bengali *bhadralok* (see Chapter 2).

One striking feature of dinner is that about 55 percent of Bengali-American households serve rice every day, and most serve it at least three days a week. One second-generation female respondent was the only exception, consuming rice only about twice a month—close to the Anglo-American standard. She usually prefers pasta. This is one of the spheres where a dramatic difference will open between the generations. Children often prefer pasta and hamburger sandwiches to rice and fish. Adult second-generation members are typically equivocal about their choices among rice, pasta, and bread, but for *first*-generation Bengali Americans, pasta and bread are not considered filling staples.

Equally interesting is the rate of consumption of fish. About 40 percent of households serve fish three times a week or more. Forty percent more serve it once or twice a week. Only about 10 percent eat it rarely. In other words, almost half of the respondents consume fish at a rate that would be considered exceptional by any mainstream Anglo-American household. Equally striking is that half of the households that consume fish prefer to buy it whole rather than filleted or in steaks—something that distinctively marks a Bengali. The Bengali American's portion size of fish has also almost doubled, perhaps in keeping with the greater importance of animal protein in American cuisine and rising incomes.

Bengalis in Bengal prefer freshwater fish. Almost 80 percent of the catch in West Bengal is from inland waters, and there is a common prejudice against saltwater fish that is probably related to Hindu taboos about the sea. Nevertheless, the most popular kinds of fish among Bengali Americans are catfish, shrimp (considered a fish in the Bengali lexicon), salmon, carp, shad, trout, whitefish, *hilsa,* orange roughy, perch, cod, smelt, *rohu,* bass, red snapper, butterfish, and flounder, in that order of preference. The typical whole "fish" are shrimp, trout, perch, smelt, butterfish, and red snapper. *Hilsa* and *rohu* are the typical Indian fish bought by almost 10 percent of households from Asian specialty stores.

Bengalis also dress their fish differently from Americans. Steaks are a close approximation to some of the cuts, but Bengalis (like the Japanese) are more particular. As the cookbook author and commentator Chitrita Banerji describes:

> Once the head and the tail together with the last . . . 4–5 in. of the body are removed and set aside, the cook decides which portion of the body will be used for the *jhol*. The body of the fish is cut lengthwise, the front or stomach portion being called the *peti* and the back being called the *daga*. The *peti* is preferred for almost any dish since it is oilier and tastier, but the bony *daga* is ideal for the medium of the *jhol*. Whatever the portion chosen, it is then cut horizontally into

pieces . . . 3/4–1 in. in thickness. Since most families are unable to buy
a whole fish, it is common in Bengali markets for the fishmonger to
portion his fish and to cut it to specifications of the client. (Banerji
1997: 46)

It is next to impossible to get the fish cut in that particular way in the
United States unless one buys it from, say, a Bangladeshi store in New York
City. Even if a whole fish is bought, it is difficult to carve in the preferred
way using a handheld knife; a special kind of Bengali cutting implement
called a *bonti* is required. The *bonti* cannot be used without squatting on
the floor, and in most American kitchens, that is awkward and inconven-
ient. For some Bengalis, the transition from the floor to the countertop is
less a sign of willing Americanization than a grudging reorientation to a
new domestic architecture. Others are willing to sacrifice a little in taste
for the convenience of countertop slicing and dicing.

Rice and fish are considered quintessentially Bengali. From marriage
rituals to mortuary rites, rice and fish anchor a Bengali. Both rice and fish
are consumed in the United States with a frequency that is foreign not only
to mainstream Americans but also to Calcutta Bengalis (especially for dinner). The average upper-class Calcuttan typically eats rice every day of the
week for lunch, along with dal, vegetables (curried or sauteed), and one
two-ounce slice of fish in a curried sauce. (The average per capita daily
consumption of fish for the highest-expenditure household in Calcutta in
1970 was about 60 grams, or 2.118 ounces). If we adjust for upper-class
consumption patterns in Calcutta, the proportion of households consuming fish for dinner does not exceed one-third. In contrast, almost half of
Bengali-American households eat fish at dinner on an average weekday.

Thus, the traditional lunch has vanished for Bengali Americans, and rice
and fish have migrated from lunch to dinner. For dinner, 81 percent of all
Calcuttan households serve *rooti* (71 percent for the upper class) with dal,
curried vegetables, and sometimes a glass of milk. Some of them serve both
rooti and rice as the principal staples. *Rooti* has been replaced by rice as the
carbohydrate anchor of dinner in the United States. Clearly, the reason is
convenience. *Rooti* is probably the most labor-intensive ingredient of a
meal, and its preparation is typically assigned to servants among middle-
class Calcuttans. In the absence of servants, *rooti* has effectively vanished from
Bengali-American meals.

Given that pattern, a better comparison would be between Calcuttan lunches and Bengali-American dinners. Table 9 (Appendix 2) shows that Bengali Americans have effectively transformed Calcuttan lunches into expatriate dinners while adding more meats, pasta, and salads, which are all second-generation preferences.

The Daily Cycle of Meals

Earlier I said that, while breakfast has dramatically changed for Bengali Americans, dinner has remained "traditional." Now it is time to complicate that claim. It is an exaggeration to say that dinner remains wholly "Bengali" in any meaningful sense. It would be more accurate to argue that dinner is *perceived* to have remained traditional while in reality significant changes have occurred. To illustrate that argument, I provide a seven-day menu for a family of five in Appendix 3 and a thumbnail sketch here.

Take, for instance, the appetizer for the Saturday night dinner listed in Appendix 3—ground turkey *pokora* (croquettes) with cilantro (coriander leaf). Turkey is hardly a traditional Bengali ingredient, yet it is cooked in a typically Bengali form—*pokora*—with ground turkey replacing ground goat meat. Any meat in Bengali cuisine is usually cooked with the trinity of wet spices—onion, ginger, and garlic. This is so in the case of the *pokora*.

The cilantro in the *pokora* provides a glimpse of the syncretic twist in the repertoire. It appears not only in the croquettes on Saturday night but also as an herb in the dal on Monday and in the fish curry on Tuesday. Although cilantro is a popular South Indian herb, it rarely appears as regularly in Bengali cuisine as it does in the food of the household discussed here. Just as the turkey in the *pokora* hints at a process of creolization on a global scale, the use of cilantro suggests the making of a syncretic national Indian cuisine in the diaspora.[5] Much like diasporic Hinduism, a pan-Indian cuisine is emerging among expatriate communities (Vertovec 1995).

Then there is the more explicit intermingling of American and Bengali cuisines on Thursday night, when the menu is roast chicken legs, steamed rice, American-style salad, sauteed bittermelon, grapes, and apple juice. Monday's repertoire (steamed rice, curried shrimp, and a mixed-vegetable stew) is typically Bengali—with the exception of strawberry shortcake and grape juice. On Wednesday, the menu features ground beef simulating goat meat. On Friday, dinner is at Red Lobster—hardly a classical Bengali option.

Nevertheless, there is a pervasive Bengaliness in all this mixing up. Rice continues to be the core of the meal. The animal protein—usually two large pieces of fish or a small portion of meat (small by American standards)—is important but remains a (relatively) fringe item in terms of the calorie contribution to the whole meal. The complex-carbohydrate core and the animal-protein fringe is paired with the third defining element—dal. The legume soup is sparsely spiced, often with a few roasted cumin seeds. The animal-protein fringe, in contrast, is highly spiced, as is typical in Bengali cuisine.

The spices and herbs are drawn mostly from within the Bengali repertoire of turmeric, mustard, *panch phoron,* cumin, coriander seed, onion, ginger, and garlic. The processes of cooking are also limited to sauteing and stewing or braising—basic Bengali notions of "cooking."

Further, we see the greatest change in the elements that are peripheral to the Bengali conception of the "meal"—that is, turkey replacing goat meat in the appetizer, juices and soda replacing water, and strawberry shortcake simulating *sandesh* (a dessert made from farmer cheese). It is perhaps because the most radical changes are confined to the accompaniments to the meal—the drinks, the dessert, and the appetizer—that the "meal" as such can still be defined as Bengali. Hence, in spite of rampant creolization of ingredients, dinner is perceived as the realm of traditional Bengali cuisine.

What might encourage the perception of the Bengaliness of dinner is that it is truly so, though in a peculiar way. In fact, dinner for Bengali Americans in the United States is perhaps even more determinedly Bengali than a typical Calcuttan's dinner in terms of both the frequency of consumption of rice and fish and the quantities consumed.

Perhaps a Bengali would not be a Bengali without consuming rice and fish in one of the main meals of the day. As dinner has come to be the most important home-cooked meal, Bengali Americans feel compelled to partake of ingredients (and cooking techniques) that anchor their Bengaliness—steamed rice and fish *jhol.* Thus, we can conclude that dinner has changed in two directions: new ingredients, such as turkey, have been absorbed into the old culinary paradigms; and the use of old constituents, such as rice and fish, is insisted on. One absorbs change, and the other reiterates tradition.

As shown earlier, breakfast has changed equally dramatically, but in other directions.[6] The primary reason is convenience. Yet convenience cannot carry the weight of the whole argument. If convenience were the only concern, dinner should have changed equally dramatically, because a Bengali dinner is more demanding than breakfast on a woman's labor. Yet to serve Western food for dinner would be equivalent to serving sandwiches for supper in an Anglo-American household—not a "proper meal," as Mary Douglas learned from her household (Douglas 1975: 249–50).

With breakfast and dinner, Bengalis appear to have divided the day into what they characterize as moments of modernity and moments of tradition, both perceived as good and necessary in their separate places. This duality toward the "modern" and the "traditional"—the former imagined as embodied in something as mundane as breakfast cereal and the latter embodied in rice and fish—is central to the identity of the *bhadrasamaj*. The Bengali *bhadrasamaj* has long been both threatened and seduced by the promise of modernization and has acted on those concerns in organizing its food practices in the United States.

Octavio Paz, who spent almost a decade in India as Mexico's ambassador, has noted that middle-class Indians have an ambiguous relationship to their past (who doesn't?), seeing it as an obstacle to modernity, yet exalting it in the hopes of salvaging its strengths (Paz 1997: 80). For Indians, the future to be realized implies a critique of the past. In contrast, argues Paz, the United States was founded "on the notion of creating a common future. To be an American is to turn one's past into a quaint holdover while focusing almost exclusively on the future. In the U.S. the past of each of its ethnic groups is a private matter, the country itself has no past" (Paz 1997: 79–80). Bengali Americans are in the process of becoming Americans by privatizing their ethnicity. In individualistic societies, the private sphere displaces the public, and food—especially food at home—provides a convenient locus of a privatized identity for Bengalis in an American world.

This separation of the "modern" public sphere and the "traditional" private sphere is also a construct of the nationalist discourse, as pointed out by Partha Chatterjee (1993). Breakfast faces outward into the public sphere, preparing the Bengali to head into the American world. Dinner faces inward, marking the time of rest and recuperation and leading eventually to the bedroom, the sanctum sanctorum of the bourgeois home. Breakfast and dinner are liminal daily rituals that mark the boundaries of the two worlds—one individualized and industrialized, the other communal and artisanal.

There are a few other points to be made about pre- and post-immigration meal patterns. First, the average Calcuttan consumes two principal and two supplementary meals a day from the household kitchen. In contrast, on a weekday the average Bengali American consumes only one supplemental (breakfast) and one principal meal (dinner) from the household kitchen. Lunch is eaten at work for those who work outside the home, and leftovers make up the meal for those who work at home.

Second, the late-afternoon snack is much less pervasive in the United States. That is, it does not have a fixed menu. Most Bengali Americans have a cup of tea when they return from wage work along with a cookie, a piece of fruit, or puffed rice with a spicy mix of fried dals and nuts. Often this supplemental snack is consumed in front of the TV, usually while watching the local news. As it does in Calcutta, the snack marks the transition from the world into the home (here underlined dramatically by the news on TV) and from the individualized lunch to the collective dinner by way of food that is consumed in the presence of other family members but not eaten with them.

Third, Bengali Americans' menus vary much more dramatically than do Calcuttans' between workday and weekend. On weekends, the breakfast becomes more elaborate and is often cooked rather than served cold; lunch becomes more Bengali; and a few American inflections are added to dinner, such as desserts. Sometimes on weekends, dinner is eaten out at a restaurant. This is an intriguing inversion, where normal weekday dinners point toward the private sphere; Sunday dinners look out toward the workweek.

Fourth, the Calcuttan menu changes more dramatically than the Bengali-American menu over the seasons, primarily for reasons of availability, price, lack of refrigeration, and the cycle of the local growing season. Generally speaking, summer (April–June) prices are higher than winter (December–January) prices in the Calcutta market. In particular, perishable food items such as fish, vegetables, and fruit are available at a lower price in winter in Calcutta. In general, American markets, following a temperate growing cycle, have more perishables available in the spring and summer than in the winter months. As incomes are generally low and food prices are high in Calcutta, seasonal fluctuations in price become more important there than in the United States. Furthermore, because of slower transportation systems and lack of refrigeration, Calcutta markets are much more localized than the metropolitan American markets. In contrast, greater disposable income, cheaper food, industrialization of the food industry, the power of the dollar, and more efficient market systems have helped

Bengalis smother the seasonal cycle in the United States. Thus, while tighter work schedules and greater constraints on time increase the variation in Bengali-American menus over the week, larger purses and more efficient markets decrease seasonal variations.

Seasonal and Life-Cycle Rituals

We witness a complex process of selection, syncopation, and elaboration of seasonal and life-cycle rituals by Bengali Americans. Everyday rituals associated with the seasons but unrelated to high Brahmanic rites have decayed dramatically. On the American landscape it would be difficult to replicate the Bengali association of the first day of the monsoon season—barsha—with khichuri (stewed rice, dal, and vegetables), or eat the short-lived ata fruit (called cheremoy in American supermarkets) as a marker of autumn. The ritual preparation of the pickled table mustard called kasundi on the third day after the new moon of the month of Baishak is effectively dead among Bengali Americans, as are almost all forms of pickle making. Nevertheless, this trend was already visible among Calcuttan Bengalis in the 1970s, and none of my respondents made pickles at home either before or after migration. Much of that skill has eluded them.

Foods associated with barsha—the monsoon season—are difficult to transplant because of the changed seasonal context, although on a few wet evenings in America Bengali-American women cook khichuri. This has been turned into an aesthetic rather than a strictly seasonal marker of the passage of time. It is on such days that the ilish is missed sorely but compensated for with a piece of salmon. But just because some practices have decayed in the new context does not mean that they have been forgotten. Past rituals have sedimented sensory and emotional experiences in the body, evoking much nostalgia, especially of the ideal kind that generates "narratives of gemeinschaft" (Sutton 2001: 54).

The autumnal festival of Durga Puja is the most important seasonal/ sacred ritual that reinserts the Bengali American in the Bengali calendar. According to tradition, the Ashtami meal was vegetarian for all the households I observed, and Navami was marked by a meat stew. Bijoya Dashami was important for the older generation, and there was much exchange of sweets and rounds of visiting. Kali Puja, which closely follows Durga Puja, was conducted in the basement of one household to which a number of other families were invited. Another household marked the coming of spring with Saraswati Puja, and the offering to the goddess, as per tradition, was mostly fruit.

In general, it appears that secular rituals and folk rites associated with "little traditions" have eroded faster than Brahmanic rites. Some scholars, such as Timothy Smith, have noted that migration intensifies the psychic basis of religious commitment because of "loneliness, the romanticizing of memories, the guilt for imagined desertion of parents and other relatives, and the search for community and identity in a world of strangers" (Smith 1978: 1174). At moments of crisis, the annual round of religious observances provides needed comfort. Oscar Handlin noted the same pattern almost half a century ago when he wrote in *The Uprooted*:

> The more thorough the separation from other aspects of the old life, the greater was the hold of religion that alone survived the transfer. Struggling against heavy odds to save something of the old ways, the immigrants directed into their faith the whole weight of their longing to be connected with the past. (Handlin 1951: 105–6)

It is arguably the classic American way to eventually abandon language, food, and lifestyle but to retain one's religious identity. It remains to be seen whether Bengalis will replicate that pattern. But we do see a subtle theologizing of Hindu Bengali Americans. That is in all probability why the Brahmanic rituals have retained their coherence over secular or folk ones. Sacred things are by their nature denser than profane routines; thus, they take longer to unravel. Sometimes they never really unravel but are adapted to the new context and given a new coherence.

New secular rituals have also been appropriated by Bengali Americans. Among them, the North American Bengali Conference (NABC) is perhaps the most interesting and important. In creating an institution such as the NABC, Bengali Americans have invented a new seasonal ritual, held annually on the Fourth of July weekend in an American or a Canadian city. The conference is typically a three- to four-day affair. In 1994, it was attended by about 5,000 Bengali Americans, and by the year 2000, attendance had doubled. The conference is held in a large hotel or at a convention center in a major city that can accommodate a gathering of this size. It requires enough space not only for panel discussions and staged theaters but also for a continuous bazaar of saris, books, music, and software programs.

This yearly gathering of Bengali families in North America was initiated in 1981. For years, it was preceded by regional events organized by Bengalis in the major metropolitan regions, such as Kallol of New Jersey, which was established in 1975 and organized the first Durga Puja in 1977. It was in the mid-1970s—about a decade after the new immigrants started entering the United States—that most Bengali regional organizations were formed. Today, most of these organizations, which list anywhere from 200 to 1,000 households each, are quite active in religious and linguistic–cultural activities such as language schools for children. The climax of the long process of institutional formation and the yearly cycle of festivals is marked by the NABC on the weekend of the Fourth of July. In the year 2000, the conference was held in Atlantic City.

Throughout the three- to four-day festival, one finds linked together what Victor Turner (1986: 42) has characterized as sacred and secular rituals, dance, song, architectural symbolism, ritualized feasting, and the enacting of mythic or heroic plots drawn from the written and oral tradition. The repertoire for most of the music and dance dramas at the NABC is derived from the work of Rabindranath Tagore and Kazi Nazrul Islam. About 80 percent of the performances are amateur; the rest are performed by troupes from West Bengal and from the largest metropolitan areas in North America. Every evening leads to a finale of professional performances that runs late into the night (midnight to 2 A.M.). By this time, many of the younger children are asleep in the hotel rooms. The older children attend their own English-language programs, which include debates, quizzes, and charades, ending in a dance social with disc-jockey mixes of Bhangra, Bombay film music, and Indo-rap. This is one of the few moments when children age ten and older are left unsupervised by Bengali parents, who are otherwise known to be overly protective.

There is much sartorial display, too. About 10 percent of men wear traditional Bengali upper-class attire of strikingly white, starched *dhooti-punjabi*—a wrapped, unstitched garment worn under a long shirt. Another 10 percent put on a *kurta* (long shirt) over a pair of trousers. The latter, common attire for middle-class men on Calcutta streets, is convenient and simultaneously modern (the pair of trousers) and traditional (the *kurta*). Both kinds of clothing are worn not with shoes, but with sandals. The rest of the men stick with trousers and shirt; very few wear suits. No second-generation boys or men wear the traditional upper-class attire. They are mostly in young American men's attire, more preppy than hip-hop (although by the Los

Angeles NABC in 2003, hip-hop clothing was beginning to trump the other types, and was read as unfortunate by most first-generation adults).

Almost 80 percent of women wear the traditional sari, which is typically made of richly colored silk in vermilion, yellow, and peacock green, with elaborate borders decorated by Bengali motifs such as the fish and the teardrop. The rest wear *salwar-kameez,* a North Indian variant of drawstring trousers and long shirt. Once again, a pan-Indian aesthetic is emerging in the diaspora that transcends the more localized linguistic cultures of India.

Rare is the first-generation woman who wears Western clothing such as trousers or skirt. Culture is clearly a gendered thing. Among Bengali Americans, nostalgia for the nation is eroticized. The love of nation is displayed by bodies, especially women's bodies. As Sunaina Maira notes about the urban second-generation in New York City: "The classical dance performances by young women, which are given pride of place at the opening of cultural shows, underscore the role women play in representing 'authentic' tradition" (Maira 2002: 149–50). Women's attire is a national script, even when women are not on stage. In fact, many women I had previously seen in Western attire had, for the NABC, reverted to traditional Indian, if not Bengali, clothing. The women are also divided almost equally between those who wear their hair long, in the traditional Bengali fashion, and those who wear it short, in the Western fashion—identified by the English word "bob" in Bengali. Adult second-generation women also wear saris, while girls wear silk *salwar-kameez* or skirts and top. Although culture is inflected through the prism of gender, generation matters, too.

For members of the first generation, the heart of the conference is what they call *adda*—a somewhat masculine version of gossip. This is a gloss on a complex institution that Dipesh Chakrabarty has written about with great eloquence; a practice that translates the European coffeehouse to the Bengali context by situating it in the interstices of the private and the public sphere—the front porch and the corner paan shop (Chakrabarty 2000: 180–213). At the NABC, *adda* is rampant. It is almost the whole point of the get-together. *Adda* continues into the wee hours of the morning in small groups in hotel rooms. In only a few of these groups is there any drinking of alcoholic beverages. The drink, if present, is almost exclusively whiskey. At the NABC, there is almost no public drinking, although there is much public eating.

Middle-class Hindus have an inordinate sensitivity toward alcohol consumption. The irrepressible Nirad Chaudhuri linked that sensitivity to the influence of Brahmo-Puritanism on the Bengali middle class:

> The Brahmo Samaj began its moral crusade with a practical programme. It attacked four vices which it found to be very widespread in the society at the time in which it came into being (ca. 1820). They were sensuality, drunkenness, dishonesty, and falsehood. In Bengali society, particularly among the middle class with which Brahmoism mainly concerned itself, none of the vices could be said to have reached criminal proportions, far less diabolic. . . . All the same, the tameness of the vices did not redeem them. (Chaudhuri 1951: 213–14)

The humorless and indiscriminating intolerance of small "vices," such as "sleeping in the afternoon," "infatuation with female beauty," and "drunkenness," was carried forward by Hindu revivalists such as Swami Vivekananda, who appears to have had substantial ideological influence over the expatriate Bengali community (partly because he spent time in the United States at the turn of the nineteenth century as a delegate to the Conference of World Religions). The extremely middle-brow litany of wrongs was appropriated from a Protestant worldview where both Brahmoism and Hindu Revivalism internalized the British Christian critique of the Hindu work ethic.[7] From the historical evidence, it appears that alcohol consumption was much more widespread among the elite and the poor than among the middle classes, and for precisely that reason a moral critique of small "vices" among "pre-modern" classes provided pleasures of middle-brow righteousness and hints of a modernizing ethic without challenging colonial political and property relations that were at the heart of the so-called decay of Hindu society.

Among most of the expatriate Bengali middle class, such a perspective persists, embroiling any consumption of alcohol between the polarities of guilt and titillation. Thus, at the NABC there is very little public drinking among the first generation but much private imbibing of alcohol, especially in heterosocial (male and female) groups. Hotel staff often set up temporary bars on the first day of the conference in the hope of generating substantial sales, as one would expect from any "normal" reunion. But very few Bengali Americans buy alcoholic beverages. One beer and two whiskeys in all were sold to the 350 attendees at the 2003 NABC banquet in Los Angeles. The desires of the second generation provide an exception to that kind of public restraint. At the Atlantic City meeting in July 2000, four separate bars were set up on the night of the young people's "dance," and at each, crowds waited fifteen to twenty minutes for a drink.

The conference organizers usually provide two meals per day at an additional charge beyond the standard registration fee. About 50 percent of the participants eat these meals. At the Atlantic City and Los Angeles conferences, all of the food stalls were contracted out to vendors; the organizers did not provide any meals. The remarkable thing is that, although much of the conference "celebrates Bengali culture," in the words of its organizers, very little Bengali food is served. The primary reason is the very success of the organization in gathering Bengali Americans: The numbers outstrip the capability of the few small Bengali caterers, if they exist at all, in the host city. Most caterers of Indian food serve Punjabi–Mughlai or Gujarati food and cannot replicate Bengali food in such large quantities, partly because Bengali cuisine is among the least commercialized and hence has not developed efficient banquet systems that can be transplanted quickly. The 2003 conference promised "authentic Bengali food for the first time" at the NABC, which turned out to be one vendor plying *ilish paturi* (*hilsa* steamed in banana leaf) and *tel koi* (climbing perch in mustard oil). Unfortunately, by the middle of the first day most of the authentic food had begun to smell and turn sour, which effectively discredited the innovation; by the second day, there were no more takers of authentic Bengali food. Another reason for the eclectic nature of the food at the conference is that the second generation is suspicious of much of the Bengali cuisine, with the exception of some finger foods such as *samosas* and *pokoras.*

At the Atlantic City conference there were six separate vendors at the "Food Court." Three served Indian food, and the other three served pizza, sandwiches, and pretzels. The three Indian vendors were staffed and managed by non-Bengalis and were called Bombay, Tandoor, and Rajbhog—non-Bengali names. Their menus were mostly South Indian (*idli, vada,* and *sambar*), western Indian (*bhelpuri*), or North Indian (*nan* bread, vegetable curries, rice pilaf, goat-meat curry, *bhatura,* pickles, and *samosas*). The only concession to Bengali nomenclature was that *samosas* were parenthetically listed as *singara,* although the spices and filling used in the *singara* were distinctively North Indian. Similarly, all four of the vendors at the Los Angeles NABC in 2003 served generic Indian food. As noted earlier, the one vendor who provided a sideline of "authentic Bengali food" unfortunately did not survive the ordeal. That vendor also had a non-Bengali name.

Nevertheless, at most of these meetings, rice is the staple, and most of the desserts (such as *rosogolla, sandesh,* and *ladikini*) are Bengali. There is no *rooti,* but sometimes *puri,* the deep-fried bread associated with festive occasions, is served, although it is more pan-Indian than Bengali. (The typical Bengali version is called *loochi.*) At the Chicago meeting in 1994, fish was served at only one meal in three days. There was none at Atlantic City. The spice repertoire is typically the pan-Indian garam masala rather than the more subtle *panch phoron* that distinguishes Bengali cuisine. The techniques used are all moist, stovetop cooking, typically curries and stews. The vegetable curries include potatoes, *paneer* (farmer cheese, which Bengalis call *chāna*), peas, eggplant, and zucchini. All of these, once again, are identified more with pan-Indian cooking than with Bengali cooking.

The Fourth of July get-together is in most senses an "invented ritual"— somewhat like Kwanzaa. John Coggeshall (1993: 37) observes that ethnic performances speak at a number of levels: some apparent to insiders but not to outsiders; some understood only by outsiders; some obvious to members and non-members; and some symbols remain hidden from view entirely. For Bengalis, the NABC is an insider affair. It is rare to see a non-Bengali among the 5,000 to 10,000 attendees. In that sense, the NABC is not an ethnic festival staged for outsiders. It is a reunion, a *puja,* a bazaar. For insiders, the conference becomes a strictly Bengali space, where performances are used to celebrate themselves by rearranging space, time, and cultural symbols, which "create a liminal period, a subjunctive mood separate from the indicative mood of normal social activity" (Turner 1986: 41–42). It is possible to become wholly Bengali for a weekend and turn a clearly non-Bengali public space into a *haat,* bazaar, or *puja pandal* reminiscent of the crowded streets of Calcutta. Just as polka dancing and beer drinking are not necessarily ethnic behaviors in themselves but become so within the boundaries of Octoberfest, eating generic Indian food at NABC turns the conferences into markers of Bengalihood for the Fourth of July weekend.

Thus, as Americans, Bengalis mark the Fourth of July weekend with a signature Bengali get-together. Picnics and barbecues are rare. The NABC *mela* is becoming a common destination for one in four Bengali-American households.

Other seasonal rituals borrowed from mainstream American society are also being adapted by Bengali Americans. Thanksgiving and Christmas are the most important. In general, households without children are the slowest to adopt these celebrations. With children in school comes pressure to mark these enormously important ritual moments.

Thanksgiving is turned into an elaborate Bengali feast, mostly without the turkey. As stated earlier, whole roasted meats are alien to Bengali culinary culture; thus, most families make do with chicken cooked in the Bengali style. There are none of the other American markers of a Thanksgiving dinner, such as pumpkin pie and cranberry relish. The missing bird on "Turkey Day" is one of the ways that Bengali families underline the fact that they are not fully American. That is how children learn that they are a little different from their compatriots in school. Some members of the second generation reflected on how that missing ritual gave pause to their belief in themselves as Americans, which they otherwise assumed naturally. For a few, it was a source of embarrassment following the holiday, when much of the discussion at school was about the meal, leading them to pressure their parents to become more symbolically American.

What Bengalis do on Thanksgiving is analogous to, although less elaborate than, what is done in some Chinese-American homes, as depicted in David Wong Louie's poignant story of Americanization, *The Barbarians Are Coming*:

> When the Chins invited us to our first-ever Thanksgiving feast . . . they served all manner of poultry. Huge poached hens. Deep-fried squabs. A mallard stew. But no turkey. . . . As the next Thanksgiving approached, my sisters and I lobbied hard for a proper celebration. In response my father simply parroted his friend's low opinion of *fuo gai ngook*. "Only stupid Americans eat turkey." No further explanation was forthcoming, nor did I expect one. (Louie 2000: 134)

Eventually, someone bought a turkey roasted in Chinatown. "No thought was given to home-cooked turkey because Chinese didn't use their home ovens for anything but storage; they prepared everything—boiled, steamed, fried—on the stovetop" (Louie 2000: 135). The turkey was even served in Chinese style, "chopped into inch-by-two-inch chunks, . . . parked next to bird's-nest soup, mung bean threads, sautéed abalone. . . . The spread looked nothing like it was supposed to, nothing like Thanksgiving on TV, the turkey brought whole to the table, drumsticks wearing paper crowns, keeping company with stuffing, canned yams, celery sticks, cranberry sauce, pumpkin pie" (Louie 2000: 135).

For Hindu Bengali Americans, Christmas poses different problems from Thanksgiving. Many Bengali-American families now add a Christmas tree to the living room, with its associated ritual of gift giving, while skirting its religious significance. The secularization of the Christmas ritual, with Santa Claus replacing Jesus Christ as the predominant icon, has aided in its appropriation by Bengali Hindus.

The enactment of life-cycle rituals is even more complicated. *Anna-prasanna* (the weaning ritual) retains its hold among Bengali Americans, probably because it is a relatively simple, hour-long rite restricted to the home. The child is fed *dudh-bhat* or *payas* (both made of rice and milk) to mark his or her transition to solid foods. As mentioned earlier, *dudh-bhat* is also the ritual first meal of the spirit of the recently dead. (This parallels the Anglo-American ritual in which the corpse is diapered partly for technical reasons and partly to return the body to its original state as a child [Frese 1993: 99].)

In contrast to *anna-prasanna,* mortuary rites that can go on for almost two weeks in Bengal are dramatically shortened among Bengali Americans. Among Brahmins, the majority of my respondents, funerary rites traditionally continue into the thirteenth day. The full extent of the ritual includes cremating on the banks of a river, bathing in the river by the male members of the bereaved household, and the wearing of unstitched clothes for thirteen days. U.S. law prohibits cremating on a riverbank, and bathing is next to impossible in most places without drawing undue attention. However, cremation has become more accepted and technically more feasible in the past few decades—a contrast to the choices available to, say, Punjabi Americans in California in the first decades of the twentieth century who in spite of their wishes had to bury their dead in "Hindu lots" in the Mexican Catholic sections of local cemeteries. Karen Leonard (1993: 147), for example, cites the Imperial Valley newspaper *El Centro Progress,* which reported an instance of county officials stopping Sikh farmers from lighting a funeral pyre on August 13, 1918.

A half century ago, Robert Park (1950) noted the hesitation among migrants to display some of their ethnic rituals in public. Bengalis fulfill his expectations when they replicate Hindu mortuary rites in the United States. Cremations are done in crematoriums rather than outdoors. Wearing unstitched clothes to work, a must for Bengali Brahmins, is next to impossible. (The shortening of this ritual is also apparent in Calcutta, which marks it as a modern rather than an ethnic trend.) For Bengali Americans, mortuary rites are turned into a one-day ritual.

The dietary restrictions are also difficult to enact. The *habishanno*—the ritual meal of rice, ghee, and beans—is considered too restrictive. Those who are troubled by this break from tradition generally fast through the first day of mourning and then come home to a simple, home-cooked vegetarian meal on the next twelve days. From what I could gather from the few instances I witnessed, for most the ritual now involves a one-day dietary restriction.

Mortuary rites are most affected because in the United States it is next to impossible to find the right kind of *agradani,* or "degraded," Brahmins who can be fed the *pindas* (the essence of the dead relative). Regular temple Brahmins would lose their caste if they partook of this ritual. Thus, the *pindas* are fed to birds. One respondent commented that at the Chicago temple, the Tamilian Brahmin priests could not even be persuaded to add fish to the rice *pinda*; thus, the *pindas* contained rice and beans, a surrogate for the flesh of the dead. According to tradition, the eleventh-day *shradhdha* meal remains vegetarian, without even the addition of onion and garlic, which are considered "foreign." As the traditional ritual requires, a number of Brahmins are fed, but the cycle is quickly completed so they can return to work.

A similar problem is faced in marriage rituals. Despite its over-arching Sanskritic structure, Hinduism is highly localized. Bengali Hindus have some difficulty in finding ritual specialists trained in their sectarian "little tradition," and they make do with any Brahmin priest available at the local temple. Furthermore, marriage is rarely consecrated in temples in Bengal; it is largely a domestic ritual. But in the United States, the trend is to move the ritual to the temple. As the journalist and writer Sandip Roy notes:

> Some of the rituals have been changed a bit in deference to the New World. "This is the point where the bride usually touches the groom's feet," says the priest. "But in America we just have them do a *namaskar* to each other." But [the priest] is not really the master of the wedding. Neither are the bride's parents. It is the videographer and photographer who call the shots, yanking small wandering children out of the way to make sure nothing will mar the picture perfect wedding video. "Do that again," they order. Never mind if the couple have already exchanged their garlands. They oblige the photographer. (Roy 2003: M4)

Many of the non-Sanskritic *stri achara* (women's rite) discussed in the previous chapter have also been syncopated. Married women in the family no longer roast the popped rice that is fed to the fire god during the ritual; the rice is now bought at ethnic stores. Nevertheless, the blessing of the hearth, the smearing of turmeric on the bride and groom, and the presentation of the whole fish to the bride was continued in two out of three marriages that I observed. The last ritual of marriage is still called *bou-bhat*, but the bride only symbolically cooks the meal, much of which is catered. The wedding banquet continues to be a sumptuous affair, but the number of fish dishes has been reduced while meat dishes have been expanded. No beef was served at any of the marriage banquets I attended, and in talking to others I found that to be the norm.

Beef and Alcohol

If mundane, religious, and life-cycle rituals bring the community together, food taboos draw the outer boundary of the community. What has happened to the major food taboos of Bengalis in the United States?

A remarkable fact about Bengali-American consumption patterns is that more than 80 percent of households eat beef. Beef in the Brahmanic view is, of course, taboo; in fact, all meat is suspect, as shown by the avoidance of meat during important ritual occasions such as a *puja* and mortuary rites (although the dead are symbolically ingested—not that far-fetched if you consider the import of the communion). In Calcutta, only about 11 percent of the households serve any meat (among whom many are Muslims). Meat for the Hindu majority usually comes from the goat—mostly from a *khashi*, or castrated male goat. In theory, castration stems the accumulation of "heat" in the carcass, which might otherwise overheat the body of the consumer. Even those who do consume goat meat—mostly upper-class Hindu men and Muslim families—do so in very small quantities by American standards, about 3.5 ounces per meal or 0.35 ounces per capita per day. (A typical U.S. restaurant steak in the 1990s weighed about 8 ounces and was growing.) The average daily per capita consumption of beef in Calcutta adds up to only about 4 grams, or 0.14 ounces.

Among those Bengali Americans who do consume beef, a little more than one-half follow some restrictions. For example, 13 percent reported that they eat beef only in the ground form, mostly as hamburgers served to children, and 21 percent reported eating beef only outside the home, thereby avoiding pollution of the domestic hearth, the locus of Vedic gods.

About 10 percent said they serve beef only to children, and 16 percent of the women who served it did not eat it. Thus, beef is somewhat contradictorily an infantile *and* a masculine food. The paradox dissolves if we see beef as "uncultured" food (in Bengali eyes), fit for boys and men but not for women who are the burden bearers of "Culture."

Further, it must be noted that a third of the first-generation adults—men and women—reported consuming beef rarely (once or twice a year), while another third said they eat it once or twice a month. Only about a third consumed beef as often as once a week. These are dramatically low figures by American standards. Yet most of the respondents did not think of beef as taboo. Most claimed that they do not prefer beef for reasons of taste and health. Something interesting is happening here: A taboo is slowly turning into an aesthetic choice, partly because taboos are considered "old-fashioned" and unenlightened.

Alcohol consumption outside the home appears to be an even greater problem than beef at home. As mentioned, the taboo on alcohol can be traced back to the relatively recent, nineteenth-century influence of Brahmo-Puritanism (recent, that is, compared with the beef taboo, which can be traced back to about 600 B.C.). About two-thirds of households acknowledged consuming some alcohol. Among the consuming households, about a quarter drank regularly (daily to thrice a week); a quarter drank once a week; and more than half drank only on special occasions. Thus, at least one person in two-thirds of the households drank occasionally. Usually, it was the man of the household; only a handful of women reported drinking alcoholic beverages. Alcohol, even more clearly than beef, is thus a gendered comestible. Of course, unlike beef, alcohol is not infantilized. Furthermore, as the NABC evidence shows, most alcohol is consumed in private by the first generation.

For the first generation, drinking at home—usually a glass of wine or a few shots of whiskey—appears to be less taboo than going out to bars. Almost none of the first-generation respondents said that they ever went to bars. In fact, almost a third of the responses to the question in the survey consisted of an exclamatory "NO!" Yet almost every respondent with adult children acknowledged that those children visited bars on occasion. (These are parents' assumptions about their children's behavior and thus must be treated with caution, but at the same time, parents have no incentive to exaggerate their children's tabooed behavior.) This, as with the frequency of beef consumption, is one of the areas where generational differences show up dramatically.

Expenditure on Food

On average, Bengali-American households (comprising 3.5 food-consuming people) spent $91 per week at the grocery store and $14 more per week at a specialty Asian grocery store, totaling $105 per week in 1995–96. The proportion of expenditure is about 87 percent in regular grocery stores and 13 percent at ethnic stores. The average annual household expenditure on food at home is $5,447. Nevertheless, there is a wide range of variation around this average. Low-expenditure households (about one-quarter of all households, at $2,400 per annum) spent about half of the average. Low-expenditure households also spent a smaller proportion of their food budget at the ethnic grocery store (down from 14 percent to 10 percent of the home food budget). High-expenditure households, constituting another quarter of all households, spent almost twice the average—specifically, $11,400. High-expenditure households spent about 14 percent of their home food budgets at the ethnic grocery store.

The average annual expenditures for eat-out and take-out food for Bengali-American households were $3,277 and $1,142, respectively. Thus, the annual average expenditure on *all* food—that is, food cooked at home, taken out, and eaten out—was $10,570. As a proportion of average annual pre-tax income (which for my cohort was about $100,000), food consumed about 10 percent of household income. How do these figures compare with the American average?

In 1995, the median American household income was $35,082 (U.S. Government, Census Bureau 1997: vii, table A) and an average household spent $4,505 annually on food (U.S. Government, Census Bureau 1998: 464), thereby spending about 13 percent of their budget on food. This is a little higher (in terms of percentage) than the average Bengali-American food budget. Nevertheless, some analysts hold that affluent Americans (defined as the top 20 percent of households), with an average income of $70,000 or more in 1996 dollars, spent about 50 percent more on food than the average household (Heath 1997). Adjusting for upper-income class would bring up the American expenditure on food to about 10 percent of income.

Since most Bengali-American households are not only more affluent than the average American household but also live exclusively in major metropolitan regions, a better comparison with the real figure (rather than percentage) would be with Americans of comparable income living in metropolitan areas. Among the major metropolitan areas in the United States, those who spend the most on food come from households in New York's Nassau and Suffolk counties, otherwise known as Long Island. They spend an estimated $5,700 annually on food at home (Mogelonsky 1996: 22). That is effectively the same as the Bengali-American average of $5,447.

On average, Bengali Americans spend about 48 percent of their food budget on eat-out and take-out foods and 52 percent on food at home. These figures are close to the national American trend. In 1996, the average American household was spending 54 percent of the food budget for food at home and 46 percent for food out of the home.

Food is important for Bengali Americans, especially because they have migrated from a context where food is scarce and higher social status is demonstrated (to oneself, one's family, and visitors) through the consumption of quantitatively more and qualitatively more expensive foods. In Calcutta, the consumption of almost every food item continues to increase with rising income, making it clear that demand for even the most basic items such as rice, wheat flour, and dal is unfulfilled. Further, the consumption of high-status items such as fish, milk, meat, and fruit increases dramatically with rising income, often multiplying two to four times between the poorest and the most affluent households (see Chapter 2). Professional Bengali migrants with comfortable earnings in the United States make sure that their pantries are well stocked and indulge in quantities of fish, milk, and fruit that they could only imagine prior to migration.

B y following the various cycles of Bengali-American food-consumption patterns through the day, the week, the year, and the life cycle, I have shown how Bengalis negotiate between the siren song of modernity and the nostalgia of tradition. I have also hinted at how Bengali Americans re-enact larger concerns about community and individuality on the gastronomic stage. (I will have more to say about that in the next chapter.) Breakfast and dinner sets the Bengali out on different paths, one toward retaining a grounded identity and the other straining to break out toward a wandering cosmopolitanism.

I have also elaborated on the process of assimilation and the recoil from it. There is nevertheless a bigger story here than that. Assimilation will eventually happen, but the more interesting thing to study is what happens on the way there. Let me give one example of the complexity of the process of gastronomic adaptation. It is generally assumed that more recent migrants consume more of their native food than those who came before them—that is, the more time people spend in the United States, the more they eat like "Americans." That is true if we are counting generations, but it is not necessarily true over the life cycle of the *same* immigrant. In one of the Pulitzer Prize-winning stories in *Interpreter of Maladies* (1999), Jhumpa Lahiri's collection of expatriate Bengali tales, the unnamed male protagonist says: "In the end I bought a carton of milk and a box of cornflakes. This was my first meal in America. I ate it at my desk. . . . I ate cornflakes and milk morning and night, and bought some bananas for variety, slicing them into the bowl with the edge of my spoon" (Lahiri 1999: 175–76). "Single Indian men," explain Judit Katone-Apte and Mahadev L. Apte (1980: 355), "have a difficult time providing traditional types of foods for themselves since they often have neither the knowledge nor the experience necessary for meal preparation." Middle-class Bengali men are particularly inept at cooking. In Bengal (as in most of India), there is no traditional equivalent to the American barbecue (or all-male hunting and fishing camps), where men and boys learn to cook and display their culinary skills outside the feminine kitchen. When Arun, a graduate student at an American university, and the protagonist of *Fasting, Feasting,* is encouraged to make "Indian food" by his American host, he "cannot tell her that he has never seen his mother cook," so he improvises and does the following:

> He turns on the faucet and runs water over the lentils, washes them. With Mrs. Patton watching, admiringly, he sets the pot on the stove and adds spices she hands him, without looking to see what it is he is adding. Their odours are strong, foreign—they should be right. They make him sneeze and infect him with recklessness: he throws in some green peppers, a tomato, bay leaves, cloves. (Desai 2000: 193–94)

In the end, "Arun sits in front of his bowl of dhal. He stares at it, nauseated. He quite agrees with Melanie: it *is* revolting. He would much rather chomp on a candy bar than eat this" (Desai 2000: 193–94). It is no surprise, then, that Lahiri's male protagonist lives on a diet of corn flakes and bananas for six weeks until his wife, Mala, joins him from Calcutta. On the day Mala arrives, he cooks rice and egg curry with unpeeled potatoes for her. She eats, peeling the curried potatoes with her fingernails: "We ate with our hands, another thing I had not yet done in America." The next day, Mala asks for a few dollars: "When I came home from work there was a potato peeler in the kitchen drawer, and a table cloth on the table, and chicken curry made with fresh garlic and ginger on the stove" (Lahiri 1999: 193). He continues:

> Although we were not yet fully in love, I like to think of the months that followed as a honeymoon of sorts. Together we explored the city and met other Bengalis, some of whom are still friends today. We discovered that a man named Bill sold fresh fish on Prospect Street, and that a shop in Harvard Square called Cardullo's sold bay leaves and cloves. (Lahiri 1999: 196)

He concludes poignantly,

> We are American citizens now, so that we can collect social security when it is time. Though we visit Calcutta every few years, and bring back more drawstring pajamas and Darjeeling tea, we have decided to grow old here. I work in a small college library. We have a son who attends Harvard University. Mala no longer drapes the end of her sari over her head, or weeps at night for her parents, but occasionally she weeps for our son. So we drive to Cambridge to visit him, or bring him home for a weekend, so that he can eat rice with us with his hands, and speak in Bengali, things we sometimes worry he will no longer do after we die. (Lahiri 1999: 197)

This pattern is replicated by other Bengali Americans. Specifically, single Bengali Americans (especially men) in the first few years of their lives in America consume very little Bengali food. That changes with marriage and a family, which is when they return to Bengali food, often with a vengeance. This transformation takes anywhere from a few months to five years. It is often said among Bengalis that "it takes a wife to tame the hearth."

Katone-Apte and Apte (1980: 357) provide another explanation for this reversal of the assimilative process: "[It] may be that many Indians who have been away from India for a long time find traditional values slipping away and make an attempt to hold on to their lifestyle by celebrating Hindu holidays, taking an active part in ethnic voluntary organizations, and consuming traditional foods." One of my respondents noted such a reversal in the acculturation of her husband using the following words:

> I came to the USA ten days after I got married. By that time I knew my husband very little, including his food habits. On one Sunday, he said he would make me a tasty dish for lunch and told me to relax. I had great expectations. He made a lettuce salad with anchovies on top. I was surprised that he expected me to survive on a salad!
>
> Then I thought maybe he is used to eating the American way, all the more because his first wife was an American girl. So I was trying to cook accordingly and get adjusted. My husband appreciated that, but I continued to cook Bengali lunches and some dinners.
>
> After a couple of weeks I found that when I cooked American food he would look at the food and say he wasn't hungry. I thought, maybe the food I cook is not up to his expectation. Then I thought, let me try something different. I started cooking regularly our Bengali fish, rice and vegetables. Then he was not only relishing the food, but started to call me in the afternoon and order foods of his choice. Then one Sunday afternoon I cooked typical *moorighonto* [fish head cooked with rice], that day he was so happy which I cannot describe. He suddenly said, "You do not cook bloody American food! I don't know how many years I have been craving for this kind of food after leaving Calcutta!"

Katone-Apte and Apte (1980: 357) also point to the gendered nature of this trajectory of assimilation: "Marital status affects both men and women, but in opposite ways. Married men acculturate more slowly than single men. However, married women seem to acculturate faster than single women." I might add: Married women sometimes appear even more willing to embrace "American" culinary culture than their spouses. In particular, married women who work outside the home appear to have greater exposure to American home cooking; they can get past the hamburger–hot dog syndrome and hence are more willing to experiment with recipes provided by American friends and acquaintances, albeit with ethnic twists. A number of female respondents who worked outside the home showed familiarity with a wide range of American foods, such as casseroles, baked potatoes, baked beans, roast chicken, pork chops, and so on, that they sought to replicate at home (more on this in the next chapter). They said that their children often loved these innovations, especially the older children, which drew married women toward American cooking. In addition, the conveniences of American cooking are an important factor in the attraction of women with double burdens. Unfortunately, however, their menfolk typically did not like these adaptations, so they had to cook two different meals—one for their spouses and the other for their children. So we may have an interesting bifurcation here: Married men with children tend to become more ethnic while married women become less so in their food preferences.

Children often drive the process of adaptation. Katone-Apte and Apte (1980: 357) note that "couples with school-age children, especially children of the ages of 10 to 16, acculturate faster than those without children." Almost all of my respondents had children living with them or had raised children in the recent past. Most agreed that it is children who drive the consumption of hamburgers, hot dogs, pasta, and pizza. Peer pressure among them is considerable, and they do not want to stand out in their consumption patterns. Children prefer fewer spices and less rice and fish, the distinguishing elements of Bengali cuisine for the first generation. One woman wrote:

> Most of the Indian children I know do not eat typical Indian food most of the time. At our Indian Society of New England meeting, I was typically asked to bring food "for the children" for this reason— they like and are most used to American food. While an Indian meal is prepared for the adults at these gatherings, the children are usually served macaroni and cheese or pizza, cake or brownies for dessert.

In this chapter I have also shown how some Bengali traditions have been invented in the United States, while others have been retained with particular stringency. I will address the reasons behind both in the next chapter and in the concluding chapter. There, I interpret the *mentalité* of Bengali Americans as revealed by food consumption and, in particular, investigate how Bengalis in the United States address one of the central problems of modernity: finding one's place in an ever changing world.

CHAPTER 4

Gastroethnicity

Reorienting Ethnic Studies

*It is probably in tastes in food that one would find the strongest and
most indelible mark of infant learning, the lessons which longest with-
stand the distancing or collapse of the native world and most durably
maintain nostalgia for it.*

PIERRE BOURDIEU, *DISTINCTION* (1984: 79)

"Whatever is not Japanese, Korean, Chinese, Indian, American,
French, Italian cooking, is ethnic," announces a Japanese informant (Ashkenazi and Jacob 2000: 46). He goes on to clas-
sify food into three categories: his "natural" Japanese food (*nihonjin*); familiar foods that are not his own (those listed earlier); and unfamiliar food (or
"ethnic"). This is as good an illustration of what "ethnic" food means to
people as any, although the details of the Japanese perspective are a little
different from the American one.

A survey of ethnic restaurants conducted in 1999 by the U.S. National
Restaurant Association identified twenty different cuisines that Americans
consider ethnic. Pizza places were excluded from the survey for having lost
their ethnic affiliation. The survey also noted that "some cuisines are becoming so in-grained in the mainstream of US culture that they are hardly considered ethnic any more. This applies especially to certain forms of Italian,
Mexican, and Chinese (Cantonese) cuisine" (NRA 2000: 5). This echoes
the sentiment of the Japanese respondent. Paraphrasing his words, one could
say that for most bicoastal Americans there is American food, then there is
Italian and Tex-Mex food, and the rest is ethnic. Of course, there are regional variations in this theater of consumption. In addition, there are changing temporal patterns. Maybe in a few decades we will be able to add

Chinese to the intermediate category—not completely of the self, but neither of the other. That is an optimistic view, because we might have trouble there both with race and ideas about essentially different cooking—
think pasta and lo mein and their resonances.

Ethnic food is other peoples' food. That is congruent with the idea of
"ethnicity"—derived from the Greek noun *ethnos,* meaning nation or people—which is used to refer both to people in general and "other" people
in particular. English usage of the word continues to carry that same
ambivalence. In American culture, "ethnic food" carries a range of meanings, from "different food" and "spicy food" to "food we do not regularly
eat but love to try." Ethnic food is what half a century ago used to be characterized as foreign food—different food, but a little different still from "soul
food," with its singular association with African American identity in the
American imagination. All this, of course, is from the perspective of the
Anglo-American resident. Everybody else since the Irish (1840s) carried
first the taint of difference and now the romance of it. In spite of the recent
popularity of ethnic food—maybe even because of it—ethnicity has largely
been imagined from the outside in. What happens when we turn the concept inside out and let ethnics define the mainstream as an ethnicity, which
it surely is?

Drawing the Gustatory Boundary

Probashi (expatriate) Bengalis in the United States define themselves in
opposition to three other identities—Bengali in Bengal, Indian in the
United States, and American. The first distinction—in opposition to Bengali food in West Bengal—is relatively muted in most cases and explained,
usually with regret among the first generation, as the result of ecological
constraints and the market context. Yet about 10 percent of my respondents asserted, with delight, that their food practices are more syncretic and
adventuresome than Calcuttan practices. A few of the same respondents
said that their food practices are healthier and more creative than those of
Bengalis in Calcutta. Thus, at least one in ten *probashi* households seemed
to relish the opportunity to break out of the straitjacket of Bengali culinary practices. Those households experimented with, combined, and ate
out at many kinds of ethnic American restaurants that they might not have
encountered in Bengal, such as Vietnamese, Japanese, or Thai.

Probashi Bengalis also define their gustatory identity in opposition to non-Bengali, Indian American food. I cannot fully elaborate on that opposition here because of the unavailability of any work on the food practices of other Indian ethnic communities in the United States. That has to await its own sociologist. Nevertheless, what can be asserted is that the main axis of that definition is not focused on breakfast, which appears to be cereal or toast for most Indian Americans (including Bengali Americans), nor can it be defined around lunch, which is a similar mix of American and Indian practices for all. It is dinner where Bengaliness is asserted against non-Bengali Indian Americans, especially in the inordinately frequent consumption of fish and rice by Bengalis in opposition to the vegetarian diet of many non-Bengali Indians.

Not surprisingly, given the context, most *probashi* respondents assert their culinary Bengaliness primarily in opposition to American food. Here we reach the meat of the matter, so to say. The quantity, quality, and nature of meat cookery appear to be the most important markers of American ethnicity for Bengalis. American food is imagined in astonishingly negative terms, perhaps echoing subconscious Hindu revulsion toward meat, especially red meat. Most of the negative stereotypes about American food centers not only on meat cookery but also on market versions of it, such as hamburgers and hot dogs. I heard numerous colorful stories about the "shocking appearance of 'uncooked' hamburger and its smell." One woman said, "Steak looks barbaric!" Another explained that "getting used to cold meat took me a long time, especially beef," and still another recoiled from "cold turkey sandwich" and "cold milk." One said, "I have never tried to eat hot dogs. The very sight and smell turns me off." Another exclaimed, "I was shocked by the appearance of a medium rare steak—to see how uncooked it was." To the (probably leading) question, "Do you think 'Cornflakes, beefsteak, and salad' would be the correct way to describe American food?" 65 percent answered in the affirmative, and only 30 percent disagreed. Among those who disagreed, some mentioned a whole range of domestic American foods, such as casseroles, stews, baked potatoes, baked beans, pies, soups, corn-on-the-cob, and so forth. But many who disagreed with the stereotypical characterization could not name any American foods other than the predictable hamburger, hot dog, and so on. I was told many an apocryphal story, one of which went this way: "When a Bengali came to America, he really wanted to try a typical American food to be able to talk about it when he returned to Bengal. A friend took him to a hot-dog stand. This man had never seen a hot dog before. When he saw it, his appetite was gone. However, he still wanted to try, so he asked, 'Do you have any other parts of the dog?'" (Note how this story distances the Bengali American both from the American with his terrible foods and the provincial Bengali who knows no better.)

Another set of distinguishing American practices, according to Bengali Americans, centers on the fact that "they" do not serve proper meals at get-togethers—a conception obviously centered on ethnocentric notions of a "proper meal" and the "proper occasion" to serve such meals, of which I heard numerous versions:

> An American couple, a friend of my husband, invited us to a party. I thought we would have a full dinner, like our style of hospitality. I found quite a big crowd and they offered us some drinks, crackers, vegetables with dip and some cheese. That's it! My husband after coming home at 1 o'clock in the morning had fish and rice and then went to bed cursing Americans for their lack of hospitality.

Another respondent, Sharmista, wrote:

> We went to an American family's house for dinner one time. They had chips and drinks for appetizer. It was O.K. For dinner they had salad (basically lettuce), bread and spaghetti (no meat-sauce). They thought Indians don't eat meat. To this day, I don't like salads. To me it is what we call "cow's food." Anyway, I had a couple of bites for manners sake. Then comes the spaghetti and tomato sauce. I could only visualize how delicious our cooking of noodles is. I could not eat that spaghetti. All I had was a piece of bread.

These diatribes against others help construct generous narratives of their own past. In other words, American notions of hospitality are considered inadequate in comparison with an idealized vision of their own generosity and that of other Bengalis. Here Bengali Americans appear to reflect certain ambivalence toward "American culture," which Katone-Apte and Apte (1980: 343) characterize as the following:

> While it is conceded that opportunities for economic betterment are many and varied, it is also felt that the sociocultural environment is

somehow corrupting. Thus, there is reluctance to acquire typical American values and attitudes, and the dominant behavioral patterns that go with . . . middle class life [including notions of hospitality and proper meal].

This ambivalence is not exceptional to Bengali migrants but shared by many migrants since the end of the nineteenth century, as made evident by Louie's "Only stupid Americans eat turkey," quoted in Chapter 3. "Food exchange," writes David Sutton (2001: 53), "provides a metonym for the community values that many people feel are under threat from the forces of modernization." Real or imagined stories about one's hospitality are nothing more than what Sutton (2001: 54) aptly calls "narratives of *gemein-schaft*." Such competitive evaluations in the case of my respondents are both a sign of nostalgia for an imagined time of simple reciprocal exchange and a repressed cry of anguish about the loss of that imagined community.

Continuing the discussion of Bengali-American perceptions of American food, one man said:

The main characteristic I noticed about American food was the serving size. It was really big, and I would inevitably exclaim, "It's so much food!" . . . Initially, I tried to eat all the food because that is what I was told by my mother, but I ended up getting sick. Then I realized you could ask to take the leftovers home in a brown bag.

Then we have the usual misunderstandings and miscommunications, some of them quite funny. One woman wrote:

I was surprised to see submarine sandwiches. . . . When I ordered a sandwich, the clerk asked me whether I would like it on a six-inch sub or a foot-long. I had never imagined sandwiches in inches or feet!

Madhumita noted:

Within a week of my arrival I was at my husband's workplace—a hospital. In the evening a nurse offered me what she called "chili." She asked me, "Do you like chili?" I said yes, but that I did *not* want any. Yet, the bowl she held in her hand showed no evidence of chili peppers and she kept offering it to me. I was a trifle amused that she would be offering me peppers and that there was no sign of them. And what the hell did she mean, anyway?

I heard a number of statements like the following: "Initially I thought that a hamburger is made of ground ham," or "I mistook lettuce for cabbage and cooked it like cabbage, but it shrank a lot." Another interviewee told me:

> When I first came to this country, my cousin accompanied me to a Burger King. I felt intimidated by all the choices on the board, especially because they did not make any sense to me. So I waited until he ordered a Whopper, and I ordered the same. I quite liked the taste. So the next time we went to a McDonald's, and my cousin asked what I would want. I confidently stepped up to the cashier and ordered a Whopper!

There is a close parallel in another story:

> When I was here during the first months, I had no idea about salad dressing, so when we went to an Italian restaurant the waitress asked my choice of dressing—my mind went blank. I had no idea what kinds there were to begin with. So I asked her what she had. She rattled off the usual ones: Ranch, Blue Cheese, Thousand Island, house, etc. I didn't know what to say. Finally I chose French because it sounded familiar and was the easiest to remember.

Beyond the negative stereotypes and the miscommunications, many Bengali Americans acknowledged shuffling up to American food with trepidation but eventually coming to like it. Many explained how and why they came to like American food:

> First Thanksgiving dinner we saw the whole turkey and panicked. " 'We are supposed to eat that?!' " But with black pepper and a little curry powder that our host offered made it quite good.

Another noted:

> My first summer in Ohio in 1989—we were invited to a "Pig Roast" at a friend's place. Seeing the pig hanging upside down on an elec-

tric rod, I was put off. My host informed me that for people like us
they had potatoes and chicken. But I couldn't spot them. Then when
the pig was taken off the spit—out came the potatoes and chicken
from inside the pig—very well cooked in the pig's fat. To tell you the
truth, they were the most delicious chicken and potatoes I've had till
today.

Others described their transformation in less dramatic terms:

Here breakfast and lunch are all ready-made; we have to cook only
our family dinner. Cooking and cleaning is also very easily done because of conveniences such as dishwashers. So we have become accustomed to eating cereal and milk for breakfast, soup, salad and *chapati*
[what Bengalis typically call *rooti*—flat bread] for lunch, and self-
cooked food for dinner. Because of the environment and availability
we have adjusted our food habits according to this country's style.

Some talked about how things have changed with the recent increase in
Indian immigration into the United States. An older woman, respond-
ing to questions about changes in Bengali cooking in the United States,
said:

I think you should ask that question of the younger generation that
has come recently. In our day there were very few Indians and so there
was a constant interchange of ideas and food between the two cultures. My husband was a student then and we went to a lot of international functions. Further, the change in food habits came gradually
without our being aware of it.

Along similar lines, another wrote:

I learned cooking after coming to the U.S. by eating at friends' houses
from all over India and also by following some Bengali recipe books.
Twenty years ago, many things were not available; now almost everything, including fish from Bangladesh, is available in big cities. Also
many Indian restaurants and catering services that are available now
have changed my experience with food. . . . When I invited guests for
dinner, I used to spend two to three days preparing various items for

dinner and sweets. In India, we always bought sweets from outside. Now you can order many items by phone.

Another pointed to similar changes and to the reasons she has made the transition to American food:

> Twenty years ago when I came to the U.S., the non-American foods—Greek, Italian, Chinese, Thai, Middle Eastern or Indian, which are popular and common nowadays—were not available in all areas. The original American foods—hot dogs, burgers, soups, salad, sandwiches, etc.—appeared tasteless and bland to me at that time. But I did not have much time left in my hand after managing my job, a family of four with two kids, to prepare Indian food for all of us starting from breakfast to dinner. Therefore I realized that I had to choose at least a few of the American foods for our survival here. I desperately tried most of the common American foods and finally picked up a few of those that suit our taste.

The next commentator pointed to something a little different from the rest. She complicated the notion of American food by referring to her experience with sushi while talking about her food experiences in the United States. She said:

> I was very reluctant to try sushi. My daughter introduced me to that. First she learned how to make it and then tried to get me to eat it by using cooked curried tuna in the sushi rolls. She said they serve it in Japanese restaurants as spicy, curried tuna rolls. The thought of raw fish was initially atrocious to me, but now I enjoy it. It is quite delicious if it is fresh. However, I have not been able to convert my husband to a sushi eater.

This comment points to the complexity of what has been considered the unproblematic, "American" mainstream so far. As Yvonne and William Lockwood have pointed out, "The new cultural configuration of immigrants draws not only from 'mainstream' American culture, but from that of other immigrant groups as well. Groups previously arrived from other countries are emulated" (Lockwood and Lockwood 1991: 3). Newly arrived Eastern and Southern Europeans in Detroit "Americanized" their Serbian

names from Obradovic and Dragic to O'Bradovich and O'Dragich, emu-
lating the Irish. Similarly, by the end of the nineteenth century Finns in
Michigan's Upper Peninsula had appropriated the Cornish pasty, a turnover
with a variety of fillings, as an authentic Finnish American dish (Lockwood
and Lockwood 1991: 5 ff). Hence, *probashi* Bengalis appropriately identify
spaghetti and bagels as mainstream American food (given the primary areas
of my research—the Northeast and the Midwest). Generally, that characterization does not extend to Chinese American and Japanese American foods.

Another *probashi* named Jhumpa provided an example of American
children reaching toward Indian food:

> I teach elementary school children ages 6 to 9 years—most of them
> are fussy eaters. They like to stay with peanut butter sandwiches. We
> tried a special lunch for Thanksgiving with ham, turkey, cranberry rel-
> ish, corn, potatoes, fruits, etc. I made a basmati rice pilaf and the chil-
> dren enjoyed it very much. I was surprised that it was their favorite
> and that they preferred it to every item, other than the corn!

As there are Bengali Americans who dislike "American" food, and those
who don't particularly care for it at first but come to enjoy it eventually,
there are equal numbers who outright love it. There is the *probashi* woman
who responded to my questions cryptically: "Can't stand Indian cooking—
too laborious. . . . Developed taste for other foods." Another wrote, "We
were invited by an Indian husband and his American wife. She prepared
marinated, breaded and roasted pork chops—that was the first time I tasted
pork—and it was delicious. Since then I make similar pork chops at home."
There were a variety of responses along the same lines:

> When for the first time I went to the grocery store in the U.S., I was
> elated to see so many foods and ingredients. Most of those things were
> unknown to me. Gradually, I learned to cook with these ingredients.
> From that time I am almost addicted to the grocery store. If I see any
> new item, I try to taste or cook it.

A Chilean woman married to a Bengali wrote: "My most favorite food
upon arriving in the U.S. in 1965 were hamburgers with ketchup and
milkshakes. I found them delicious. . . . I now find them fatty and taste-
less." A man who arrived recently wrote:

I never had any problems adjusting to American food. I was open to everything. I feel very fortunate to be here in a sense that I am able to taste food from so many countries around the world, which is not possible in India.

A number of respondents were delighted with pizza. As one of them said:

Being vegetarian I thought pizza with cheese and vegetables looked good when I first came here. And I was right. A friend of mine took me to a pizza joint and ordered thin crust cheese pizza. I loved it and have enjoyed pizza thoroughly since.

Anamika wrote a paean to the hamburger:

It was the day after I arrived to this country in the mid-seventies. My sister-in-law and her husband were visiting my home. I became quite attached to my brother-in-law who is a professor and a gentleman. My sister-in-law was visiting somebody else that day and my husband was at work. My brother-in-law said in a conspiratorial voice, "*Boudi* [respected sister-in-law], I am going to get a special treat for you." Within fifteen minutes he came back with a bag full of many Styrofoam boxes. He opened a box with huge buns layered with lettuce, tomato and a brown patty along with some fried potatoes. I ate the delicious sandwich with Coca-Cola. In the meantime my sister-in-law walked in and yelled at him, "You are feeding *Boudi* these unclean stuff?!" We exchanged conspiratorial looks. I knew I had been introduced to Americana by a friend for life and by Burger King!

Another woman wrote along similar lines:

My first experience with American food was when I arrived in this country back in 1974. I remember going to a Ginos fast-food place in Langley Park, which is KFC now, and eating cheeseburger and french fries for the first time. I took a bite of that cheeseburger, and since that day I always look forward to taking the kids to KFC or a Burger King. I have a sudden urge for cheeseburger and fries and I am so grateful for experiencing one of America's most beloved

foods. . . . I can eat any kind of food when I am outside of my house.
But at night for dinner I want my Indian food—rice, dal, vegetables,
and chicken or fish curry. One meal I must have my own food.

The lowly Jell-O seduced others:

> I was fascinated with Jell-O—its shimmering shape. I told everybody
> about it. When I was married in India, my friend sent me Jell-O
> packages—but I couldn't make it because I had no refrigerator!

Then there are views from the other side, especially from the twelve
American women (among 126 respondents) who were married to Bengali men. Through these respondents we can again change the angle of
vision and reorient the discussion by moving out of the insider group.
A self-defined "former Episcopalian" American woman married to a Bengali man wrote:

> His mother knew British as well as Bengali cooking . . . was very smart
> and competent. Her meals were varied and kids never got fried food.
> We repeat too much, have fewer "courses," cut corners, do the easy
> and utilitarian thing. For example tonight. . . I filled this [survey] out,
> while my husband made *masur* dal with onion and cumin, *chochori*
> with cumin, black onion seed, turmeric, swiss chard, potato, spinach,
> yellow squash and broccoli and served it with *chapati* heated over the
> gas burner. (My son tried leftover chicken curry and rejected it,
> returning later for two scoops of . . . ice cream. My daughter is sleep-
> ing over at a friend's whose dad is Bengali and mom is American and
> vegetarian.) There was no *raita,* or fried eggplant (different texture to
> contrast with the rest) and no attention to the ayurvedic principles
> of bitter, pungent, salty, sweet, astringent, sour and the last one I for-
> get—the seven tastes that should be present in a meal. . . .
>
> I had a shock going to India the first time. First, I was offered
> *sandesh* and *gulab jamun* [fried cheese balls in syrup] and *rosogolla*—
> never had I encountered so much sweetness. Then lunch was served—
> a huge mound of rice with a watery yellow dal. I bravely tackled it,
> not realizing that fish, meat, and vegetables were on the way. Chili
> would sometimes be intense. The combination of fenugreek and
> maybe *panch phoron* turned my stomach. I lost weight every time on

my first three trips to India. By the fourth, I was used to the sweets
and most foods. I can now handle food cooked with green chili much
better and I like coriander leaf (I didn't at first).

A Jewish American woman married to a Bengali wrote: "In my experience, Indian cooks tend not to experiment with other cuisines. Also they
prepare 3–6 dishes for each dinner, whereas American foods involve only
1–3 dishes per meal." She continued:

> My husband and sister-in-law, perhaps because they were 10 years and
> 9 years old, respectively, when they arrived in the U.S., have been very
> open-minded about trying different ethnic foods. Just a few weeks
> ago I visited a niece who recently (2 years ago) came to the U.S.
> Although she is considerably younger than my husband, I was a lit-
> tle surprised at how narrow-minded she was regarding trying non-
> Bengali food. Her main explanation for not liking a few of the dishes
> she has tried in the U.S. is that they "didn't taste like Bengali food."
>   The fascinating part is that this prejudice extended to *non-Ben-
> gali* foods. For example, she stated that the European style cakes she
> ate from bakeries in the U.S. were not as good as the European-style
> cakes from Calcutta! I found this quite amusing since I've had tortes
> in Europe and America and the gritty sugar frostings I had in Cal-
> cutta were not anything like the originals that they were attempting
> to imitate.

Of course, what the niece is asserting is not so much the taste per se but
its capacity to produce memories and hence identity. The past is recalled
through food, and no matter how "gritty" that sugar frosting, it was more
memorable than the best frosting one can have here and now.

A Lithuanian American woman married to a Bengali man responded
to the question, "Why is your cooking different from your mother's?" by
writing:

> I am trying to feed two kids who can't stand fish in any form other
> than fishsticks and a husband who would only eat fish if he could. In
> my mom's house we ate what she told me to make. Only my father
> could complain. That is, I cook what I learned to and compromise
> between kids and husband . . . all of whom have the right to and do

complain. I cook vegetables and use more spices. We eat less meat and less casseroles and soups. . . . The children like to eat what their friends eat: white bread and hamburgers with ketchup. Their food tastes are simpler, no complicated spices.

She concluded:

Luckily for my sake, I began this "cultural exchange" on a bout of vegetarianism. I was eating nothing familiar and trying to change my food habits drastically (nothing did taste like a chili dog!). So when I ran headlong into a man who didn't know how to cook anything but dal as vegetarian food, I was used to suffering. I ate it quietly, only spilling my guts later that dal was not my idea of a meal. We have since blended food habits and I eat all the meat he cooks and he suffers my noodles and potato binges.

Emily, a cultural anthropologist of India who is married to a Bengali, responded to the question, "Do you think, 'Cornflakes, beefsteak, and salad,' would be a correct way to describe typical American food?" with an angry "NO!" She continued: "American food is currently very eclectic, reflecting cuisines from around the world. Most people I know eat a wide variety of food and do not eat much beef, preferring chicken or fish or vegetables." Emily concluded:

I am an American of Scotch-Irish heritage who is married to an Indian. I am also a cultural anthropologist (Ph.D., 1989) and have spent more than a year living (and eating) in India. In India, I ate almost all the food that was offered to me (provided it was clean and well cooked) and enjoyed it very much. Family members and friends in India had certain stereotypical notions of what kind of food I would like—they assumed, for example, that I would like large quantities of meat, but I don't. But on the whole they did not make a big issue (nor did I) about the spiciness or "hotness" of foods. On the contrary, in the U.S. I find many Indians to be very sensitive about the "hotness" of their food, probably because of the *occasional* American who reacts strongly against it. For example, I have enjoyed and cooked Indian food for over 15 years, never once complained about the spiciness or "hotness," and yet I am still routinely asked—even by close

Indian friends—whether or not their food is too "hot" for me. While, as an anthropologist, I can understand their desire to define themselves as "Indian" and me as "American" by assuming (incorrectly) that all Americans cannot tolerate spicy foods, as an individual I find this *very, very* annoying.

I've also come to realize that many Indians in the U.S. seem to believe that it is *impossible* for a non-Indian to cook Indian food that tastes reasonable. I will not pretend that my cooking is always good, but on occasion I have made certain dishes which, when tasted by Indian friends, produce a reaction of disbelief or outright denial that I could have made them. For example, some years back a friend insisted that my husband (who *never* cooks) must have made the chicken curry we were eating. At our Indian Society of New England meeting I am routinely asked to bring food "for the children"— assuming, again, that I am unable to make anything suitable for the adults.

She ended poignantly: "Sorry if I am complaining too much—food is *definitely* used as a marker of cultural identity by Indians living in the U.S., whose identity is likely to be more vulnerable owing to separation from India itself. Perhaps I resent efforts to exclude me from the enjoyment and preparation of Indian food, precisely because I myself feel very close to Indians and India."

In dramatic contrast to all the other American women married to Bengali men, Christina was in some ways the most devout Bengali. In the section on religion and prayer in the questionnaire, she gave a most detailed description of how she had built an alcove in the living room where, on a mat, are the *murtis* [idols] of Krishna and Radha, Buddha, Shiva, and Durga; next to them are a conch shell, an incense holder, and the Bhagavad Gita. She is also exceptional as a vegetarian among Bengalis in the United States, although she cooks meat dinners for her husband. She is exceptional because, contrary to stereotypical expectations about Hindus, none of the Bengali-American households in the survey were vegetarian. Only 6–9 percent (depending on the source) of West Bengalis in India are vegetarians. Ironically, Christina was the only American who agreed with the stereotype of American food as "Cornflakes, beefsteak, and salad." She, in fact, added: "Forget the salad and add a *can* of vegetables!" (Was she being ironic?) Then she responded to the question, "What do you think is more convenient—Indian food or American food?" with, "American—open a box, turn on the microwave, it is supper! Yuck!" She continued: "Americans don't cook—they prepare things from a box, while Indians cook from scratch." She was the only respondent who considered it inappropriate for Hindus in the United States to eat beef: "The cow is sacred—like *mataji* [mother goddess]—we must respect the cow, which gives us so much." She was also the only respondent who answered in the negative the question, "Can an Indian family be considered Indian if it does *not* eat Indian food regularly?" She wrote: "No—then it is an Indian family trying to be American and forgetting their culture; food is one of the things that define cultures." It is ironic indeed that it takes a non-Bengali by birth to become the purest of Bengali Hindus in the United States. Christina in some ways contradicts the fixity that I have given to ethnicity at other places in the book. Nevertheless, as an exception she also confirms the point.

Looking at a variety of ethnic constructions of Bengali and American gustatory identity as seen through the eyes of Bengali Americans—those who love American food; those who hate it; and those who have come to terms with it—as well as the more liminal and necessarily complicated views of American women married to Bengali men, I have sought to reorient the study of ethnic groups by looking at their food practices from the inside out and from the margins in. In the next sections, I compare the food practices of Bengali Americans with those of other "ethnic" Americans, then discuss the implications of the reorientation that I suggest here.

Comparing Bengali-American and Other "Ethnic" Foodways

I discovered Jitsuichi Masuoka's remarkable study "Changing Food Habits: The Japanese in Hawaii" (1945) after my own survey was sent out. Like mine, Masuoka's study draws chiefly from 100 household records, especially of food expenditures. Masuoka noted that the food of Japanese Americans in Hawaii had changed toward the consumption patterns of upper-class Japanese in Japan: "This fact maybe noted from such casual comments as: 'Our mouths are so sweet that we are not satisfied with coarse foods any more'; and, 'We are so accustomed to *zeitakuna seikatsu* [extravagant ways of living] that we are laboring daily just to eat well'" (Masuoka 1945: 761). On returning from Japan, a salesman noted:

> When I went back to Japan, I found that I could not eat the food.
> Everything was so tasteless that I could not enjoy it. The farmers ate
> very ordinary foods.
>
> Really in Hawaii we eat as good food as a *Kencho* [a governor of
> a prefecture]. The people in my village never dream of eating raw fish
> everyday, or beef and pork three to four times a week. (Masuoka
> 1945: 761)

Comparing these kinds of statements with the picture forty years prior to
that (i.e., circa 1900), Masuoka noted the "simplicity" of the diet of a Japanese American plantation worker:

> Mr. Nakayama, who came to the plantation in 1900, recalled his daily
> menu in a boarding house. It was as follows: breakfast—steamed rice,
> *miso-shiru,* and thinly sliced dried *daikon* seasoned with *shoyu* sauce;
> lunch—cold rice, kidney beans with salt, and stew made of potatoes,
> *daikon* and *aburage*; and dinner—steamed rice, pickled *daikon,* beef stew
> and dried fish. Raw fish was had only once in a long while. (Masuoka
> 1945: 761)

Masuoka noted that Nakayama's family of seven spent about 36 percent
of their monthly income on food ($58.50). Of the total expenditure on
food, nearly 51 percent ($30.00) was spent on various non-Japanese foods,
such as white flour, macaroni, bread, pastry, oatmeal, soda crackers, beef,
pork, poultry, butter, Crisco, mayonnaise, canned produce and soups,
sweet pickles, poi, jelly, jam, baking powder, yeast, chocolate, cocoa, and
coffee.

The proportion of cash spent on cereals and animal proteins was about
61 percent of the total food expenditure, and slightly more than one-half
of this was spent on rice and fish. Comparing the food practices of his
Japanese American sample with those of other Americans and with Japanese in Japan, Masuoka drew a number of conclusions. First, the rice–fish
complex was relatively intact for the first generation (Issei). Yet the importance of rice in the basic diet was slowly losing ground, as demonstrated
by the proportionately less money spent on rice. In Japan, he continued,
the amount of money spent on rice tended to increase as income increased,
whereas in Hawaii it decreased with increasing income:

In Japan as a family rises in its standard of living, it tends to discard the use of wheat or sweet potatoes and eats *hakumai* or polished rice. But in Hawaii, as a family rises in social status it eats less rice and spends more money on American foods, such as white flour, macaroni, crackers, breads and other cereals as well as on vegetables, meats, milk and coffee.

This change came about rather slowly in Hawaii. In the beginning of the Japanese adjustment to new conditions of life, there was a definite tendency for them to discard sweet potatoes, wheat and millet from their diet. If they ate sweet potatoes, they did not mix them with rice; and if they ate wheat; they ate Quaker oatmeal. Upon their coming to Hawaii, the Japanese people took to *hakumai* or polished rice, for the eating of polished rice meant the rise in their social status. (In Japan only the very well-to-do eat *hakumai*.) Moreover as polished rice became a basic food for all, it lost its traditional status value among the Japanese in Hawaii. (Masuoka 1945: 762–63)

Next, according to Masuoka, fish was eaten in Japan only rarely among small farmers in 1945, while Buddhism and their prohibitive price discouraged the eating of beef and pork. In Hawaii, as living standards rose so did the consumption of beef, pork, poultry, and fish, which were a daily or weekly rather than occasional ingredient in main meals. Some of this transition was aided by the fact that planters provided beef for plantation laborers in the early years. In 1945, Masuoka found only a few "old women" in his sample who still abhorred the idea of eating beef or pork.

Third, Masuoka noted that with the next generation (Nisei), rice gradually lost its status value and in fact was often associated negatively with Old World traditions. Eating American foods got status more readily.

Fourth, he found the most conspicuous changes in the breakfast menu. Food such as bread, butter, coffee, chocolate, and fruit juice had taken the place of the traditional *miso-shiru* and rice. Every family in his study bought these "American" items. In particular, the children preferred them, as did the men who worked in higher-status jobs in the offices of the mills. In contrast, laborers in the field ate rice in addition to their bread and butter.

Fifth, he found that, in contrast to breakfast, the other meals of the day remained relatively unchanged and there was substantial continuities in the manner of preparation primarily because Issei women did the cooking.

Meats were still prepared as *sukiyaki* or stews. Farmers ate *sukiyaki* rarely in Japan, but in Hawaii it became a weekly dish. Yet none of the families ate roast beef, pork or chicken. The fish was also "cooked in the traditional fashion: fried, boiled, or eaten as *sashimi*. When fried, fish was eaten with *shoyu* sauce; when eaten as *sashimi,* it was sliced thinly and eaten raw with shoyu and mustard sauce; and when boiled, fish was seasoned with *shoyu,* sugar, and other condiments." In addition, the stews had more beef or pork in them and they were more often thickened with flour than was the case in Japan. Fresh vegetables were pickled (*tsukemono*) and seasoned with *shoyu* and *ajinomoto,* and when boiled were seasoned with the same along with a little beef, pork or fish.

Finally, Masuoka found that salads of all kinds were appearing on the dinner menu more often than in Japan, and yet desserts were never served. Cakes, cookies, and candies were instead eaten between meals and often served with tea to guests.

Masuoka identified generational differences as the most important factor in the transformation of food habits among his respondents. The Nisei in public schools brought home new ideas of nutrition and the proper food to eat as a result of peer pressure and direct proselytizing by educators. One Issei man noted:

> I don't say much to my children. I know that they know and understand about America better than I. My children tell their mother what foods are good for our health. They say that we must eat more vegetables and fruits and less rice. They learn this in school—American school, I mean. I believe that their teachers are better informed along this line so I do not interfere nor ignore their suggestions. I believe firmly that the children should obey their teachers.
>
> Judging from what my children tell me, nearly all the ideas that the *Issei* have are greatly different from what they learn in the school.
>
> It is impossible for us, *Issei,* to become Americanized and act and talk like the *haoles* [white people in Hawaii are called *haoles*]. We have "old heads" or set minds. Even though we know that we should be Americanized, since we intend to stay here for good, we cannot. But, we know that our children could because they know how to talk *haole* language and associate with them more freely. When we pass away, we are sure that they become Americanized. (Masuoka 1945: 765)

Masuoka then quoted a Nisei girl, a graduate of an American high school working in a *haole* family as a domestic, as saying: "I don't like Japanese foods, I don't know why. I don't like rice and fish. Fish smells bad and rice takes too long to cook. Anyway it is so troublesome to prepare Japanese dishes." On that note, Masuoka concluded that, "with the passing of the *Issei,* much of the Japanese foods will pass out of the picture" (Masuoka 1945: 765).

I was astonished by the parallels between my conclusions and those of Masuoka. Each of his conclusions can also be drawn for Bengali Americans: the rice–fish complex is relatively intact among the first generation; more fish and meat is consumed in America than in the original site of the culture; breakfast has changed dramatically while dinner has not; salads are rarely eaten, as are desserts; and the second generation is clearly moving away from the food practices of the first generation, probably for the same reasons: schooling, peer pressure, work schedules. I need to add only two qualifiers: First, among my respondents of the first generation there appears to be no decline in the consumption of rice, as Masuoka noticed among his respondents (although there is such a decline among the second generation); and second, very clearly what has changed is the context where ethnicity is no longer—at least, not at the present time—seen as something to be shed by the larger American community. Thus, Bengali Americans can afford to be much less defensive compared with the tone of the Issei father quoted by Matsuoka. He had to face the onslaught of American institutions, including teachers and nutritionists, on his daily practices as retrogressive holdovers from the Old World. The defensive tone may also have something to do with the class profile of Masuoka's respondents compared with the predominantly middle-class professionals among mine. Today, status is acquired not by abandoning ethnicity but by claiming it ever so loudly, even when very little of the original practice survives.

I will now move on to a comparison with Italian Americans—one of the most studied groups in terms of migrant food practices in the United States. No study of Italian American food habits can begin without engaging the work of the remarkable sociologist Phyllis Williams, who published *South Italian Folkways in Europe and America* in 1938. She compares pre- and post-immigration practices of Italian Americans in the realms of housing, diet, dress, religion, marriage, and mortuary practices. In the realm of dietary practices, she identified the main Southern Italian ingredients of pasta, cornmeal, bread, signature vegetables (including red peppers and mush-rooms), melon and sunflower seeds, *caffe* (made of roasted ground grains rather than coffee), and *vinello* (wine diluted with water) as markers of culinary ethnicity. She noted that the main foods were bread, cheese, beans, potatoes, greens, salads, and fruit, with "*maccheroni*" served at least once or twice a week. She also noted two fast days a week. The main changes wrought by migration were largely a product of higher standards of living (*pace* Masuoka). There was more cake, candy, real coffee (rather than *caffe*), and meat. There was also more spaghetti and sauce, the main repast of the day, served three or four times a week. She concluded:

> The first-generation Italian wants to live as did his fore-fathers. He makes what immediate adjustments he has to, especially in occupa-tion, dress, and living quarters, but will often pay a premium to get some familiar dish. In the search for the same victuals they had eaten abroad, immigrants found that some of their native fruits and veg-etables grew or could grow naturally in New England, but others had to be brought from the warmer parts of the country or imported. Merchants established stores stocked with articles shipped over by *paesani* [townsmen] and even relatives of the local Italian commu-nity. The basic food habits of Italians have been, therefore, preserved. The modifications that took place represented efforts to emulate practices of the better classes in Italy rather than of Americans. (Williams 1938: 62)

Williams argued that the adherence of Italians to their native cooking ves-sels, such as implements to make *passatelli* (a fine noodle) and coffee roast-ers, further delayed dietary adjustments, as did Italian taboos against canned goods, especially canned meat. In addition, according to Malpezzi and Clements (1992), Italian Americans were insistent about using certain items that were considered more Italian than others, such as peppers, onions, endive, eggplant, beets, spinach, fava beans, Swiss chard, zucchini, squash, carrots, broccoli, cauliflower, garlic, parsley, basil, fennel, grapes, figs and wal-nuts (see also Bianco 1974; Gambino 1974; Williams 1938).

Judith Goode, Karen Curtis, and Janet Theophano (1984a, 1984b) make a number of claims about the relationship between food and ethnicity that takes the analysis of Italian American food practices further. Their first major contention is that most studies of ethnic foodways have been based on frequency of distinctly marked items used by a group—for instance, pork by Southern blacks and spaghetti by Italians. Noting that the use of such distinctly marked ethnic items tends to decline over generations, those studies erroneously concluded that the ethnic content of a group's meal pattern declines over time.

Goode and colleagues contend that such an analysis tends to overstate the process of assimilation because it misses the ethnic structure (not content) of menus and weekly, annual and ritual cycles that persist even when the use of distinctive items may have declined. For instance, the frequency of consumption of pasta, tomato-based sauces, certain cheeses, and distinctively Italian herbs may decline over time, but there is a certain "Italianness" to the structured alternation between gravy (or one-pot) meals and American platters. In many Italian American households, particular days of the week—in some, Wednesdays, and in others, Thursdays—become gravy or one-pot days, and on other days of the week, such as Mondays and Fridays, American platters are served. Gravy or one-pot dishes are a wet, saucy, slow-simmering mixture and connote Italianness, while dry, segregated platters imply Americanness. Gravy and platter nights are somewhat analogous to "boiling" nights and "frying" nights among African American migrants to Northern cities. The Sunday dinner, for Italian Americans, remains an elaborate gravy dinner even when breakfasts and lunches may have become completely Americanized. Even dinners on many a weekday may be completely Americanized, with no distinctive ethnic markers; nevertheless, the Sunday dinner acts as a paradigmatic ethnic "feasting" meal from which all other eating events are drawn. One of the forms of the typical feast is the "elaborated Sunday dinner which contains more courses than the paradigmatic Sunday dinner. One or more antipasto courses, a soup course, whole roast course, multi-dish dessert course, and an ultimate course of nuts and fruit can be expected. The meal is served to a seated group" (Goode et al. 1984b: 77). Richard Gambino (1974: 20) also underlines the importance of the evening and Sunday *pranzi* (dinner) to Italian American identity.

Friday dinners are equally marked by ethnic considerations and yet are inversions of Sunday dinners: They are paradigmatic "fasting" meals, which must include fish and exclude meat. It is as if, between Friday dinner and Sunday dinner, the week is punctuated by meals to separate workdays from leisure days. Between Friday and Sunday dinners comes the equally important Saturday morning breakfast, where friends and family join together at home or at a diner to make a commensal beginning of the weekend.

This is not necessarily an Old World Italian tradition but a New World invention by Italians. And the food at the Saturday breakfast maybe completely American, but the fact of gathering together on a Saturday to commune with one another is putatively Italian American.

Ethnic marking therefore is not limited to items but elaborated in menus (which may include new American items) and, most important, by the rhythm of the week and weekends. Thus, researchers who have focused exclusively on frequency of ethnically marked items miss the continuities by ignoring the rhythm of the week and the year.

Nevertheless, on certain occasions in the annual cycle, the content of the meal may also become very important—for example, at Easter, when ricotta pies and other baked goods become the paradigm of such meals among Italian Americans. "Here, the simple presence or absence of specific items *is* what is significant since no meal format rules are involved" (Goode et al. 1984b: 77). Similarly, Christmas Eve is an extended Friday format where an odd number of typically meatless dishes must be served; Lent is another extension of the Friday format.

Generally, researchers have argued that while mundane meals become Americanized, ritual meals remain ethnic much longer, but Goode and colleagues contend that even this is not necessarily true. In fact, the highest-level feasts, such as those served after weddings, may in fact be completely American. Ironically, their case study shows that "Italian items are more important in a disapproved marriage to an outsider than in a highly approved marriage between those with strong identities. For insiders, format and item choices had more to do with social status and prestige than ethnicity" (Goode et al. 1984a: 213). Furthermore, the lowest-level feasts, such as Sunday dinners, remain the most Italian. Intermediate-level feasts, such as meals associated with first communions, confirmations, and funerals, and slightly lower-level feasts, such as birthdays, anniversaries, and graduation, generate the greatest variability in format and content. The repertoire in these meals often depends on the taste and preference of household members, the politics of menu negotiation, and the nature of the guest list. Goode and colleagues found no pattern for these middle-level feasts. They contend that "stability in pattern was not necessarily more significant for major ritual events than for more routine events" (Goode et al. 1984a: 146).

Third, Goode and colleagues show that the rules of menu negotiation, even when the meal is not particularly Italian, may have a distinctly Ital-

ian flavor. The primacy of the preferences of the senior male and the heightened sociability within the community where members of the extended
kin network gather together regularly to eat and commiserate are two
major markers of ethnicity:

> The frequency with which this group celebrates special occasions
> and the emphasis on hospitality and food exchange for each cele-
> bration accounts for the way that the repertory of food formats
> remains a continuing focus of discussion, gossip, interest, and manip-
> ulation among the women. The female peer group and the intricate
> linkages between households accounts for the shared traditions and
> the shared innovation. (Goode et al. 1984a: 212)

There are differences between households, but many of these variances are
predictable according to such variables as the composition of the household, stage in domestic cycle, generational cohort, and labor-market-
participation rates of the primary female.

My work confirms most of the contentions of Goode and colleagues.
For instance, among Bengali Americans, as among Italian Americans, the
content of breakfast and lunches has been dramatically Americanized,
mostly due to new work schedules. Further, breakfasts and lunches vary
along cooked-uncooked as well as hot-cold dimensions among both Italian Americans and Bengali Americans. On weekends and when guests are
present, breakfasts and lunches are cooked and hot—omelets, *rooti,* curried
vegetables, and so forth—while less significant meals are cold and uncooked,
such as cereal. Further, the popularity of one-pot stews has clearly declined
for the young, both among Italian Americans and Bengali Americans.

Another parallel between Bengali Americans and other American "ethnic" groups is the relative decline in the significance of religious and folk
health ideologies. Informants in both groups—Italian American and Bengali American—could state some shared beliefs, such as those surrounding
"hot" and "cold," but they were not very significant in daily food choices
(other than in cases of illness).

Most important, my work underlines the importance of analyzing various cycles of consumption in making any judgment about ethnic reten-
tion or assimilation. In particular, I have pointed to the importance of the
weekly cycle in the Bengali consumption pattern. Goode and colleagues
argue:

The level of a group-shared food system is indeed evasive to the observer unless he looks specifically for it and looks at the highest level of analysis, the meal cycle. . . . Items and recipes are very significant for truly isolated and closed communities like the Amish, for isolated subsistence-oriented farm communities, and *for the migrant group in the arriving generation.* However, contact with supermarkets, communication media, restaurants, school lunches, and industrial workplaces tends to lessen the importance of content and increase the importance of the structure embedded in the meal cycle as a marker of group-oriented systems. The issues of continuity and change cannot be explored without a focus on meal formats and meal cycles instead of items and dishes. . . . The week, the weekend, and the seasonal and life-cycle feasts all must be investigated. (Goode et al. 1984b: 85; emphasis added)

Almost all of my *probashi* respondents were first-generation migrants who came to the United States after 1965. For first-generation migrants, ethnic items and recipes still play a crucial role in the performance of ethnicity. Fish, rice, various spices, flavors, fats, cuts of fish and meat, cooking utensils, and methods of cooking are central to ethnic claims. Content matters for insiders. Early immigrants had the greatest difficulty in acquiring some of the defining elements of their cuisine (such as green chili and spices such as asafetida, fenugreek, and coriander seed). In some peculiar ways, that very scarcity triggered a deeper association between Bengaliness and the missing ingredients. The memory of long ago and of another place was kept intact, just as Proust could associate the madeleine with his Combray childhood precisely because he had not tasted a madeleine since. Most ingredients are today available to *probashi* families, if not at the regular grocery store, then at specialized Asian stores. Only a few items, such as freshwater fish, high-quality mustard oil, and a few exotic field greens, are not available in the United States. Goode and colleagues may be right: For subsequent generations of Bengali Americans, items and recipes may become less important than meal format and cycles as more and more of the marked items become available in American grocery stores, but that is not the case yet.

Bengali Americans are a small and a dispersed community, numbering about 30,000,[1] and still considered highly exotic by the larger American society. They do not have the market presence yet to influence stocking of items exclusive to their cuisines, such as the pith of banana stems, banana blossoms, and jackfruit. They may not have that kind of power in the marketplace for a long time. But the ingredients of their cuisine that intersect with the cuisine of others, such as rice, green chilies, and coriander leaf (cilantro), have become relatively easily available, especially in and around big cities.

What Goode and colleagues ignore is the continuing importance of certain marked ingredients even for long-established and integrated groups, such as pasta and tomatoes for Italians, crawfish and peppers for Cajuns, and collard greens for Southern blacks. It is unclear whether Bengalis will retain that kind of long-term attachment to certain items or whether they will ever be large enough as a group to generate such stereotypes. All we know for now is that the first generation does identify its attachment to particular ingredients with its ethnicity. The emperor may not have any clothes on, but the kind of clothes we imagine him to be wearing matters.

Hasia Diner's *Hungering for America: Italian, Irish, and Jewish Foodways in the Age of Migration* (2001), the most comprehensive comparative work on ethnic cuisines to date, is a cogently argued, beautifully written, and a highly readable book, composed with a social historian's eye for the perfect little picture—drawn from memoirs and works of fiction—that illuminates big ideas. The book is crafted around two telling questions: first, what is the fundamental difference between pre-immigration and post-immigration foodways of Italians, Irish, and Eastern European Jews; and second, why did the Italians and Eastern European Jews develop an American identity around the specificity of their "authentic" foods while the Irish did not?

The most important difference between pre- and post-immigration foodways, Diner notes, is abundance. As Rosolino Mormino, a resident of Napoleonville, Louisiana, wrote to his brother in Italy with telling eloquence, "In America bread is soft, but life is hard" (as quoted in Diner 2001: 48). Diner elaborates:

> Immigrants never believed that the streets of America were paved with gold. Instead, they expected that its tables were covered with food. Newcomers knew that they would have to work hard, but that was nothing new. The difference was that arduous labor before migration had gotten little food, while in the United States equally hard work in factories, mines, mills, railroads, and farms would be rewarded with tables sagging with food unimaginable to them back home. (Diner 2001: xvii)

A dietary study of Italians around Chicago, conducted in the 1890s by the U.S. Department of Agriculture and Hull House, reported that "Italian oil, wine, cheese, which even the poorest families use, are all imported, and of course expensive. . . . They consume a great deal of macaroni" (as quoted in Diner 2001: 56). Olive oil seemed to become essential to Italian identity, as did meat. "In Italy few from the lower classes ate [meat] more often than three times a year. In America meat appeared regularly on their menus" (Diner 2001: 56). Dishes that kept their Italian names, such as "*minestra* (vegetable soup), *ciambotta* (mixed vegetables), *scarola* (escarole), *cocozza* (squash), and the like," became richer and more complicated. "Pizza in Roseta Valforte [Italy] was a flat, thin disc of bread with salt and oil. In Roseto, Pennsylvania, tomatoes, onions, and anchovies gradually covered the dough. In Carneta, Pennsylvania, the addition of meat transformed the fare of Foggia's poverty to that of Italian American abundance" (Diner 2001: 53). Migration effectively elevated the cuisine of the poor Italian to that of its elite.

Class elevation also occurred with Eastern European Jews after immigration. "The formerly poor started to eat *blintzes, kreplach, kasha-varnitchkes, strudel,* noodles, *knishes,* and, most importantly, meat every day. Their once meager cabbage or beet *borschts* now glistened with fat pieces of meat" (Diner 2001: 180). Marcus Ravage, a Romanian Jewish migrant in New York in 1900, noted with astonishment, "In New York, every night was Friday night and every day was Saturday [sabbath], as far as food went. . . . Why, they even had twists instead of plain rye bread, to say nothing of rice-and-raisins (which is properly a Purim dish) and liver paste and black radishes" (Ravage 1917: 75–76). Diner elaborates:

> Immigrant parents and their children blended the familiar with the new, the eastern European Jewish and the American. They continued to eat certain familiar foods of pre-immigration Europe and still talked about herring, dark bread, *borscht, gefillte* fish, *tzimmes,* and *kugel.* The first three, along with potatoes and cabbage, they ate pretty much all the time in America. But increasingly dark bread was pushed aside in favor of white and rye. Furthermore, evening meals began to consist of meat stews, meatloaf, and meat soups, along with old familiar dishes. Jewish consumers did not so much reject older foods as make them secondary to newer, decidedly richer ones. (Diner 2001: 194)

Furthermore, a "national" cuisine was born in the diaspora that eventually de-emphasized regional styles. Immigrants came to America, Angelo Pellegrini (1971: 31) wrote, "ignorant of cuisines beyond their own regions. In the Little Italy of the American metropolis the Southern Italian ultimately learned about *osso buco* and *veal scaloppini,* and his neighbor . . . from the north met up with pizza and eggplant Parmesan." Diner (2001: 225) concludes astutely:

> Much of the food world, which immigrants from up and down the Italian peninsula constructed in America, was new. That they called the foods they ate "Italian" was new. . . . [T]he fundamental details of their American consumption represented a break with the past. But no matter how great the chasm between what had been and what they achieved in terms of food in America, they believed that they were behaving in traditional ways. They invested the foods which they ate in America with the aura of authenticity.

Niccola de Quattrociocchi (1950: 30), a native of Palermo, wrote about the 1920s: "One evening [while strolling in New York], we went to an Italian restaurant where I was introduced to two very fine, traditional American specialties called 'spaghetti with meatballs,' and 'cotoletta parmigiana.' . . . I found both extremely satisfying and I think someone in Italy should invent them for the Italians over there." Other new elements crept into their repertoire, such as the drinking of beer with their food rather than wine (Diner 2001: 60).

Food played such an important role in Italian American identity that surprisingly, according to Diner (2001: 80), "even children expressed little interest in transcending the food boundaries of their families and communities. Memoirs . . . never mention the temptation to eating out in restaurants serving other than Italian foods. Few described the pleasures of visiting with friends and co-workers from other ethnic groups and sharing their foods." She continues:

> They pushed the limits of their foodways but only within a constructed definition of "Italianness." In the evolution of an Italian American food culture based on a fusion of certain iconic Italian foods, pasta and sauce, olive oil and distinctive cheeses, with American

foods, particularly meat, Italian Americans created a distinctive way of life in America. While they no longer ate as they had back home, neither did they eat like other Americans. Yet they evinced little personal anguish or familial discord over the distance between standard American fare and their own. (Diner 2001: 81)

Of course, there was much pressure from the mainstream to abandon ethnic foods. Earlier I cited Masuoka's observations about such pressures. Only a few Italian Americans have talked about such compulsions; Jerre Mangione (1978: 15), for instance, wrote about being embarrassed by his Sicilian family's public Sunday meals at the park. Another confessed that "we seldom took our home prepared lunch to school, although we much preferred Italian bread and Italian food" (Covello 1944: 343). Expressions of shame were limited to the public sphere while children relished their ethnic foods at home.

Of course, there were difficulties between the generations, especially around notions of obedience and cultural loyalty, but very little of that spilled into the realm of food. Diner (2001: 82–83, 226) writes: "Although opting for American furnishings, American popular culture, American clothing, they kept to their own food, invented though it may have been in this country. . . . As a group often stigmatized by the dominant culture for its low aspirations and violent character, Italian Americans pointed to an area of public culture where they claimed superiority and a contribution to their new home." She is probably right to argue that "the Italian story may best represent the experiences of most immigrants" (Diner 2001: 26). But I think it is an exaggeration to conclude that "the Irish and Jewish stories were too laden with inner conflict, too fraught with problems to be paradigmatic" (Diner 2001: 226).

The generational dissonance was graver among Jewish Americans than among Italian Americans partially because of the greater symbolic importance of *kashrut* in keeping the Jews a "nation apart." In fact, a group of traditionalists lamented the embrace of American food as "*treyf.*" While most, especially the young, viewed "America as eastern Europe's antithesis and saw their old world limited, narrow, a modern-day Egypt, shaped by persecution and scarcity, America meant freedom and food" (Diner 2001: 180).

Nevertheless, I suspect that the contrast she builds between the "food fights" within the Jewish community and the "food fest" within the Italian community may be overdrawn. She writes: "Food seemed to cause

[Italian Americans] no problems. Families did not fight over it . . . and all agreed upon the Italian American food consensus that emerged" (Diner 2001: 225–26). In my judgment, that would make the Italian American community exceptional to the point of being turned into a caricature. Just as there were serious generational contentions over *kashrut* among American Jews, there surely were similar fights over Catholic fast days among Italian Americans. The appearance of greater disagreement among Jews may be an artifact of the greater volume of memoir literature produced by that group than by any of the other groups. Diner's bibliography lists about forty-five works of fiction and memoirs for about 2.5 million Jewish immigrants and their progeny, and only thirty-one sources for 4 million Italians and their descendants. More voices are prone to be talking at cross-purposes rather than generating a consensus.

In the Irish story, Diner tends to over-generalize with statements such as:

> The vast majority of Irish also subscribed to a particular religious system, a distinctive form of Catholicism that made little room for religious celebration by feasting. Instead, it emphasized fasting, total as well as periodic abstentions from meat, eggs, and milk products. . . . After the Famine a devotional revolution swept through Ireland, and the culture of fasting intensified. No religious festivals brought food into the church to complement the joyous world of sacred time. Abstention from food, it seems, heightened Irish spirituality. (Diner 2001: 86)

I find that assertion extremely bold but ultimately unconvincing because: (1) the Italians seem to have done fine in spite of all their fasts (just as Hindus and Muslims have created a rich celebratory tradition with food in spite of substantially more fasting days in a year); and (2) it would make the Irish quite a pathological exception in their inability to celebrate with food. In fairness, it must be noted that the specificity of Irish Catholicism is only one of six kinds of argument Diner makes about why the Irish could not or did not develop a gustatory identity (other than in the realm of drinking).

Another reason for the Irish disdain toward their own food, according to Diner, is that such a memory is interwoven with English/Protestant colonization and their accursed imposition of the potato—the only food most poor Irish Catholics knew. Furthermore, the stark social separation of the ruler and the ruled in Ireland made it impossible for the Irish poor even to imagine the food of their elites, which is usually the model for emulation during times of plenty. The starkly antithetical relationship between the Catholic Irish and the Protestant English that the preceding points posit is largely a figment, I think, first of imperialist and later of nationalist rhetoric. The real lived experience of people in colonized Ireland was more complicated than that.

British imperialism in India is perhaps the closest parallel to the fate of the Irish, and I am familiar with the real, rich, corrupt, and bastardized culture that was born in the cross-fertilization of British imperialism and Indian everyday life that could not be easily ignored by either the most virulent racist or the most rabid nationalist. Nevertheless, in the Indian case few foods other than toast with jam, mulligatawny soup, and curry powder traveled from the English elite to the Indian elite. Of course, we Indians did emulate the English in the realm of drinks, such as tea (with cream and sugar), whiskey, gin, and punch (in the last case, the name went in the opposite direction from the drink, as the English drink came to be known by an Indian name). The English appear to be singularly incapable of culinary imperialism, contrary to their transatlantic cousins. That, of course, is an altogether different issue.

The Irish did not model their cuisine after the English not because the Irish poor and the English elite had so little in common, and the little that was shared was tainted by brutal power, but because the discursive field of Irish nationalism (which remains a dream today for many in Northern Ireland) did not and still does not allow such modeling. Independence for Northern Ireland is still a dream deferred and hence that much more powerful than the dream fulfilled in the Indian case.

In addition, Diner (2001: 223) says, the

> inability of the Irish to use food for the construction of ethnicity was compounded by their widespread employment in domestic service. The Irish women who took their first American steps through the back doors and into the kitchens of Yankee homes were hounded and ridiculed for their lack of skill at the stove and table.... Having to cook someone else's food, under someone else's supervision, and according to someone else's rules drove another wedge between Irish culture and food culture.

Plausible but unconvincing in the face of the example of black women's association with food in more than 300 years of white American history. The
problem for the Irish, in fact, may not have been their servitude in Yankee
homes (in spite of which a black culinary culture developed) but the insid-
ious and inevitable comparison with the black experience. We must remember that the period of largest Irish migration (1840–1924) was also the great
arc of controversy about black identity that took us through secession, Civil
War, and Jim Crow laws. Poor, white Irish immigrants were quick to invest
in their whiteness in the developing social drama, and hence they were more
interested in pointing to their cultural similarities (including food) to the
Anglo-German elite than to their distinctive differences, which were burdened with race (see Ignatiev 1996; Roediger 1999). In the process, Irish
Americans never elaborated their culinary culture as a badge of distinction.

Finally, Diner (2001: 223) writes: "Not that they did not eat and enjoy
food. But the foods consumed could not embody the idea of Irish identity.
Inasmuch as the Irish understood Ireland as a repository of hunger, they
could not enact identity by means of food. This made them unique among
immigrants to America." Here Diner is closest to the truth. It is not that the
Irish had a peculiarly restrictive Catholicism to contend with, or that they
were cursed by the potato, or that there were a million dead from the
famine. Not even their domestic servitude can explain their inability or
refusal to develop a gustatory element to their identity. Others have done
so under much greater constraints. If Indians could develop such an identity in spite of about 12–30 million dead through the "Late Victorian Holo-
caust" (Davis 2001) from 1876 to 1896, then the Irish surely could have produced a gustatory identity. If African Americans could develop a culinary
tradition in spite of their brutal servitude, then it is unconvincing that the
Irish could not. Instead, the Irish under the influence of Irish nationalism
and literary convention developed a discourse that made Irish identity syn-
onymous with hunger and famine, which also affects the sources that Diner
uses. The memoir literature that Diner cites for the Irish is, in volume, less
than one-half the size of the literature for American Jews, although there
were twice as many Irish. This partly explains the paucity of reference to
food among Irish Americans. Even more important, the Irish novelistic convention, with its leading role in high modernism, developed masculine
tropes of nation, class, religion, and modernity, giving short shrift to the quotidian details of domestic life, such as food. The noise about alimentation in

Irish literature is confined to dialogue between men in dark, smoky pubs. Thus, it is not that the Irish do not enjoy a good meal; neither is it that they do not know how to celebrate with food. They are just too busy talking loudly about other things to let anybody get a word in edgewise about what is cooking at home.

In the larger context, my criticisms are quibbles compared with the essential truth and elegance of Diner's study. With absolute historical fidelity, she concludes:

> The linkage between food and migration remains valid at the end of the twentieth century, in terms not so different from those recorded for eras long past. . . . [I]mmigrants were historically women and men who experienced want of work, want of money, and hence want of food. Their hunger propelled them outward. When they settled in new places they recreated elements of familiar foodways, at the same time that they embraced novelty and enjoyed greater abundance. The history of each immigrant group entails a particular negotiation between the memories of past hunger and the realities of new foods available in greater quantities than previously encountered. (Diner 2001: 10)

True, but my own story is a little different precisely because the Bengali Americans under discussion are more affluent both in their native contexts and in the New World.

The hagiography of American abundance among Irish and Eastern European Jews, or even the muted critique of American foods and tastes by Italian Americans, stands in sharp contrast to the attitude of my Bengali-American interlocutors. Only two of my respondents even mentioned abundance. Bengali Americans appear to carry far more uncritical nostalgia about their homeland than Italians or Irish or Eastern European Jews. That is mostly because of where they came from and how they crafted an identity that left behind the hunger of their poorer compatriots.

Implications of the Reorientation

Much has been written about the disparaging observation from the mainstream about the food practices of arriving migrants. Among others, Donna Gabaccia (1998), Harvey Levenstein (1988, 1994), and Laura Shapiro (1995) have written extensively about the treatment meted out to Eastern European and Italian migrants by social workers, nutritionists, and cooking-school experts at the turn of the nineteenth century. Typically, nutritional scientists told the unmanageable "new immigrants," as recorded by Levenstein (1988: 103–4), that the essence of European economical cooking—the *minestras* and *pasta-fagioles* of Italy; the *borschts,* goulashes, and *cholents* of Eastern Europe—required uneconomical expenditures of energy to digest. He noted:

> Strong seasonings that made bland but cheap foods tasty were denounced for overworking the digestive process and stimulating cravings for alcohol. Nutritional science reinforced what their palates and stomachs already told them: that any cuisine as coarse, over spiced, "garlicky" and indelicate-looking as the food of central, eastern and southern Europe must be unhealthy as well. (Levenstein 1988: 103–4)

The New York Association for Improving the Conditions of the Poor, the largest private relief agency at the turn of the century, held an exhibition in lower Manhattan that condemned the "complexity of combinations" in the most common Italian dishes as "a real tax on digestion" (Levenstein 1988: 104). Mexicans repeatedly have been referred to as "pepper bellies" since the Alamo. Doris Witt shows in her incisive book *Black Hunger* (1999) how Aunt Jemima was created as a trademark after a 1889 vaudeville performance connected black culture to food and stigmatized it by association with chitterlings and watermelon.

What is more intriguing and less studied is the attitude of immigrants toward the host culture and, in particular, their reading of American food. There is much in the fictional literature and first-generation autobiographies and memoirs that points to the view of immigrants as seeking to emulate American cultural norms. For instance, Yezierska, a Jewish migrant who wrote in the early decades of the twentieth century, identified "Jewish eating" apologetically with herring and onions. American food, by contrast, is identified as "spinach, salad and chops" by Sara Smolinsky, the protagonist of Yezierska's autobiographical *Bread Givers* (1925). When she finally gets a job as a *teacherin,* Sara buys an expensive dress from a fashionable Fifth Avenue store, travels on the Pullman, and orders a proper American meal of "chops and salad" in the dinning car.

Americans are repeatedly identified with affluence and as individuals with their own personal forks, napkins, towels, and toothbrushes, something unthinkable for poor migrants on the Lower East Side of Manhattan in the early decades of the twentieth century. They are also credited with a certain cool smartness that eludes grasping new migrants such as Max Goldstein in *Bread Givers*. Bengali migrants today express a similar envy of the easy sociability and cool confidence of the "American," and they can often be heard urging their sons to be a little "smart" like the Americans.

But that goes hand in hand with a certain disdain for American culture, which is seen as normless and easy. That is why among every migrant cohort today "to be like an American" is considered an epithet that reeks of hedonism, irresponsibility, and the decay of proper gender roles—an astonishing attitude given the broader historical pattern.

American food is seen as an immediate reflection of that loss of culture. As Donna Gabaccia (personal communication, 2000) says, "the evidence is spotty, but it is there, lurking in the Italian immigrant's disdain about hurried American eating and the inferior quality of American bread. At the turn of the twentieth century, Italians also associated the use of corporate and prepared foods with lazy American housewives who had abandoned their proper gender and family roles." Arlene Voski Avakian, a first-generation Armenian migrant, has written about how she often heard in her family that "Americans didn't know the taste of their own mouths. On the rare occasions that my family shared food with Americans they went on and on about how the Americans loved the food, and the implication was clearly that they had now tasted real food and could, with the help of Armenians, learn the taste of their own mouths" (Avakian, personal communication, 2000; see also Avakian 1992, 1997).

I draw attention to this insider conversation about "Americans" because, first, it gives us a window into the self-conception of beleaguered food cultures and their payback to mainstream disdain. I do not believe that marginalized communities, even at the height of the food fights of the early twentieth century, were completely colonized. They often met disdain with disdain. Insider caricatures of dominant outsiders are an important resource in the fight for cultural survival. It is a classic "weapon of the weak." Bengalis deploy it today, and surely Italians did so 100 years ago.

Second, I think that the civil-rights and nationalist movements have changed the very terrain of cultural politics. Post–1965 immigrants are entering into a context that is much transformed. They can play out the Orientalist argument in reverse: "You have technology and economy, but look at us: We have Culture." I see that attitude among Bengali Americans today. I am not so sanguine that such an attitude existed among the 1880–1924 cohort of immigrants. I do not see much evidence of it in the work on Italian Americans, Jewish Americans, Irish Americans, or Japanese Americans that I have cited.

Of course, there is a problem here for the historian: Ethnic insiders in the first generation write and publish very little about food (as Gabaccia shows, although Diner makes excellent use of what has been written). The best documentation is done by the dominant institutions of the state and the church, which attempt to reform migrant eating practices. Thus, we need nuanced reading of the suggestions, the tonalities, and the silences to uncover such an attitude, if it did exist. It may have always been there but invisible to researchers who were typically outsiders—or, at least, were seen as such.

Nevertheless, about Bengali-American attitudes I can say a few things. The moral economy of the crude materialist American is constructed with great unreflexivity. Among cosmopolitan Bengali professionals this sense of superiority is heightened by their own success. The market economy was one sphere where the West had to be conceded its superiority. Indian reformers acknowledged that more than two centuries ago. Swami Vivekananda, who was otherwise convinced of the ethical superiority of the Hindu, acknowledged the "mercantile virility" of the Western man. Hindu reformers, when confronted with the proof of colonialism as a sign of Western superiority, hoped to use the domestic realm to hold the line against the invasion of bourgeois modernity. Many Bengali Americans now feel that they have not only stemmed the tide in the domestic realm but have also joined the battle in the public sphere. They believe that their success in the professions derives from their strength in family life. Conservative American commentators' nostalgia for "family values" for these Bengali professionals is dramatic proof of the acuity of Hindu reformers who said as much: Protect the family from the ravages of modernity and thou shall inherit the kingdom of heaven.

Of course, such an assertion is possible only because West Bengali Americans are neither burdened by limits of class nor by language, which makes them naïve about the historical possibilities of the American dream and sometimes terribly self-righteous. Currently, Bengali-American identity sits uncomfortably within a series of unsettled polarities. Bengalis feel their racial intermediacy as not white, not black, and not Asian, either; their religious identity as not Jewish, not Catholic, not Protestant, and not Muslim;

their class location as not working class and not elite. In addition, they are numerically few and linguistically invisible to Americans, apolitical (they are not a pressure group yet), and, unlike most recent immigrants, Anglophone. Thus, they face the problem of trying to affirm difference without being too antagonistic to what they see as the mainstream culture. Hence, domestic cooking is the perfect place where their cautious middleness gets deployed as a private, hesitant, ornamental identity—an identity commensurate with a consensual rather than a conflictual view of America. They hold a very middle-class view of an ascriptively alien American—an identity that can be murmured, along with the rhetoric of science, progress, and opportunity, through private consumption, which is the ultimate affirmation of American values.

Assimilation has long been understood as a process where people come to America with much cultural baggage, which they eventually lose. In the long run, that is a relatively accurate description. But in the medium and short run—which is to say, between twenty and sixty years—more interesting things are happening in American food practices.

The pattern of consumption among migrants is more complicated than either assimilationists or romantic ethnics would have us believe. Breakfast and lunch would provide fodder for assimilationist arguments, while dinner would confirm the expectations of those who insist on ethnic survival. Different meals of the day and the week may be used to portray contradictory objectives of the migrants. Migrants have in them both the hope of assimilation and the aspiration to retain their ethnicity. That holds true at least for the first generation. By the second generation, the pace of assimilation accelerates dramatically for complex reasons of intent, convenience, mixed socialization, and the slow dissipation of an ethnic memory.

There are further complications, such as when Bengali-American children consume syncretic foods on an everyday basis for dinner in the privacy of the home, and yet these same children are compelled to eat more Bengali foods when the audience is the *probashi* public, as in dinner parties within the community. In the even more "public" public sphere of parties to which "Americans" are invited, the children revert to American food. This is the reverse of what one would expect from reading Erving Goffman's rendition of insider–outsider relations:

Since it is not necessary to retain social distance or be on guard before those who are one's colleagues in occupation, ideology, ethnicity, class, etc., it is common for colleagues to develop secret signs which seems innocuous to non-colleagues while at the same time they convey to the initiate that he is among his own and can relax the pose he maintains towards the public. (Goffman 1959: 192)

True, but not the whole story, because masks of appearance are also important for the symbolic exchange within the community. That is so because the consolidation of identity receives its greatest charge from the elaborate staging of ideas and ideals in and through the insider community.

There is an embrace of "otherness" or recoil from it depending on the context and the contingent intentions of the performative self. All of this is underlined by an ambiguity about identity, where complementary duality is tolerated. Like everybody else, Bengali Americans have the rounded attributes of characters in time, where identity is repeatedly undermined by possibility.

There are innumerable explicit and implicit rules about how to play the role of an "ethnic" among both insiders and outsiders. Among insiders, playing that role is a matter of "blood" and "spirit"; to outsiders, playing the role is often a metonymic caricature where one aspect of an ethnic culture is exaggerated and made to represent all of it. This happens particularly in the sphere of food consumption, where the French come to be called "Frogs"; the English, "Limeys," and so on. There are no gustatory caricatures specifically about Bengalis yet, primarily because they do not matter as much, given their small numbers and middle-class invisibility.

Metonymic shorthands are used not only by dominant cultures but also by ethnic subcultures in identifying the mainstream. I have provided a number of examples of how this process of identification occurs in the realm of food habits. Bengali Americans make explicit and implicit comparisons between "American food" and "Bengali food." In identifying their own food they point to specific ingredients and cooking processes. The boundaries are drawn in contrast to what are seen as "American" ways. Hidden inside these broad patterns are a range of particular stories that cannot be easily classified.

The broad patterns of *probashi* foodways are comparable especially to those of other first-generation migrants, such as the Japanese in the 1920s and Italians in 1940s, who were at about the same level of adaptation and generational dynamic at that point in time as Bengali Americans are today. (I will say more about that in Chapter 6.) The difference lies in their class background and in their reception by the mainstream. Earlier cohorts had to face much stronger pressure for assimilation, which was underlined by class and ethnic disdain.

Predictably, over time and generation there is clearly increasing adaptation to the new context. What has changed since the 1940s is that ethnicity is valorized today, especially the ethnicity of middle-class professionals, and particularly by outsiders. One could hypothesize that, under these changed circumstances, the diacritical features that people look for and exhibit to show ethnic identity will persist longer because they are fashionable. Yet that very comfort might undermine the need to retain a distinctive subculture as more and more Bengalis are accepted within the culture of the professional middle class (unlike, say, working-class Italians a century ago). Only poor working-class Bengalis from Bangladesh, the butt of jokes on *Late Night with David Letterman,* could vitiate that smooth ride to assimilation for professional Bengalis. With rising tides of nativism, Bengalis could be misread by the American mainstream as completely alien and hence potentially hostile, despite their best attempts to dissolve into public invisibility by way of their middleness. Which way it will go remains to be seen.

CHAPTER 5

Food Work

Labor of Love?

A woman well set free! How free I am,
How wonderfully free, from kitchen drudgery
Free from the harsh grip of hunger,
And from empty cooking pots,
Free too of that unscrupulous man.

SUMANGALAMATA (BUDDHIST NUN, INDIA),
SIXTH CENTURY B.C.

O ur understanding of other people is dependent on our conceptions of their gendered roles in the making of the household. The heart of my research is about food consumption and its place in the construction of identity. Yet I cannot construct a compelling picture of food consumption without some observations on food work. I focus on a few questions. First, who does what food-related work in Bengali-American households? Second, how has migration affected the distribution of that work? Third, how does that compare with what "American" women do? Finally, what does the division of labor tell us about distribution of power within the household?

Any discussion of food work must begin with the dramatic fact that 65 percent of Bengali-American women have professional credentials, or at least a master's degree. That violates assumptions that "ethnic" women have less education and hence are willing to do more housework. Nevertheless, many Bengali-American women are underemployed. It is not unusual to find a Bengali-American woman with a master's degree staying at home and raising children or working as a bank teller. One woman with an medical degree classified herself in the survey as a "housewife," while another was a physician's assistant; another woman with a Ph.D. stayed home. Although more than 70 percent of the women are in full-time or part-time employment, at least one-half of them hold "jobs" rather than pursue "careers"—"waged job complementary to that of the husband, and compatible with it, and almost always performed in a minor mode" (Bourdieu 2001: 108). Here the figure of the subservient woman returns.

Yet there is nothing particularly Bengali about this distribution. Although Italian American women typically have fewer degrees, almost the same percentage hold "jobs" and choose "career" paths (Theophano and Curtis 1991). In interviews it became clear that among Bengali American women, some of this is driven by choice (related in most cases to child-rearing) and some by insider expectations about a woman's role. A few women were upset that various disruptions in employment brought about by pregnancies and long summer breaks (so that the family could visit India) had effectively destroyed their opportunity to move up the career ladder. Yet most appeared reconciled to their familial role.

Groceries, Cooking, and Cleaning

In most Bengali-American households, women do most of the cooking. When asked about the responsibilities of cooking, 10 percent of respondents held that husbands and wives equally share the responsibility. Another 20 percent held that husbands cook about once a week, and another 20 percent said the husbands cook occasionally.

These figures look quite respectable in terms of men's participation rates compared with what I would have predicted from anecdotal information and from ethnographic observation. Other evidence also suggests that middle-class Bengali men are particularly unskilled at cooking. Most do not have any experience of cooking before migration. Before marriage, mothers, sisters, aunts, grandmothers, and servants do all of the food-related work in the most strictly gendered division of labor. After marriage, food work becomes the wife's exclusive responsibility.

Cooking, in middle-class male Bengali eyes, is tainted by burdens of gender at home and class in the marketplace. When a young man sets out for the New World, he survives on packaged cereals and cafeteria food until his wife joins him. As noted earlier, there is no tradition in Bengal even of outdoor men's cooking, as is common in the United States. Hence, it is surprising that the survey data provide a figure that is close to the broad American pattern—that is, 10 percent of men cooking regularly, and 40 percent cooking occasionally.[1] Are Bengali men learning to cook after migration and marriage? Or are anecdotes about Bengali men's ineptitude in the kitchen just that? We will have to wait for other studies to affirm or undermine these figures.

Cooking is largely a feminized task, but what happens to grocery shopping, which is a masculine task in the pre-immigration milieu? Sixty-percent of households shop for food once a week. Another 35 percent shop more often, usually once every few days. Adult women shop by themselves in almost 50 percent of the households. In addition, in about 40 percent of households the husband and wife shop together for food. Only in about 10 percent of the households do the men do groceries on their own. Thus, women are involved in shopping for groceries in about 90 percent of the households. This is the exact opposite of what happens in Calcutta, where men shop for groceries on their own (Dutt 1988).

So 90 percent of the women are shopping for groceries, and 90 percent are cooking regularly. Are there any justifications provided for this relatively skewed division of domestic labor? According to the scriptures, household work is an aspect of a woman's *dharma* ("religion"). Traditionalists postulate two categories of worship: the cooked-food sacrifice offered to the domestic fire, and the oblation sacrifice offered to the sacred fires. Fire, water, and ghee are essential elements of a sacred sacrificial performance, as is the participation of a male priest who knows the proper words in Sanskrit (Embree 1988: 24). However, household offerings of cooked food are presided over by the women of the household, preferably married and fertile. Everyday offerings of food to the divinities have come to be managed by women who control the kitchen—the heart of the sacred geography of the home.

According to Pika Ghosh (1995: 21–25), the preparation of food is regarded as an act of worship similar to but not of the same order as rituals performed by a priest.[2] Women assume the responsibility of conveying the transfer of divine beneficence that occurs during the offering and blessing of food. A woman who does the cooking serves it to family members as if she were a priest:

The household rituals that women perform derive their authority from their marital status and fertility. In Bengal, the notion of both sacredness and auspiciousness is intimately associated with women. The newly married woman is introduced to her husband's house as a deity, not just as a wife. Bengali terms for wife are applied to Lakshmi, the goddess of wealth and prosperity, and the Bengali woman is described as being Lakshmi because she is the embodiment of the virtues of the goddess. (Ghosh 1995: 23)

In general, what Judith Walsh (1997) calls "the discourse of devotion" to the husband and the family seems to be intact among first-generation Bengali women, as shown, among other things, by their exclusive responsibility for cooked food. Such a "traditional attitude" is surely one source of inequity in the division of household labor. Nevertheless, the justification of such a "tradition" gives some women the room to appropriate a certain amount of symbolic power.

Reconfiguring the Sexual Division of Labor

Table 10 (Appendix 2) provides a quick overview of the daily hours of food-related work for Bengali-American women. In almost 70 percent of the households, women work for at least one-and-a-half to three hours a day shopping for groceries, cooking, and cleaning.

Of course, much of this work is interwoven with other chores, such as infant care, dropping off and picking up children from school, and swimming and tennis lessons for older children; hence, it is difficult to estimate in terms of clearly defined hours of work. Nevertheless, figures for Bengali-American women's food work are comparable to average American figures (see Table 11, Appendix 2).

In Bengali-American households, men and children help most often in washing dishes. Many clean and cut vegetables; some reheat food, take out the trash, load the dishwasher, and set the table. In Calcutta, some of this work—washing dishes, cutting vegetables, and taking out the trash—was clearly women's work, usually done by women within the household or by paid female servants. Thus, some parts of the food work, especially setting the table and cleaning and disposing of trash and leftovers, has been masculinized and infantilized in the United States. (It appears from the ethnographic data that children, both boys and girls, are generally expected to help set the table and put away leftovers in the United States. That is hardly the case in middle-class Calcuttan households, where boys are effectively excused from household work.)

Some parts of the domestic labor process related to food production but not wholly part of it, such as gardening, have become masculinized. Bengali-American men appear to be much more involved in gardening than I have seen in Calcutta. Higher incomes, larger homes with bigger yards, and middle-class American notions of recreational work may have brought out what was always latent in Bengali men. Nevertheless, in the same constrained context of Calcutta, Bengali women did raise gardens, often containing nothing more than a Holy Basil (*tulsi*) or a flowering plant, both intended as offerings to domestic deities. Gardening was clearly women's work. After migration, in contrast, men appear to be more involved in gardening, recalling a practice followed by Italian American men in planting fig trees, tomatoes, eggplant, and fennel (Malpezzi and Clements 1992: 241). In the case of Italian men, this propensity to garden at the turn of the nineteenth century was often explained as a link to their peasant past. That cannot be the reason for urban, middle-class Bengali men. The sources of middle-class Bengali men's affinity for gardening lie elsewhere.

In contrast to gardening, other parts of the domestic-labor process have been feminized. The most dramatic example of feminization, as mentioned earlier, is doing groceries. Further, the transportation of food and children to and from the household has also been feminized. In Calcutta, it was the men of the household using mass transit systems who were primarily responsible for that. One reason is gendered expectation; the other is low private automobile ownership—fewer than 1 percent. In contrast, in the United States, with private automobiles and multiple-car suburban households, Bengali wives have become the primary conveyors of children to and from school, sporting events, and doctors and dentists, in addition to hauling unprepared food home. Further, in Calcutta, aspects of work, such as infant care, babysitting, and cooking, were shared with other women of the household or with paid help. In the United States, paid help is either considered too expensive or too culturally aberrant. Extended kinship networks rarely exist. (It is interesting to note that the increase in average family size in the United States to 3.32 members typically increases housework for the homemaker, but any increase beyond that reduces work. In large families, other family members or nonfamily helpers take over some of the tasks of the mother; see Bryant 1996: 365.)

Thus, one could conclude that, in all probability, middle-class Bengali-American women are doing much more housework in the United States than they did in India. Most respondents said so. For middle-class Bengali-American women, the most important transformation in the domestic labor process is the absence of servants. That is something Harriet Beecher Stowe saw coming long ago when she wrote, "This want of servants is the one thing that must modify everything in American life" (as quoted in Fussell 1983: 12).

For some Bengali-American women, totally novel responsibilities such as pet care has been added. Most middle-class households in Calcutta did not have pets in the 1970s. Other burdens, such as laundry, have increased. In Calcutta, laundry was handled in three different ways: It was done by a servant at home, farmed out to a *dhobi* (launderer), or done by the wife and mother at home. In the United States, all the laundry is done by the homemaker. Furthermore, Bengali Americans have many more clothes in the United States. For example, a typical middle-class professional man in Calcutta has four to five shirts in all, whereas in the United States the wardrobe of a professional can include 15–30 formal-wear shirts and half that number of trousers. Further, the laundry is done more often in the United States, because of both higher incomes that increase the size of the wardrobe and higher standards of cleanliness. For instance, in Calcutta, a shirt is often worn two to three days in a row without washing, while in the United States a newly laundered shirt is the norm for professionals every day.

The same logic increases work in the kitchen, especially in dishwashing and storage. There are many more pots, pans, dishes, and silverware. The house is also bigger, leading to more work to keep it clean, although most houses in the United States require less dusting than do those in Calcutta. Some other kinds of work have also decreased in the United States. Craftwork of quilting and ritual painting with rice flour has vanished. Few grind spices in the United States—another chore usually done by servants in Calcutta. The food processor has replaced the servant but has to be assembled, used, disassembled, cleaned, and put away. Perhaps one area where housework has dramatically and clearly increased is in storing large quantities of produce in multiple freezers and refrigerators and cooked food in containers. A consequence of freezing and storing so much produce is that it takes a lot more planning and strategic thinking about "first in, first out" systems, times to be allowed for defrosting, menu planning to use ingredients that are dated, and so on. In contrast, in Calcutta fresh produce was purchased daily.

Most of the changes in housework parallel the experience of American women over the past three generations (Bryant 1996). What is distinctive about the experience of Bengali-American women is the telescoping of these changes within their life spans. What has taken the typical American women at least three generations to get used to, the Bengali-American woman must adjust to in her lifetime. That, of course, is the fate of all immigrants.

One area in which labor may have been clearly *reduced* is in the cooking process. Instead of three hot meals a day, most Bengali-American households eat one cooked meal a day, and most women do not cook all the courses daily. Often, the main animal-protein item, and sometimes even the dal, is cooked a few times a week in large quantities, frozen or chilled, and then reheated in small amounts. But the main carbohydrate anchor for dinner—rice—is cooked daily. Many households use rice cookers, which have eliminated the difficult labor of cooking in large stock pots with excess water that needs to be watched over and drained when steaming hot. Nevertheless, some of the food work may have increased due to the bifurcation of preferences between the generations, making it necessary to prepare different food ensembles for the same meal. Children prefer certain items in their meals, such as hamburgers and pasta, that adults—especially adult men—will not entertain for dinner. Commenting on American households, Shapiro (1997: 38) notes that "the refrigerator would 'help' the housewife prepare in advance and store two separate meals, one for the adults and one for Junior. The grown-ups, for example, would have meat loaf and pie. . . . Junior would have a hamburger and a cup of pie filling. Miraculously, 'cooking' had been made more time-consuming without in any way affecting the amount or quality of the food." In Calcutta, adults and children typically ate the same meal.

The most complex part of food work may be managing the whole process of feeding the family while taking into consideration the needs and demands of each member. Some of the most recent work on household labor shows that even if we accept the optimistic figures showing a decline in the hours of housework over the past six decades, the total hours for "marketing and managing" have increased (Bryant 1996).

Power and Household Labor

In their work on Italian Americans, Janet Theophano and Karen Curtis (1991: 171) hold that "through the food system, women express and maintain their social positions in the community." This is a revisionist reading of women's role as gatekeepers who control the flow of goods into the household and regulate the channels through which food reaches the table (McIntosh and Zey 1989). Bengali-American women do express and maintain their social position in the community through food work. They are the ones who are primarily responsible for managing systems of reciprocity among households. They keep account of friends and neighbors who have invited them for dinner and the number of times they have been invited. They decide when it is time to reciprocate and to what extent—a formal dinner or tea and snacks? That is what Micaela di Leonardo (1992) has called kin-work. Bengali-American women maintain these networks of reciprocity, as is the norm in every other community.

In spite of some degree of autonomy and substantial power that comes from kin-work and the right to make strategic household management decisions, women have to keep their eyes on the collective needs of the household rather than on their individual self-interest. Within the household, the adult male's preference takes some precedence in designing a menu, in part because of the husband's economic predominance, and perhaps more important, because of the discourse of devotion around which the feminine self is constructed.[3] The wife's job is to keep the husband happy, especially about food. Yet it is not at all clear that this is only a matter of individual power, as made evident by the attention given to the taste and health of relatively "powerless" children, who sometimes take even greater priority in a mother's meal planning than the husband. Nevertheless, children can be disciplined and taught what is good for them (and their mothers), but husbands cannot (in most cases).

By desiring a female-labor–intensive dinner—symbolically the most important meal of the day—the Bengali man's sense of loss and homelessness, engendered by migration, is compensated for by reaffirming what he thinks is patriarchal control over the domestic hearth. Lest we confuse this patriarchal dream as an Oriental holdover, it must be made clear that there is nothing peculiarly Bengali in this division of labor. The U.S. data affirms that. A study by Nickie Charles and Marion Kerr (1986; 1988) of families in the north of England found that the women also had the main responsibility for buying, preparing, and serving food. A later study carried out in Manchester by Alan Warde and Kevin Hetherington (1994) underlines the same gendered division of labor for food-related tasks. In the Manchester studies, women predominated in preparing meals—especially "proper meals" of roasted meats, two vegetables, and a dessert—and men participated in recreational cooking such as beer and wine making and barbecue.

Similar patterns emerge in M. Ekström's (1991) work with 348 Swedish families. Ekström divides feeding work under four headings: planning meals, shopping for food, the preparation of breakfast, and the preparation of dinner. Planning is overwhelmingly the mother's work. Shopping, although a joint activity, is primarily the responsibility of women. For the main meal of the day—dinner—59 percent of Swedish households rely entirely on the mother. Breakfast is the only meal for which fathers and other family members take substantial responsibility.

Nickie Charles's contention that men eat more and higher-status food (Charles 1995) is generally confirmed by my ethnography in the United States and the 1970 data from Calcutta. But it needs a few important qualifiers. Since all my respondents were from affluent families, there was no significant difference in the quality of the diet by gender or generation. In fact, in many households, foods defined as the freshest and best are consumed by children. Milk products and fresh fruit—often considered the most valuable—are prioritized for children's consumption. Men, by contrast, often snack on what is considered the lowest-quality food, such as leftovers, stale fish, and overripe mangoes. If children are the best fed and the weakest, it creates a problem for the traditional feminist assumption that greater or better consumption equals more power. It could be that men's power also constrains men's action because of the accompanying responsibility. Powerful men may be looking at family resources from the perspective not of individual acquisition but of collective social reproduction.

Although women eat less in general, their relationship to power may not be inversely related to consumption. If we can extricate ourselves from contractual assumptions and analyze gastropolitics as a redistributive or gift-giving system, then it may be possible to imagine that those who feed others may be more powerful than those who gorge themselves.

Furthermore, the vision may be one of shared responsibilities rather than individual needs, a vision driven by what Bourdieu, in an uncharacteristically short postscript to *Masculine Domination,* calls the mystical possibilities

of love—the capacity to suspend the symbolic violence of male domination, "binding men through the magic of the attachments of passion, making them forget the obligations linked to their social dignity, bring[ing]
about a reversal of the relation of domination" (Bourdieu 2001: 109–10).
Yet, he says, this is merely a miraculous truce in the context of war, a truce
that makes possible momentary lapses into disinterestedness and disintru-
mentalized relations; a truce that must endlessly guard against the return
of egoistic calculation through mere routinization. It is a gift of the self,
where the self recognizes the other as another self and in perfect reflexiv-
ity seeks a contingent communion where "two beings can 'lose themselves
in each other' without being lost" and share the burdens of raising a family (2001: 110–11).

Karl Polanyi (1980) has shown that in reciprocal and redistributive systems, power accumulates not with the greatest accumulator of material
things but with the greatest giver of goods (and hence the receiver of moral
and political beneficence). The modern household may be one of the few
spheres where such noncontractual relationships survive and, in fact, even
thrive. Yet there is one problem with that characterization: Although the
powerful have often been gift givers, they have rarely been the ones who
work the hardest physically, and we do know that women do most of the
work at home. Historically, those who work—in particular, those who do
physical work—are at the bottom of the social order. In contrast, those who
do ritual work have greater stature; that is, priests, medicine men, and other
ritualists are often found at the top of the status hierarchy. So it is important to ask whether women's work in the household is seen as mere physical work or ritual work, work that preserves a community. Here we come
up against an alternative conception of housework as domestic ritual, as
discussed earlier. If the preparation of food is regarded as an act of worship, of "the cooked-food sacrifice offered at the domestic fire" analogous
to rituals performed by a priest, then the issue of power looks very different from the feminist-materialist perspective. The issue may be particularly
important when a people migrate and seek to sustain cultural ties. Is this
so-called traditional conception just a convenient sleight of hand by men
to keep their wives subservient? Maybe, but those who make such arguments are all women. Is that just "false consciousness"? Maybe. Yet ideas
matter, and how one conceives one's role in the division of labor and how
others see it—*pace* ritual work—determines to some extent whether one
is empowered or powerless. The symbolic element is crucially important

in the distribution of power, as Bourdieu has shown in his long-standing and ongoing critique of the narrow materialist interpretation of domination. We should be careful lest we pour all the meaning of domestic labor into the Manichean mold of patriarchy. As Theresa Devasahayam (1997) notes, women do a number of things as they work in the household—they resist, maneuver, change, express, and even reinforce the social asymmetry. Food work is characterized simultaneously by cooperation and competition, by guilt and gratification. In a capitalized world of cash nexus and instrumental individualism, food work can be both one of the most challenging and fulfilling emotional and work experiences. Thus, it must come as no surprise that an overwhelming number of female respondents in the survey argued that they enjoy cooking for their families, and they insisted that they do not see food work as oppressive or even as an unfair division of labor.

As two-thirds of adult Bengali-American women either hold part-time employment or are full-time homemakers, Bengali-American women take on greater responsibilities at home. Among those who study family issues, this perspective is often characterized as the "time-availability" model or the "resource-exchange" model, in which housework is divided either according to the time each spouse has available or is exchanged for wage work (Atkinson and Huston 1984; Berk 1985; Coltrane and Ishii-Kuntz 1992; Coverman 1985; Pleck 1985). Research supports that claim directly, noting that when some of the women's commuting and work hours are long, their husbands appear to do much more housework, including some of the cooking. There is also substantial difference in housework hours between women employed part time and those employed full time. Furthermore, in a typical household the total hours spent in household labor by women ranges from thirty to forty hours per week, which is equivalent to the typical workweek of the man (Marini and Shelton 1993: 377). Yet when women spend an almost equal amount of time at paid work as their husbands (34 hours per week for both), there is no equitable distribution of work at home (34 hours per week for women; 20 hours per week for men), which is what should happen if the time-availability model is to work fully (Marini and Shelton 1993: 377).

Many of the female respondents considered dinner—the most labor-intensive part of the daily meal cycle—to be very important in keeping the family together. According to Marjorie DeVault (1991), women's work of feeding the family, of creating and staging the family-meal-as-event, can be seen as counteracting the centrifugal forces that the activities of individual family members, each with his or her own schedule, generates. In this sense, feeding literally produces the family. Bengali-American women do see the commensal dinner as counteracting the fissiparous tendencies of their kin. It is also the time to reinvent tradition, not only for Bengali men, but also for Bengali women in the United States. Inundated by the mythology of the collapse of "Western" families, the Bengali woman idealizes dinner as the "traditional" family huddle. In a rice-and-*jhol* dinner, she creates a memorable tradition. Through the creative consumption of commodities, tamed as food at the domestic hearth, the Bengali woman affirms a ritual that denies the limitations of time and place—limitations that inevitably confront a migrant. The assertion is that the Bengali dinner can be re-enacted any place and at any time, as long as she is willing to work.

From this discussion it should *not* be concluded that all my respondents were happy with the division of labor at home. I have perhaps labored a little too hard to seek explanations for why so many women find the division of labor at home workable, even when it is apparently so inequitable. In the process, the difficulties and the frustrations of such an unfair division of labor may have been given short shrift.

Recent research that might explain the relative lack of trouble in many families shows that

> non-traditional attitudes to gender roles are associated with dissatisfaction with the division of housework, while traditional attitudes are associated with satisfaction with the way the housework is organized between partners. Women who believe that people should adhere to traditional gender roles are more satisfied with the division of the housework than women with an egalitarian view of gender roles. (Baxter and Western 1998: 113)

It may be that most of my female respondents just have "traditional" attitudes toward housework and that, to the great consternation of many a modernizer, they need to be "forced to be free." Socialization, or the performative construction of gender, is used to explain why only a minority of wives desire their husbands to do more even though they do most of the housework. Mothers often voice concern over giving up authority over child care. Some have argued that women's reluctance to give up family work is based in part on the sense of purpose they derive from being needed by their children and husbands (DeVault 1990; Thompson and Walker 1989). They have also shown how and why mothers and fathers collude in making relatively unfair divisions of parenting appear "natural." The dominated, argues Bourdieu (2001: 30),

> are condemned to give at every moment the appearances of a natural foundation to the diminished identity that is socially bestowed on them: they are the ones who perform the long, thankless, tedious task of picking up from the ground the olives or twigs that the men have brought down with a pole or an axe; they are the ones who, delegated to the vulgar preoccupations of the everyday management of the domestic economy, seem to take pleasure in the petty calculations of debt and interest to which the man of honour does not stoop.

In addition, it has been shown that the most important predictor of a woman's satisfaction with the household division of labor is not her husband's equal labor but his efforts in nontraditional activities—that is, feminine chores. If he does a little more cooking than men usually do, if he does the laundry once in a while, and if he does a few more household chores, it is fine with the woman that he works much less in aggregate. Janeen Baxter and Mark Western (1998: 113) contend that

> for most women it seems that the benchmark against which their own household arrangements are judged is not some ideal which men and women contribute equally to domestic labor (and against which almost all households fall short), but a pragmatic assessment of reality, in which men do much less and in which there is a pronounced gender division of labor. Against the yardstick of a highly traditional gendered division of domestic labor, any consistent participation by husbands in non-traditional male activities is better than the alternative, and hence is associated with increased satisfaction amongst women.

The division of labor within the household is so deeply entrenched and universal that migration barely has any effect on it other than in the reallotment of some work, such as grocery shopping to women and dishwashing and gardening to men. In addition, middle-class Bengali women bear greater burdens in the United States primarily due to the loss of servants. Otherwise, the domestic division of labor stays remarkably inequitable and yet parallels (with some minor variations) what is going on in most households in the United States, Great Britain, and Sweden. Contrary to popular assumptions, there does not appear to be a dramatic difference between First World households and Third World middle-class migrant families in terms of the gendered division of labor.

What does this inequitable division of labor tell us about power within the family? That is probably the most difficult question to answer. There is certain validity to each of the arguments made earlier—namely, "discourse of devotion," "resource exchange," and "time availability." What matters in the final analysis is whether the women concerned feel disempowered, and if they do, what would they want to change? That does leave the issue to the vagaries of ideational systems (what men and women think about fairness and why). Ideas matter, and what women think about the relationship between the household division of labor and power is central to the issue.

The issue of power is framed within a different optic if we shift to the emic (insider) conception of the problem. If rites are sacrifice and sacrifice is work (*shram*), then household work is a sacrifice and a devotion. Sacrifice and devotion, like gift giving, are reciprocal relationships of bondage. Mary Douglas (1990: ix) writes, "There are no free gifts; gift cycles engage persons in permanent commitment." The commitment deepens if the gift is internalized—as with cooked food. All bonds are limiting. Power comes from recognizing that simple truth. In contrast, *mukti* (liberation) and *ananda* (happiness) are otherworldly phenomena that can be achieved only by doing one's duty in this constrained and bonded world—an unreal world, an unfair world.

Nevertheless, Bourdieu (2001: 46–47) has cautioned us that masculine domination is not only a matter of consciousness and will but an embodied disposition—a historical, collective unconscious; a somatization of the relation of domination—that is affirmed by both men and women by the familiar, continuous, ordinary, repetitive, and monotonous toil, physical and cognitive, that is performed out of sight and out of mind in the darkness of the house. The dominated, argues Bourdieu (2001: 32–33, 35), apply categories constructed from the point of view of the dominant, thus naturalizing the latter's viewpoint:

Although it is true that . . . recognition of domination always presupposes an act of knowledge, this does not imply that one is entitled to describe it in the language of consciousness, in an intellectualist and scholastic fallacy which, as in Marx (and above all, those who, from Lukács onwards, have spoken of "false consciousness"), leads one to expect the liberation of women to come through the immediate effect of the "raising of consciousness," forgetting—for lack of a dispositional theory of practices—the opacity and inertia that stem from the embedding of social structures in bodies. (Bourdieu 2001: 40)

Yet it is also true that the kitchen is a source of feminine power. Although she acknowledges that the first time she had to do "real day-to-day meal-after-meal cooking," she found it to be "the longest, most discouraging week," M. F. K. Fisher nevertheless concludes,

> The stove, the bins, the cupboards, I had learned forever, make an inviolable throne room. From them I ruled; temporarily I controlled. I felt powerful, and I loved that feeling.
>
> I am more modest now, but I still think that one of the pleasantest of all emotions is to know that I, I with my brain and my hands, have nourished my beloved few, that I have concocted a stew or a story, a rarity or a plain dish, to sustain them truly against the hungers of the world. (as quoted in Gioia 1999: 50)

And what hungers they are! Of home and homeland, of a corner in the world. As women resist and reinforce the social asymmetry in the kitchen, they cook up a world and show us innovative ways of reimagining it. They provide us with a heterotopic reality where we labor not only for money and fame but for our own pleasures and to minister to the needs of others.

In Bengal, in America, and all over the world, that is primarily a feminine gift. "The gift cycle echoes Adam Smith's invisible hand: gift complements market in so far as it operates where the latter is absent" (Douglas 1990: xiv). Without gift giving, no social relationship can survive. Without the gift of her labor, no household can work. It is left to the rest of us to reciprocate. But her gift being the original gift is unrepayable, around which are built narratives of devotion.

CHAPTER 6

Meals, Migration, and Modernity

I, Saleem Sinai, possessor of the most delicately gifted olfactory organ in history have dedicated my latter days to the large-scale preparation of condiments. But now, "A cook?" you gasp in horror, "A khansama merely? How is it possible?" And I grant, such mastery of the multiple gifts of cookery and language is rare indeed; yet I possess it. You are amazed; but then I am not, you see, one of your 200-rupees-a-month cookery johnnies, but my own master. . . . And my chutneys and kasaundies are, after all, connected to my nocturnal scribblings—by day amongst the pickle-vats, by night within these sheets, I spend my time at the great work of preserving. Memory, as well as fruit, is being saved from the corruption of the clocks.

SALMAN RUSHDIE, MIDNIGHT'S CHILDREN (1980: 38)

Salman Rushdie writes about the "chutneyfication" of the world. I in turn draw your attention to the world of chutneys. What happens when the chutney goes global? This is not about McDonald's or Coca-Cola; neither is it about "ethnic" restaurants in metropolitan centers. It is about home-cooked ethnic meals in the metropolis. It is a particularly intriguing pattern to study because it focuses on everyday domestic cooking, which is relatively under-studied, and it reverses the usual trajectory of globalization. Most studies of the globalization of food address either the "McDonaldization" of the world or the great "multicultural" flowering of "fusion" and "ethnic" restaurants in global cities.[1] Mine is a different story.

Globalization accentuates the modern problem of engendering a sense of stability in the context of rapid change. As Marshall Berman (1982: 6) put it in *All That Is Solid Melts into Air,* modernism is "a struggle to make ourselves at home in a constantly changing world." It is a problem about which Mark Twain, with characteristic irony, reportedly said, "I am all for progress, but it is change that I cannot stand." Middle-class migrants run into that problem with particular directness, and food is one of the arenas where Bengali Americans grapple with modern issues of home and away, progress and tradition.

For the middle-class Bengali migrant, all the trouble with food has to do with two things: home and heritage. Both are about defining one's self in terms of a place and a past, and that makes the middle-class Bengali migrant a quintessentially modern subject. In the process of showing that, I take nostalgia seriously and critique the assumption that migrants are somehow more traditional than others. I will illustrate that point by drawing attention first to Bengali Americans' project of finding a place of their own by way of the kitchen garden.

Place

Satan, being thus confined to a vagabond, wandering, unsettled condition, is without any certain abode; for though he has, in consequence of his angelic nature, a kind of empire in the liquid waste or air, yet this is certainly part of his punishment, that he is . . . without any fixed place or space, allowed him to rest the sole of his foot upon.

DANIEL DEFOE, *THE POLITICAL HISTORY OF THE DEVIL* (2003: 73–74)

Food locates us. Discussions about place steer us homeward, and home inevitably leads to the hearth—the *focus* of the household. The household fire is also the site of sacred oblation to the Vedic Hindu. The hearth, which is one of the manifestations of Agni, god of the sacrificial fire, is among the earliest loci of deification among Indo-Aryans. Yet the homebound quest for the hearth is not an exclusively Vedic virtue. We are told in Homer's *Odyssey*, which Milan Kundera (2002: 7) characterizes as "the founding epic of nostalgia," that the protagonist "would give anything for the mere sight of smoke rising up from his own land" (Rieu 1946: 26). We know that it would take much misadventure and circumvention to get him to his hearth and the self-sacrificing Penelope.

Joseph Rykwert (1991: 51) may be accurate in stating that cooking, which is one of the earliest forms of taming fire, is the origin of culture:

"Hearths and middens, kitchen-refuse heaps, are some of the earliest traces of human habitation—the very notion of home seems to have grown around the hearth." Home is where the most important meal of the day is eaten, at the same hour, in communion with the same people, day in and day out. Or so we would like it to be.

Food is particularly potent as a place-making practice because it links the land to the hearth and the hearth to the heart through the mediation of produce. As Alice Waters, noted chef and culinarian, says: "If you see the same ingredients every place you go you lose a sense of time and place. Then nothing is special" (Waters 1999). That is exactly why immigrants crave some of the distinctive products of their homeland, notwithstanding time or place.

The link among produce, land, and homeland is evoked most directly by the kitchen garden. If we are to read the landscape around the home as a text, then we come up with a number of intriguing patterns. Beginning with the obvious, we can note that all landscaping around Bengali-American homes (for that matter, all modern homes) is divided between the front and the back—that is, kitchen gardens and front lawns. The front seems to be appropriate only for lawns, flowerbeds, and non-functional plants— things that are appropriate for display (Simmel 1991 [1908]). In contrast, kitchen gardens are functional insofar as they produce products that are subsequently prepared as food, such as eggplants, tomatoes, and green chilies.

This replicates what was self-evident to many Italians in Brooklyn almost a hundred years ago. One Italian American boy felt that gardens marked Italians as strangers in America: "There was another difference between us and them. We had gardens, not just flower gardens, but huge gardens where we grew tomatoes, tomatoes, and more tomatoes. Of course, we also grew peppers, basil, lettuce and squash. Everybody had a grapevine and a fig tree" (Oblate Sisters of the Sacred Heart of Jesus 1990: xxi). And often in the middle of the garden was a religious statue—St. Francis blessing the crop. According to Donna Gabaccia (1998: 52), "Men in Greenbush did much of the kitchen gardening, their children remembered, but as a strenuous 'hobby, a means of providing for their families and a labor of love.' "

Further, the layout of these gardens conveys substantial symbolic meaning. Bengali-American kitchen gardens are laid out along three patterns (if I am allowed to be precise). The first type is circular, with the outermost arc marked by American fruit trees such as plums, peaches, and bushes of

berries close to the outer boundary of the backyard. There is an intermediate stretch of lawn, then a concentric ring of tomatoes and eggplants.
Finally, there is an innermost ring of chilies and *tulsi* (the sacred basil). The
most Bengali of plants—*tulsi* and chilies—at the center of the landscape
underlines the idea of a soul, which is both hidden and valued. (The identification of chili as essentially Bengali, given its post-Columbian dispersal, tells us much about the fictions of authenticity we create.) The duality
between the body and the soul reflects the duality between the world of
sensation, which is individualized, and that of conception or morality, which
is collective. What fig trees were to Italian migrants, the *tulsi* is to Bengali
Americans. The world, so to speak, is arrayed around the "authentic" core,
recalling the design of temples around the orienting axis. A fixed point, of
course, is central to all notions of space and time.

This basic pattern is similar in structure to sacred diagrams in Indian
folk art. Temporary tattoos (*mehndi*) and rice-powder paintings on the floor
(*alpona* in Bengali) begin with a circle or an eight-petaled lotus flower as
diagrams to contain and direct the power of the supernatural. Nirad Chaudhuri, who is sometimes considered the nemesis of the expatriate Bengali
community and at other times their representative, recalls from his childhood days at Kishorganj in East Bengal:

> The girls took the powders in handfuls, closed their fist, and released
> the colours through the hole formed by the curled little finger, reg-
> ulating the flow by tightening or loosening their grip. It was won-
> derful to see how quickly they filled up the space. The sun was a star-
> ing face about two feet in diameter, the moon slightly smaller. The
> first was laid out mainly in red and black, producing a fiery effect,
> while the moon was for the most part in rice powder which very
> successfully brought out its blanched appearance. The floral decora-
> tions were of course *motifs* on which Bengali women had practiced
> no one knows for how many generations, and they came out as
> quickly and neatly as if they were being done from stencils. (Chaud-
> huri 1951: 18–19)

These protective charms are executed daily at dawn and at dusk, which
connects them to the sun. The diagrams are also drawn at rites of passage
such as marriage, birth of a son, or a boy's investiture of the sacred thread
(see Barnard and Beeche 1995; Boner 1990). In a backyard in Chicago, the

circle on the ground is fractured into an arc, but the cycle of life continues, just the context has changed. The universe rotates in endless cycles,
and the job of humans is to replicate that cosmic pattern. That is why Bengalis draw circular designs on a flat world. At least, some Bengalis do.

The next pattern is one of linear rows of green chilies, eggplants, and
tomatoes in a discrete corner of the backyard, ending with trellises of
pumpkins and squash. In a world that goes round and round, some Bengali Americans seek to draw a straight line. All of this is at the greatest distance from the house. Between the kitchen and the kitchen garden there
is a stretch of lawn. In this case, there is segregation, a juxtaposition of the
Bengali and the American, of the functional and the aesthetic. Different
things must stay discrete. Things must be kept in their places. That is the
hope. That is what provides stability. Or so some Bengalis think.

In the third pattern, the kitchen garden hugs the back porch, creating
a visual field of continuity among the hearth, the home, and the land. It is
a little Bengal in the back, hidden behind the American façade. It echoes
the claim of the Punjabi migrant Hari Singh Everest, who almost a century ago could hold that Sacramento Valley was "the Land of Five Rivers"
and hence the "Punjab." To substantiate his claim, he elaborated:

> In my story the Land of Five Rivers was Sacramento Valley. The river
> Sutlej was Feather River. The rest of the four rivers—American, Bear,
> Yuba, and Sacramento. My Bhakra, the Orville Dam. My Govind
> Sagar, the Orville Lake. The city of Anandpur Sahib, the nearby town
> of Paradise. The Shivaliks, the Sierra foothills. There was Naina Devi,
> our Mount Shasta. And yes, the Jawalmukhi, the Lessen Volcanic Park.
> Obviously, I was carried away by my imagination. Yet, the reality was
> not left far behind. The water, like the water in the Punjab, had the
> same urge to run downward. The distant hills had the same charm.
> (as quoted in Leonard 1997: 126)

This is the obverse of the claim by a young white reggae fan in Birming-
ham, England, talking about his English home:

> There is no such thing as "England" any more. . . . [W]elcome to
> India brothers! This is the Caribbean! . . . Nigeria! . . . There is no En-
> gland, man. This is what is coming. Balsall Heath [in Birmingham] is
> the center of the melting pot, 'cause all I ever see when I go out is

half-Arab, half-Pakistani, half-Jamaican, half Scottish, half-Irish. I know 'cause I am [half-Scottish/half-Irish]. (Hebdige 1987: 158–59)

This young man's claim is exceptional and draws attention to the fact that it is not only those who leave home who feel displaced. Displacement *is* the modern condition (real or imagined, it does not matter). Even those who stay home have to reconfigure their relationship to their place and reinvent their landscape, much like Hari Singh Everest.

Bengali Americans do that repeatedly. When it rains a little hard, they say, "It is just like the monsoons in Bengal." When they face a crowded subway, they contend that "it is just like Calcutta." And if it gets a little too hot and humid, they sigh, "It is just like back home." "Home" and its associated landscape are "revisioned," in Leonard's (1997) felicitous phrase. Sometimes things are taken a step further, when, as for Pietro Crespi in *One Hundred Years of Solitude,* "nostalgia would transform the smell of mud and putrefying shellfish of the canals [of Venice] into the warm aroma of flowers" (Márquez 1970: 111). Bengal becomes ever more beautiful in these distant dreams, now that its troubles can be kept at an arm's length. Anthony Giddens (1990: 140–41) notes:

Modernity "displaces" . . . —place becomes phantasmagoric. Yet this is a double-layered, or ambivalent, experience rather than simply a loss of community. . . .

This is less a phenomenon of estrangement from the local than one of integration within globalized "communities" of shared experience. . . . As Joshua Meyrowitz points out, a person on the telephone to another, perhaps on the opposite side of the world, is more closely bound to that distant other than to another individual in the same room (who may be asking, "Who is it? What's she saying?" and so forth).

To work the soil is to produce a place. The problem becomes how to produce a home in a land that is not yours. Many of the immigrant generation are haunted by an acute sense of displacement and yet seem to have some difficulty in giving voice to that state of mind. Some slip into nostalgia, much as the protagonist Arun does in Desai's *Fasting, Feasting.* The novel is about Uma and Arun. Uma is the unprepossessing, unattractive, and unmarriageable sister who nevertheless seeks to "extract every scrap of living out of the marrow of her barren existence" (Roy 1999). In contrast, her pampered brother Arun, who is in the United States, the land of literal and figurative plenty, is so scared of being included that he has closed himself off to anything but homesick yearnings for Indian food. The question Desai poses is: Who is fasting, and who is feasting? It is also a statement about how nostalgia can circumscribe the limits of one's world.

The word "nostalgia" derives from the Greek word *nostos,* meaning homeward journey. According to Bryan Turner (1987), "nostalgia" originated in a Swiss medical treatise of 1688 used to diagnose the condition among Swiss mercenaries in Italy. It took the English language another three centuries to name the feeling "homesickness." Nostalgia is decisively a sentimental longing for an idealized home. Orlando Patterson (1991: 171) contends that, even before the Swiss—that is, among the ancient Greeks—nostalgia was a masculine sentiment: "Home separation was then, as it remains today, a male anxiety." Perhaps because in patrilocal cultures, women are much better equipped to leave their father's home. Home is where the marriage is. Perhaps even more appropriately, as Ifat, Sara Suleri's sister, put it: "Men live in homes, and women live in bodies" (Suleri 1989: 143).

To Suleri, home is sometimes like the *zenana khana* (the women's quarter). "We who lived on the inside of that idea were caught in that curiously constricting position," she writes. "We felt imprisoned in the very place we knew represented an area of rampant fantasy in the city's psychic life" (Suleri 1989: 47–48). Home may not be what it is cracked up to be in nostalgic longing. Nevertheless, it persists.

Immigrants have some difficulty giving voice to their state of displacement because the exile overwhelms modernist literature. Homelessness is a trope in *Moby Dick, Huckleberry Finn, Kim,* and many others major modern novels, in which "the contingent heroes of bourgeois modernity have left the homes that they felt were no longer truly theirs to wander in search of a home not for a future nation of multitudes [as in the Bible] but for their own multitudinous selves" (Hollander 1991: 40). Home is where one starts from. Home is where one endlessly seeks to return to while running away from it—from its tyrannies of being walled-in; from structuring places and times.

For some, exile is a forced political condition. For others, it is embraced for aesthetic reasons—it is a heroic posture. In contrast, travel is linked to privilege and leisure. Migration, however, is undertaken in search of a livelihood and is thus neither particularly leisurely nor heroic (see Kaplan 1996; Kennedy 1993). While the exiled author defines her individuality by her posture against the community, the immigrant stays undifferentiated—a horde. Immigrants face a certain disdain equally, from traveling elites, expatriate intellectuals, and grounded patriots, each with their own notions of the appropriate relationship with the homeland. What have been the models of expatriate behavior? What has been the arc of expectation from the Indian expatriate over the last century?

In Search of Home:
From Rabindranath to Rushdie

We are born, so to speak, provisionally, it doesn't matter where; it is only gradually that we compose, within ourselves, our true place of origin, so that we may be born there retrospectively.
RAINER MARIA RILKE

Exiles are not only homeless but also worldly, and their aesthetic creativity apparently flows from that wandering cosmopolitanism. That kind of travel or exile appears to be substantially different from the structure of feeling of a migrant. Feeling displaced and yet lacking an aesthetic model, Bengali migrants turn to Rabindranath Tagore to frame their attitude toward the new home and the loss of the old one.

Tagore (1861–1941) has almost single-handedly defined the modern Bengali aesthetic. In Bengali, twenty-eight large volumes are available comprising his poetry, dramas, operas, short stories, novels, essays, and diaries. His letters are innumerable, and his songs number about 2,500; his paintings and drawings number more than 2,000. Much of his prolific writing is widely read and performed in Bengal and in the expatriate community today.

Mahatma Gandhi called Tagore the bard of Bengal; it was Tagore who first called Gandhi "Mahatma," the Great Soul. In 1912, Tagore won the Nobel Prize for Literature. He was subsequently canonized as Bengal's greatest creative artist. As a recent biography notes, "No writer, living or dead, is today more actively worshipped in Bengal than Rabindranath Tagore" (Dutta and Robinson 1996: 1). His birthday has become a seasonal ritual in Bengal second only to Durga Puja.

In a letter to a friend, Tagore wrote in 1921 that he was the first to introduce the land of Bengal to Bengalis as a subject fit for literature (Tagore 1961; Dutta and Robinson 1997: 177; unless stated otherwise, I use the 1997 translation). Bengalis first developed a lyrical patriotism toward their land through Tagore's songs in the course of the agitation following the partition of Bengal by the British in 1905. Nevertheless, in many of his writings Tagore was in fact seeking a way out of home. Home was too confining for him, especially his ancestral home under his father's iron hand. In his memoirs, *My Reminiscences,* Tagore smarts "under the rule of the servants." The outside beckoned him:

> Caged in the house as we were, anything savoring of foreign parts had a peculiar charm for me. It was one of the reasons why I made so much of Lenu [a young Punjabi servant]. It was also why Gabriel, the Jew with his embroidered gabardine, who came to sell attar and scented oils, stirred me so; and why the huge Kabulis, with their dusty, baggy trousers and knapsacks and bundles, worked my young mind into a fearful fascination. (Dutta and Robinson 1997: 65–66)

Tagore gave voice most successfully to someone trapped at home rather than away from it. His sweetest memories of childhood were those associated with travel with his father—first to Bholpur; then to Dalhousie in the Himalayas, and eventually to England and the rest of the world in his adult life. In England, he met a group of expatriate Bengalis who he came to call *ingabangas* (after Debendranath Tagore) and drew a devastating caricature in the following words:

> To know the ingabanga—the England-worshipping Bengali—truly one must observe him in three situations. One must see how he behaves with Englishmen; how he behaves with ordinary Bengalis; and how he behaves with fellow ingabangas. To see an ingabanga face to face with an Englishman is really a sight to gladden your eyes. The weight of courtesy in his words is like a burden making his shoulders droop; in debates he is the meekest and the mildest of men; and if he is compelled to disagree, he will do so with an expression of extreme regret and with a thousand apologies. . . . But catch him with his own countrymen in his own sphere, and he will display genuine temper. . . .

Had you seen for yourself the thorough research these people put into which way up a knife or fork should be held when dining, your respect would surely be still further increased. What the currently fashionable cut of a jacket is, whether today's gentleman wears his trousers tight or loose, whether one should dance the waltz, the polka or the mazurka, and whether meat should follow fish or vice versa— these people know all these things with unerring accuracy. Their preoccupation with trivia—what is and is not "done"—is far greater than that of the natives of this country. (Dutta and Robinson 1997: 100–102)

Note especially the second paragraph, with its repeated reference to the quotidian—the knife and fork, meat and fish, waltz and polka. The rhythms, postures, intonations, and tastes of foreigners appear fundamentally alien and embodied in the gestures of the other. Being nondiscursive and a product of innumerable small, multiple, and repetitive hints over years, they become quotidian markers of difference made evident by carriage, posture, accent, style, and volubility of any recent immigrant. Hence, such "trivial" markers become the most visible signs of mimicry taken to its extreme, which threatens everyone by its capacity to dissolve the signs of difference. Tagore in his propensity to be profound dismisses all as trivia, the very things that trouble a migrant in his mundane everyday life. Intellectuals have a tough time taking embodied, everyday knowledge seriously because of a long preference for the soul over the body, mind over matter, and theory over practice. Tagore falls squarely within that tradition.

In addition, the caricature of the *ingabanga* hints at Tagore's fear of transgression in spite of the lure of travel. This is self-ridicule of the *bhadralok*, mimicking the British stereotype of the WOG (Worthy Oriental Gentleman). British Indian newspapers such as *The Englishman* poured perpetual scorn on the same figure—"the Shakespeare-quoting seditious Babu" (Raychaudhuri 1988: 120). Tagore was not particularly original in making the Anglicized Bengali the target of contempt. He firmly belonged to the tradition of Bengali vernacular literature in which figures such as Bankimchandra Chattopadhyay, who, in arguing for a masculine and virile Hindu nationalist response to British imperialism, mocked the Bengali *babu* (while proposing a preposterously masculine diet of four chickens and eight eggs a day for himself) (Chattopadhyay 1965: 11–12; Raychaudhuri 1988: 113).[2]

Some of the disdain for the Anglicized Bengali is unalloyed self-hatred in the face of racism—Bankim's *jatibaira*. Some of it is an attempt to appropriate ridicule and deflect it by owning up to it. The *ingabanga* is Tagore's less vitriolic appropriation of *bhadralok* self-mockery and terror of crossing over.

This is not to reject out of hand the critique of the *ingabanga* as a superficial mimic and a social parasite. As the conservative critics Bhudev Mukhopadhyay and Rajnarayan Basu noted, the mimicry of Englishmen meant a certain affinity for "Western luxuries" such as drinking and meat eating, as shown by Michael Madhusudhan Dutt—modern Bengal's most famous epic poet and a convert to Christianity—that was both a sad reflection of the insecurities about everyday routine that the colonized elite suffered from and particularly wasteful of national resources (cited in Raychaudhuri 1988: 32, 58). It was, of course, easier to imitate "vices than virtues," as the anti-hero of a popular Bengali farce, Nimai Datta, exemplified in Dinabandhu Mitra's *Sadhabar ekadasi* (1866). Nimai Datta was represented as a drunken, "degenerate western-educated Bengali," a character believed by many to be modeled after Dutt.

Although Tagore furthered the cliché of the *ingabanga* in Bengali literature, which outlined the limits of appropriation of Western culture, in a letter written from Java in 1927 he nevertheless hinted at an ethic of homelessness and critiqued the excessive home-boundedness of the Hindu:

> In Batavia I met Sindhi shopkeepers. Their custom is to go home to Sind once every two years. I asked them why they did not bring over their wives and children and set up house, and they said that would never do, for a wife is bound to a family life, which would be disrupted if she were taken away. I hardly think such an argument would have been advanced in the India of the *Ramayana*! (Dutta and Robinson 1997: 118)

In contrast, Tagore wrote, "Westerners are homeless, and therefore they can make their homes anywhere. . . . How can *sanatan* home-dwellers hope to hold their own against these people?" (Dutta and Robinson 1997: 118).

As a modern writer, Tagore came to valorize a certain kind of exile. He credited Kalidasa's creativity to an exile of sorts—exile from the thick and oppressive atmosphere of luxury in the king's palaces. Kalidasa's state was the obverse of his Western analogue, Socrates. It is said that Socrates refused to travel out of Athens because he knew that he would lose distance and hence perspective if he were physically distant (Khateb 1991: 136). It is the toughest thing to be distant from a distant home. But some do manage to do that. In India, the models are Mahatma Gandhi and Rabindranath Tagore, who were nationalists with a profound discomfort with nationalism. Even when they traveled far, they retained a critical distance from their tribe, a distance that they maintained on their return home. Gandhi's critique of Hinduism and violent exclusivist nationalism came from being a Gujarati, a Baniya, and a Hindu. Tagore's critique of Bengali character came from his grounded Bengali lineage.

Although Tagore's language is accessible to Bengalis, he is much too well grounded and at home in terms of class, caste, and location to fully give voice to the expatriate's sense of loss. He connects better with our wanderlust. Bengali Americans draw succor from Tagore's cosmopolitanism while policing the limits of their community by way of the caricature of the *ingabanga*. Tagore is a cosmopolitan Brahmin seeking to cross the chalk circle that Bengali Americans have already transgressed. Their own problem is to come to terms with that infringement.

At the end of a century that began with the prolific writings of Tagore, Bengalis are bemused by a figure who has hewn a different path. They are intrigued by his fame (good and ill), and rumors about a possible Nobel Prize link him indissolubly to Tagore. And they wonder where his talk— a lot of it—about home and homelessness leads. The man is Salman Rushdie. He is not a Bengali, but he connects with the troubles of the expatriate community.

Rushdie, unlike Tagore, is the transgressor par excellence. He thrives on transgression. All his novels are a teeming mix of places, high and low cultures, and languages. Rushdie's stories are lots of "different tales juggled together in a sort of dizzy whirl" (Rushdie 1991a: 16). Syncretic creation through "re-mixing" is the point. Rushdie is virulently suspicious of the "pure," anything pure—race, language, nationality, ethnicity, even food. Rushdie's reputation is that of his storyteller, Rashid Khalifa, "whose never-ending stream of tall, short and winding tales had earned him not one but two nicknames. To his admirers he was Rashid the Ocean of Notions, as stuffed with cheery stories as the sea was full of glumfish; but to his jealous rivals he was the Shah of Blah" (Rushdie 1991a: 15). Much of this nonsense rhyming and shrewd punning, Rushdie acknowledges, is inspired by the Bengali filmmaker Satyajit Ray's fabulist interpretations of his humorist father Sukumar Ray's verses for children in *Aabol Taabol* (Nonsense) (Rushdie 1991b: 107–14). *Aabol Taabol* is still the most widely read children's book in Bengal. Sukumar Ray is to Bengali children what Dr. Seuss is to American children.

Rushdie is a postmodern jinn and a long way from Rabindranath, but the same things move him. Among others, he is moved by the relationship between "the home and the world," as one of Tagore's most influential plays was titled.[3] Rai, the narrator of *The Ground Beneath Her Feet,* while in the process of abandoning Bombay notes: "Among the great struggles of man— good/evil, reason/unreason, etc.—there is also this mighty conflict between the Fantasy of Home and the Fantasy of Away, the dream of roots and the mirage of journey" (Rushdie 1999: 55). Like Tagore, Rushdie valorizes the outside, albeit in a different tone. Unlike Tagore, Rushdie does not think that "not belonging" is a particularly Western virtue and that Ormus Cama can become an artist only through his rapid disenchantment not only with "Wombay" (Bombay as a womb?) but also with "the fantasy of the West." He in some ways has to be alienated from both worlds, the East and the West, as was Aadam Aziz, the grandfather of Saleem Sinai, the narrator in *Midnight's Children.* Aadam Aziz was "knocked forever into that middle place" from where he glued together "a badly-fitting collage" of his land (Rushdie 1980: 6, 23).

Yet this "India thing" keeps drawing Rushdie back. India, Rai thinks, is "where my parents lay buried, and the smells were the smells of home" (1999: 246). Rai's boss, Anita Dharkar, refuses to leave home, Rai says, because "India was still the only place on earth to which she could imagine herself belonging, corrupt and crooked and heartless and violent as it was. She belonged. . . . She could not define herself, could not give herself any meaning, except here, where her roots had gone too deep and spread too wide" (Rushdie 1999: 246). If she left, she would be disoriented.

Almost as soon as that is out of his mouth, Rai turns the idea on its head: "But let's just suppose. What if the whole deal—orientation, knowing where you are, and so on—what if it's all a scam? What if all of it— home, kinship, the whole enchilada—is just the biggest, most truly global, and centuries-oldest piece of brainwashing? Suppose that it's only when you dare to let go that your real life begins?" (Rushdie 1999:177). Yet Saleem Sinai in *Midnight's Children* repeatedly notes: "I had been mysteriously handcuffed to history, my destinies indissolubly chained to those of my country" (Rushdie 1980: 3).

Lest all this talk about love and nation degenerates into nostalgia, the American-born *desi* (literally, native; really, expatriate), Vina Apsara, the heroine of *The Ground Beneath Her Feet,* is clear that she hates India:

> I hate India. And there's plenty of it to hate. I hate the heat, and it's always hot, even when it rains, and I really hate the rain. I hate the food, and you can't drink the water. I hate the poor people, and they are all over the place. I hate the rich people, they are so goddamn pleased with themselves. I hate the crowds, and you're never out of them. I hate the way people speak too loud and dress in purple and ask too many questions and order you around. I hate the dirt and I hate the smell and I specially hate squatting down to shit. I hate money because it can't buy anything, and I hate the stores because there is nothing to buy. I hate the movies, I hate the dancing, I hate the music. I hate the languages because they are not plain English and I hate English because it is not plain English either. I hate the cars except the American cars and I hate those too because they're all ten years out of date. I hate the schools because they're really jails and I hate the holidays because you're not free not even then. I hate the old people and I hate the kids. I hate the radio and there's no TV. Most of all I hate the goddamn gods. (Rushdie 1999: 71–72)

The joke, of course, is as much on Vina—the spoiled, American-born, confused *desi* (or ABCD, as newly expatriated Indians call them)—as it is on India.[4] Yes, the heat is impossible; the water is infected; the poor are everywhere; the rich are insufferable; the cars are old; the place is crowded. And, yes, there are too many gods, too. But, big deal! Who cares? Rushdie's irreverence is that of one estranged from his homeland yet still oddly defined by it. His perspective is much like that of the best Jewish American writers of the twentieth century, who were trapped in a place between the community and the cosmos, the old and the new, tradition and modernity—writers such as Isaac Bashevis Singer, Philip Roth, and Saul Bellow.

Food plays an intriguing role in Rushdie's work (in contrast to Tagore, who never spent much time on such a low-minded thing). "I spend my time," Rushdie says in the words of Saleem Sinai in *Midnight's Children,* "at the great work of preserving. Memory, as well as fruit, is being saved from the corruption of the clocks" (Rushdie 1980: 38). He compares the intricacies of writing with those of cooking, in particular pickling:

There is . . . the matter of the spice bases. The intricacies of turmeric and cumin, the subtlety of fenugreek, when to use large (and when small) cardamoms; the myriad possible effects of garlic, garam masala, stick cinnamon, coriander, ginger . . . not to mention the flavorful contributions of the occasional speck of dirt. (Saleem is no longer obsessed with purity.) . . . I reconcile myself to the inevitable distortions of the pickling process. To pickle is to give immortality, after all: fish, vegetables, fruit hang embalmed in spice-and-vinegar; a certain alteration, a slight intensification of taste, is a small matter, surely? The art is to change the flavor in degree, but not in kind; and above all (in my thirty jars and a jar) to give it shape and form—that is to say, meaning. (Rushdie 1980: 550)

Food authenticates the local but it also defeats time and locality in the form of pickles and chutneys. Chutneys and *kasundis* (or, according to Rushdie's northern locution, *kasaundies*) mark a place, but they do so in their mixed, corrupt forms, where even specks of dirt are a part of the recipe. Not too pure and clean and wholesome, in addition to being portable. Bombay is marked by its foods—street foods, impure, homeless foods—*chana* and *bhelpuri*. Food is also powerful in communicating states of mind. "Amina began to feel the emotions of other people's food seeping into her— because Reverend Mother doled out the curries and meatballs of intransigence, dishes imbued with the personality of their creator; Amina ate the fish salans of stubbornness and the birianis of determination" (Rushdie 1980: 164).

Similarly, the trigger to Sara Suleri's (another expatriate South Asian, discussed earlier) autobiography *Meatless Days* is the question of *kapura* put to her by her sister Tillat. *Kapura,* she had been told politely, is sweetbread:

So the next time I was in the taut companionship of Pakistanis in New York I made a point of inquiring into the exact location of its secret, first in the animal and then in the meal. *Expatriates are adamant, entirely passionate about such matters as the eating habits of the motherland.* Accordingly, even though I was made to feel that it was wrong to strip a food of its sauce and put it back into its bodily belonging, I certainly received an unequivocal response: *kapura,* as naked meat, equals a testicle. Better, it is tantamount to a testicle neatly sliced into halves, just as we make no bones about asking the butcher to split chicken breasts into two. . . . No one, however, was interested in this finesse. "Balls, darling, balls," someone drawled, and I knew I had to let go of the subject. (Suleri 1989: 22; emphasis added)

The revelation troubles Sara because she wonders how many polite lies she must have been told by her mother. "What else have I eaten on her behalf?" she wonders. "[I] had to go back to where [I] belonged and—past a thousand different mealtimes—try to reconstruct the parable of the *kapura*" (Suleri 1989: 24). The parable would also open doors into her past. Scarcities and rationing of flour, butter, cigarettes, and tea in "Pakistan's erratic emotional market" would come to mind, as would Ramzan fasting, the rich *sehri* meals designed to keep the penitent sustained from dawn till dusk, and then "the twilight meal, the dusky *iftar* that ended the fast after the mosques had lustily rung with the call for the *maghrib* prayer" (Suleri 1989: 30–31).

Suleri (1989: 34) remembered how "food . . . gave us a way not simply of ordering a week or a day but of living inside history, measuring everything we remembered against a chronology of cooks." Finally, on her Welsh mother's death in Pakistan, she "dreamed a dream" about London "that left her reeling":

A blue van drove up: I noticed it was a refrigerated car and my father was inside it. He came to tell me that we must put my mother in her coffin, and he opened the blue hatch of the van and made me reach inside, where it was very cold. What I found were hunks of meat wrapped in cellophane, and each of them felt like Mamma, in some odd way. It was my task to carry those flanks across the street and fit them into the coffin at the other side of the road, like pieces in a jigsaw puzzle. (Suleri 1989: 44)

As a parable, the *kapura* reaches its limit. Suleri then awakens "to a world of meatless days" (Suleri 1989: 44). Suleri left Pakistan because she was "hungry for flavors less stringent on my palate, less demanding of my loyalty" (Suleri 1989: 123). Now each time she returns, she realizes "that I have quite forgotten what it is, the fragrance of real tea" (Suleri 1989: 86). Here is the mirror image of Proust's nostalgia.

Recalling Proust, Rushdie (1980: 544) also notes that "the taste of the chutney was more than just an echo of that long-ago taste—it was the old

taste itself." There is no escape from home and its flavors. This is so true
that Ormus Cama's love of leavened white bread is seen as betrayal:

> There was leavened bread in Bombay, but it was a sorry fare: dry,
> crumbling, tasteless, unleavened bread's paler, unluckier relation. It
> wasn't "real." "Real" bread was the chapati, or phulka, served piping
> hot; the tandoori nan and its sweeter Frontier variant, the Peshawari
> nan; and for luxury, the reshmi roti, the shrimal, the paratha. Com-
> pared to these aristocrats, the leavened white loaves of Ormus's child-
> hood seemed to merit the description . . . the undeserving poor. They
> were nothing like the lavish loaves sitting plump and enticing, and
> for sale, in the windows of [London's] many bakeries. . . . Ormus
> Cama plunges into this new world, betraying, without a backward
> glance, the fabled breads of home. . . . East is East, thinks Ormus
> Cama; ah, but yeast is West. (Rushdie 1999: 289–90)

Rushdie's mischief with metaphors is devastating, but it lacks the despon-
dency of a migrant's state of mind. Rushdie is too much of a cosmopolite
and he is having too much fun with this business of homelessness. The
migrant is mordant. Some are. And they need a different voice. For that,
the Bengali American must turn to another eloquent expatriate, V. S.
Naipaul.

Like Tagore, Naipaul repeatedly writes about the confinements of being
home, especially the "half-made" and badly made homes of the Third
World, with all their postcolonial excuses for third-rate workmanship. Yet
his search for the self begins with the need to find a "house of his own."
The eponymous protagonist in *A House for Mr. Biswas* "was struck again by
the wonder of being in his own house, the audacity of it: to walk in through
his own front gate, to bar entry to whoever he wished" (Naipaul 1961: 8).
Nevertheless, eventually he loses the house and dies unable to find a home
away from the cloying joint family of his in-laws, the Tulsis. Naipaul told
an interviewer in 1983: "To grow up in a large extended family was to
acquire a lasting distaste for family life" (Theroux 1998: 345).

Mr. Biswas, modeled after Naipaul's father, had "yearned after the outside world" and acquired a new respect for his wife, Shama, because she had
"a packet of letters from a pen-pal in Northumberland" (Naipaul 1961: 207).
On hearing that Owad, his brother-in-law, was to be sent abroad to study,
"Mr. Biswas was overwhelmed. . . . He had never thought that anyone so

close to him could escape so easily" (Naipaul 1961: 349). Subsequently, like Tagore's *ingabanga,* Owad draws a caricature of Indians in England.

> They were a disgrace to Trinidad Indians; they were arrogant, sly and lecherous; they pronounced English in a peculiar way; they were slow and unintelligent and were given degrees only out of charity; they were unreliable with money; in England they went around with nurses and other women of the lower classes and were frequently involved in scandals; they cooked Indian food badly (the only true Indian meals Owad had in England were the meals he cooked himself); their Hindi was strange . . .; their ritual was debased; the moment they got to England they ate meat and drank to prove their modernity (a brahmin boy had offered Owad curried corn beef for lunch); and, incomprehensibly, they looked down on colonial Indians. (Naipaul 1961: 539)

The Tulsi family comes to the solemn conclusion that they are "the last representatives of Hindu culture" (Naipaul 1961: 540).

His father, Naipaul says in *The Enigma of Arrival* (1988: 111), "had dreamed of fulfillment in a foreign country." Only in the Wiltshire countryside would the junior Naipaul find himself "in tune with a landscape in a way that I had never been in Trinidad or India" (Naipaul 1988: 173). While the older people in his Asian Indian community looked back to an India that became more and more golden in their memory, his ambition caused him to look ahead and outward, to England (Naipaul 1988: 130). Driven by the colonial smallness that could not be aligned with the grandeur of his ambition, he dreamed of being in England—"a child's fantasy of a beautiful other place" (Theroux 1998: 221).

In spite of his early romance with England, Naipaul still felt out of place. Paul Theroux notes that Naipaul would repeat despondently: "I belong nowhere, I have no home." Certain aspects of the Caribbean made him nostalgic to return, but he never could get out from under the grandeur of the metropolis or the stunning quietude of the English countryside (Theroux 1998: 221). "The idea of an address—a place of his own preoccupied him sometimes to the point of obsession. Not owning a house made him yearn for one," and yet, the "more he became a householder, the stronger his sense of alienation" (Theroux 1998: 221, 230). With a tidy and secure place in central London, Naipaul continued to claim with great solemnity, "I have no country to call my own. I am placeless. . . . Exile is not a figure of speech to me. It is something real. I am an exile. . . . I can't go home. . . . I have no home" (as quoted in Theroux 1998: 230–31).

Naipaul remains stuck in some in-between place—between England, India, and Trinidad. In fact, each of these places becomes somewhat one-dimensional in his lived imagination, and all are absorbed into his moral landscape of good and bad places. Naipaul never gets sentimental, either, about India, his ancestral home, or Trinidad, his original home. "India had not worked its magic on me. It remained the land of my childhood, an area of darkness" (Naipaul 1992: 252). Yet Naipaul returned repeatedly to India, and each time he was a little less harsh but kept his cold, hard gaze on its follies. There is a wintry stoicism in his writing. He trounced India's blemishes, from the obvious "Indians defecate everywhere" to its colonial mimicry of England, its obsession with symbols and avoidance of action, its failed corrupt modernity of "traffic lights where nobody stops," and its moral deficiencies, illustrated by the fifteen different excuses for adultery in the Kama Sutra. With his eye for detail and for unalloyed truth, Naipaul hit the mark a number of times.

Naipaul's is a kind of anti-nostalgia. Or is it nostalgia for the idea of home and disappointment with particular homes? Maybe it is hatred on being home. He has to go out and see the larger, harder metropolitan world. He has to leave Trinidad. But he returns. He returns repeatedly to his ancestors' home—India—which invariably disappoints him. In part, Naipaul's problem with India is that of every migrant—the damn place doesn't stay the same. "How can I explain my feeling of outrage when I heard that in Bombay they used candles and electric bulbs for Diwali festival, and not the rustic clay lamps, of immemorial design, which in Trinidad was still used? . . . [T]he thought of the decay of the old customs and reverence saddened me" (Naipaul 1992: 36).

Naipaul has a sharp and unforgiving eye for people's weakness, including his own Hindu prejudices, which appear to involve a deep-seated racism. One cannot ignore Naipaul's racism, partly, in this case, because it connects to the diasporic Bengali imagination. The black servant at the Tulsis' in *A House for Mr. Biswas* is named simply and crudely Miss Blackie, and an unnamed "big black man" builds Mr. Biswas's shoddy house. These are the only non-Indian non-whites that Mr. Biswas interacts with, and that interaction is not much.

Add to that what Theroux reports. If he can be believed (Naipaul's subsequent novel *Half a Life* makes it plausible), the following exchange took place between him and Naipaul:

NAIPAUL: When you come to London I want you to tell my brother
that you sleep with African girls. I want you to shock him.

THEROUX: I don't get it. Why should he be shocked?

NAIPAUL: Because he's always talking this liberal nonsense. And he
was brought up in Trinidad. Yet it would not occur to him to
make love with a black woman. . . .

NAIPAUL: Do you find those African girls frightfully beautiful?

THEROUX: The ones at the bar? Some of them yes. Very beautiful.
A few reminded me of Yomo.

NAIPAUL: . . .

THEROUX: Do *you* find them beautiful?

NAIPAUL: No. No. . . . No. (Theroux 1998: 77)

Notwithstanding his own difficulties with color, Naipaul was shocked to
learn that, in spite of "all his aspirations," it was only his color that whites
saw on the boat to England. On the boat, when a "Negro" refused to be
ghettoized in the same cabin with the eighteen-year-old Naipaul, he won-
dered, "What else was there to him apart from his racial passion?" (Naipaul
1988: 126). Nevertheless, he acknowledged, "With my Asiatic background,
I resisted the comparison" with the Negro. On his return to Trinidad, he
noted that "the Negroes of Trinidad, following those of the United States,
were asserting their separateness. They simplified and sentimentalized the
past. . . . They wore their hair in a new way. The hair that had with them
been a source of embarrassment and shame, a servile badge, they now wore
as a symbol of aggression" (Naipaul 1988: 159–60).

Now listen to his thoughts in a different context. An old, white woman
came to Naipaul's Wiltshire home, looking for the cottage she had grown
up in. "I was . . . embarrassed to be what I was, an intruder, not from another
village or country, but from another hemisphere; embarrassed to have
destroyed or spoilt the past of the old lady " (Naipaul 1988: 318). Here his
compassion is boundless and touching. It is something for us in these race-
conscious times to think about. Yet this amazing sympathy for the old white
woman who had lost her past to the colored immigrant, when juxtaposed
with his derision for the colored subaltern who by way of the "Afro" was
merely reclaiming his due, is disturbing. Self-consciously, Naipaul writes:

I have been rebuked by writers from the West Indies, and notably
George Lamming, for not paying sufficient attention in my books to

non-Indian groups. The confrontation of different communities, he said, was the fundamental West Indian experience. So indeed it is, and increasingly. But . . . to me the worlds were juxtaposed and mutually exclusive. . . . I can speak only out of my own experience. (Naipaul 1992: 35)

His "experience" of race, he says, is the following:

We ate certain food, performed certain ceremonies and had certain taboos; we expected others to have their own. We did not wish to share theirs; we did not expect them to share ours. They were what they were; we were what we were. We were never instructed in this. . . . Race was never discussed; but at an early age I understood that Muslims were somewhat more different than others. They were not to be trusted; they would always do you down; and point was given to this by the presence close to my grandmother's house of a Muslim, in whose cap and gray beard, avowals of his especial difference, lay every sort of threat. . . . I saw it in their appearance, their house, their dress and presently, as I had been fearing, in their food. We were offered some vermicelli done in milk. I believed it to be associated with some unknown and distasteful ritual; I could not eat it. (Naipaul 1992: 31)

This revulsion was based on the certainty of rumor. It turns out that these people Naipaul was visiting were not even Muslims, just rumored to be so. From his Hindu upbringing he developed "a vague sense of caste, and a horror of the unclean" (Naipaul 1992: 33).

It horrified me at school to see boys sharing Popsicles and Palates, local iced lollies; as it horrifies me to see women sipping from ladles with which they stir their pots. This was more than difference; this was the uncleanliness we had to guard against. . . . [F]avourite street-corner and sports-ground dishes of the Negro proletariat, were regarded by us with fascinated horror. (Naipaul 1992: 33)

In the science class at school one day we were doing an experiment with siphons, to an end which I have now forgotten. At one stage a beaker and a length of tube were passed from boy to boy, so that we might get to suck and observe the effects. I let the beaker pass me. I thought I hadn't been seen, but an Indian boy in the row behind, a Port of Spain boy, a recognized class tough, whispered, "Real brahmin." His tone was approving. I was surprised at his knowledge, having assumed him, a Port of Spain boy, to be ignorant of these things; at the unexpected tenderness of his voice; and also at the bringing out into public of that other, secret life. But I was also pleased. (Naipaul 1992: 35)

Perhaps Theroux's African friends in Kampala were right when they said Naipaul was typically English. The English expatriates, however, characterized him as typically Trinidadian. And the Indians in Uganda called him a typical Brahmin. A number of people observed that he was a settler type, which was the worst one could say about anyone in Africa (Theroux 1998: 105).

It could be that Naipaul is merely telling the truth as he sees it. Our shock may be a response to his repeated injunction: "Don't prettify it. . . . The greatest writing is a disturbing vision from a position of strength— aspire to that. Tell the truth" (as quoted in Theroux 1998: 17). Naipaul tells the truth, the terrible truths about our terribly close-minded anxieties. Yet in the end, it is sometimes difficult to avoid Derek Walcott's judgment: The myth of Naipaul as a phenomenon, as a singular, contradictory genius . . . has long been a farce. It is a myth he chooses to encourage—though he alone knows why. . . . There is something alarmingly venal in all this dislocation and despair. Besides, it is not true. There is instead another truth. Naipaul's prejudice." Walcott goes on to say that Naipaul's reputed "frankness" and truth-telling are nothing more than bigotry. "If Naipaul's attitude towards Negroes, with its nasty little sneers . . . was turned on Jews, for example, how many people would praise him for his frankness?" (as quoted in Theroux 1998: 294).

Yet Naipaul connects with the expatriate Bengali imagination in a number of ways. First is the despair about the loss of home. There is that hankering for home and yet a recoil from it, especially from its underdevelopment, its disease, and its poverty. There is a desperate helplessness that quickly turns into anger toward the poor, the diseased, and the unlucky. Second, there is a romance with the metropolitan landscape. Sometimes it is expressed as a kind of dreamy hyperbole of snow for "a person from a tropical island for whom snow is decoration . . . never having to be shoveled or driven through" (Theroux 1998: 221). Next, there is the prejudice. Naipaul connects to a deep-seated Indian prejudice against blacks and Hispanics. The prejudice is very particular. It could be extrapolated from amazingly mundane "facts." It runs the whole range from the usual stereotypes of welfare dependence, laziness, teenage pregnancy, and criminality to even more minor "facts." Take, for instance, the "fact" that the Greyhound bus service is often erratic. Why, you ask? "Because you know the blacks run it." The minutiae of racism is endless and tiresome. Most important for our purposes, we witness something akin to the brutal sentimental Brahmanism of somebody like Naipaul, especially in his references to food: Other peoples' foods are always disgusting.

Naipaul connects with the expatriate Indian imagination by way of a certain disdain toward other people's food. References to food in Naipaul are relatively limited—that trivial thing again—and when mentioned at all are overlaid with a Brahmin's dread of transactional pollution. Generally, he uses food not as a mimetic device for representing details of everyday life but as a metaphor of otherness. It evokes visceral disgust for other people and their food, especially poor people and colored people. Never whites. Maybe that is what Naipaul is best at: expressing honestly what moves people at their core without "prettifying it."

In Naipaul we can recognize the troubled dynamic of nostalgia for cultural authenticity, which always implies culinary exclusivity, or what Michèle Lamont (1994) has called "boundary work." The search for authenticity inevitably leads to the search for a usable past, which is the other face of modernity.

Heritage

Every established order tends to produce . . . the naturalization of its own arbitrariness.
PIERRE BOURDIEU, OUTLINE OF A THEORY OF PRACTICE (1977: 164)

The search for authenticity is particularly poignant in the face of minimal standardization of Bengali-American cuisine. Much of Bengali-American cuisine is a marriage of pre-immigration memory and the marketplace. The rest is individual style. There are the bare beginnings of a print media with recipes, but most people do not depend on them to cook.

According to Ernest Gellner (1983) and Benedict Anderson (1991), national standards are dependent on print culture, which have the capacity to connect people over time and space. The nation depends on the development of the book, the novel, and the newspaper alongside a literate reading public capable of using these sources to imagine themselves as a community. Films and TV programs facilitate this process as they make possible instantaneous and immediate identification with a collective style. Anderson (1991: 6) argues that "all communities larger than the primordial village of face-to-face contact (and perhaps even these) are imagined. Communities are to be distinguished not by their falseness/genuineness, but by the style in which they are imagined."

Over the past few years, recipes have started appearing in newspapers and journals directed at the diasporic audience, such as *India Abroad* and *India Tribune*. Both of these newspapers cater to a pan-Indian diasporic community rather than to the West Bengali-American community in particular. They produce weekly Gujarati and Punjabi editions printed in the respective vernaculars, but there are no Bengali editions, primarily because most West Bengali Americans are proficient in English.[5]

The English-language edition of *India Tribune* has run a food column irregularly since 1995, and the largest circulating diasporic Indian weekly, *India Abroad* (established in 1970), carried food columns intermittently until its reorganization in 2002, after which there has been a regular bi-weekly page on food—mostly reviews of Indian restaurants written by men and recipes for making festive foods, especially desserts, written by women. Overall, the influence of the print media on the paradigm of Indian American home cooking is limited. Most of the recipes in the diasporic journals are "specials," with inordinate focus on desserts rather than representative of everyday cookery.

Yet broad parameters of Bengali-American cooking appear to develop. What we name Bengali cuisine has developed through mechanisms presumably of face-to-face contact that we do not understand clearly. Patrilocality in marriage generates some tendencies in the cross-fertilization of menus between the bride's natal and affinal homes. Recipes circulate through networks of kin. Reciprocal invitations between friends and families also lead to the sharing and shaping of each other's recipes. Finally, what is available in the marketplace provides some limiting patterns. The broad frames of reference that are established allow substantial room for sectional and individual styles.

Even the pre-immigration imaginary of Bengali cuisine is not particularly standardized. Bengali food in Darjeeling is not the same as Bengali
food in Asansol or in Calcutta. Further still, these urban centers do not
occupy the same place in the Bengali imagination. There is a clear hierarchy of style, where Calcuttan recipes are hegemonic, while the style of
cooking from Darjeeling and Asansol are considered "tainted" by Pahari
(hill people) and Bihari influences, respectively. Bengali food among *kulin
brahmins* is not the same as food among *kayasthas*. Shakta cuisine is different from Vaishnav cuisine. Working-class Bengali diets are distinct from
babu diets. In fact, Bengali food is not the same even between households
of the same caste, class, and sect.

If Bengali food is so difficult to pin down in Bengal, it is even tougher
to identify the paradigm of food for Bengali-American households. The
patterns become only vaguely visible at a distance. In the diasporic context, as collective rituals of marriages, birthdays, graduations, conferences
and even Durga Pujas disentangle themselves from their associations with
certain organic contexts, we end up with greater room for sectional and
individual idiosyncrasies. By their very nature, idiosyncrasies are difficult
to classify. Perhaps that is why we often end up with the tautological insistence that Bengali food is what *Bengalis* cook. Edward Said once told
Salman Rushdie:

> A close friend of mine once came to my house and stayed overnight.
> In the morning we had breakfast, which included yogurt cheese with
> a special herb, *záatar*. This combination probably exists all over the
> Arab world, and certainly in Palestine, Syria and Lebanon. But my
> friend said: "There, you see. It's a sign of a Palestinian home that it
> has *záatar* in it." Being a poet, he then expatiated at great and tedious
> length on Palestinian cuisine, which is generally very much like
> Lebanese and Syrian cuisine, and by the end of the morning we
> were both convinced that we had a totally distinct national cuisine.
> (Rushdie 1991b: 175)

Rushdie then asked, "So, because a Palestinian chooses to do something it
becomes the Palestinian thing to do?" Said replied, "That is absolutely
right" (Rushdie 1991b:175).

What are sometimes considered distinctly Bengali are the "exotic"
ingredients, such as rice and fish, spices, and vegetables such as *potol* and

bittermelon. Items like rice and fish get accentuated in the expatriate Bengali imagination as markers of ethnicity. Ingredients such as beef cannot fill that place, no matter how Bengali its method of cooking.

The abstraction of "Bengali equals rice and fish" becomes useful because any further specifications would inordinately complicate the definition of a Bengali American. For some, Bengali identity is associated with a particular fish, such as *ilish,* but in general it is associated with any kind of fish in conjunction with rice. In "Mrs. Sen," a remarkable story about expatriate longing for home, Jhumpa Lahiri writes: "Two things, Eliot learned, made Mrs. Sen happy. One was the arrival of a letter from her family. . . . The other thing . . . was fish from the seaside. It was always a whole fish she desired, not shellfish, or the fillets" (Lahiri 1999: 121, 123).

Rice and fish become particularly potent symbols of Bengaliness precisely because outsiders, be they other Indians or Americans, are considered unable to appreciate them or incompetent in handling the bones. Rice and fish is considered a real insider delicacy. The honored guest is served the head, and the ability to tackle it reveals the guest's insiderness.

Ecology also encourages the pairing of rice and fish. Wet rice cultivation is particularly suitable to raising freshwater fish. Anybody with a coastline can harvest fish from the sea. It is only those who are competent to raise wet rice who can bring forth a harvest of sweetwater fish. Fish links the Bengali to his ancestral land, the landscape of ponds, lakes, and rivers, with its profusion of deltaic waterways. Rice and fish literally locate the Bengali.

That is why the *ilish* is the paradigmatic Bengali fish. It begins in the ocean but ends in the estuaries, where only an estuarine civilization can tame it. It is as if the *ilish* makes a beeline for the Bengali and chooses the Bengali to consummate the relationship. (The *ilish,* like salmon, sturgeon, and shad, is anadromous—it cavorts in salt water but spawns and breeds in fresh water.) What better way to honor Bengal than to consume one of its distinctive natural elements, incorporate it into one's body?

The best *ilish* is one that is bountiful with roe. The *ilish* not only sacrifices itself to the Bengali but deposits its future generations at the altar of Bengali civilization. The *ilish* is particularly bony and difficult to eat. The pleasure is doubled because others find it unmanageable. Bengalis love narrating real and apocryphal stories about how others struggle with the many tiny bones of the *ilish.* Only a Bengali eats *ilish* with the fine but tough bones arrayed in a ring around the plate, like a mandala giving thanks for god's beneficence. Crunching through the bones, the tail, and the head and making a pile of chewed remains on the plate consecrates the real Bengali.

The *ilish,* like other "Bengali" fish, must be freshly killed. *Magur* (catfish) and *koi* (climbing perch), two other quintessentially Bengali fish, are considered spoiled if dead; they mush be kept alive until they reach the Bengali home. Live, resistant nature is brought to its heels at the Bengali hearth. That is what makes a Bengali so natural, or so the claim goes. None of the fancy packaging of the supermarket, where death is cellophaned away by the "great geometer" into steaks and briskets. It is *rakta* (shared blood) that makes a Bengali. It is shared blood and gore that makes us who we are. The food of our favorite goddesses—Kali, Chandi, and Durga—is blood, too.

The recipes for preparing these types of fish are considered by Bengalis to be simple and elemental: not too many spices, not too much cooking. The fish, simple and "natural," is to be savored with a pile of steaming rice and ghee. Rice and fish also makes a Bengali particularly "intelligent and cultured." That is one of the claims. Of course, everybody knows it is the fish—especially the fish head—that makes the Bengali so bright. It is a matter of simple logic: You eat brains, you get brains. Fish heads don't make the Bengali brave or strong, but they do turn him into a thinker. That is exactly why "what Bengal thinks today, India thinks tomorrow." That is why Bengal is the only state in India that has produced two Nobel laureates: the poet Rabindranath Tagore and the economist Amartya Sen. That is what Bengalis assert in a complex interweaving of irony and pride. And not only Bengalis but other Indians have created the stereotype of the bright (but cowardly) Bengali. On hearing that Amartya Sen had won the Noble Prize for Economics in 1998, a non-Bengali Indian friend of mine said: "You know, I think, Bengalis and Jews are God's chosen people." Yes, they are, Bengalis are convinced. And that has to do with their food.

Yet it is not just content that makes ethnicity. When Bengalis say that "rice and fish" makes them Bengali, one could retort, "What about sushi?" It is then pointed out, with a certain irritation, that "it is not the same thing" because "we" cook the fish, and we cook it differently. So, you ask, is it then the style of the curries? Yes, it is. Then what about beef curry? Is that Bengali, too? Well . . . not exactly. The qualifications multiply. If you pursue further, the question is answered, irascibly, that "of course a Bengali knows what is Bengali food." But how does a Bengali know? Because he or she has been raised on it; because it is natural to him. Or so the claim goes.

These claims are a part of what Sutton calls narratives of *gemeinschaft*—stories about another place where relationships were presumably less instrumental, although no less transparent. Nostalgia in the narratives of *gemeinschaft* is balanced by laughter at one's own traditional backwardness (Sutton 2001: 54). The precapitalist aura of "natural" things from another place are counterposed to new memories of a greater, tougher world out there—the American world. Narratives of localism play hide-and-seek with claims of a wandering cosmopolitanism.

There is also a sense that you have to keep doing it—repeat the recipes over and over and keep eating rice and fish in the Bengali style. There is anxiety that it will vanish if it is not repeatedly performed. Repetition is not replication; thus, variations abound, but within limits. According to Georg Simmel (1950), a community connotes a common set of social relations, which reinforce the practical, everyday lived culture by repetition that renders the most meaningful knowledge and beliefs unconscious habits. Through repetition, things become naturalized. Through repetition, rice and fish become the quintessence of Bengaliness. Here is a claim about the "very nature" or "substance" of Bengalis.

In the social sciences it has become a commonplace to assert that identities are performances rather than "natural" acts. Sociologists such as Erving Goffman (1959) have proposed that individuals in society are like actors on a stage who present "managed" impressions of themselves, depending on their interests and situational constraints. Nevertheless, within the first-generation Bengali-American community (and probably in every other community) there is an assumption that "we" are what our substance is "naturally" made of. When Ronald Inden and Ralph Nicholas (1977: 3) asked Bengalis to provide a definition of "one's own people," they were told that they are persons related by "blood" (*rakta*) or by the "same body" (*eka-sarira*). In these emic (insider) conceptions, there is a certain resistance to acknowledging that our identities are mere performances.

Thus, cooking and eating Bengali food naturally make us Bengali. It seems self-evident to Bengali insiders that an "American" can never replicate Bengali food or even come to really like it. What a number of my respondents point to is a certain stringency—the insistence to get things precisely and exactly that presumably cannot be replicated by any ethnic "other."

Yet under the cover of consistency a new repertoire of diasporic Bengali food is developing in the cookbooks of Bharati Kirchner (1992) and

Chitrita Banerji (1997) and on a number of websites.[6] Claims about the distinctive nature of Bengali food are insistent precisely because the substance itself is rather slippery. Cooking is nowhere as standardized as in cooking schools or recipe books, but the very absence of cooking schools and the marginality of the print media to domestic routines makes Bengali cuisine even more improvisational in nature. There is no Bengali cuisine but multiple variations along class, regional, and sectarian lines. The cut one makes depends on the eyes of the beholder as much as the substance of the matter. "Bengali food," "Bengali–American cuisine," and "American food" are relational categories that exist in a matrix of cross-cutting relationships. One cannot exist without the other. "Bengali cuisine" makes sense only as a contrast to "American cuisine" or "Bengali–American cuisine"; they make sense only in relation to each other, and that is as analytical abstractions. That is, of course, what semioticians have taught us for a long time—signs make sense only in a system of signs, and identity is wholly a function of difference (Saussure 1983). Furthermore, not all signs are created equal. Some, such as "rice and fish," have greater valency than others.

If authentic food authenticates the Bengali, the idea of authenticity pulls in two unresolved directions. One is toward a Bengali identity, with its internal complexities of caste, class, and gender hierarchies; the other is directed outward, toward the American.

Let us first turn to the problem of internal differentiation. The West Bengali–American community is particularly homogenous in terms of class background because of the workings of immigration laws. The main wage earner in 96 percent of my sample households had earned a master's or a more advanced degree. Almost all were employed as professionals—engineers, doctors, or academics. There was very little class stratification within the imagined community of *probashi* West Bengali Americans.

In terms of caste, the story is more or less the same. Among those who were willing to identify their caste, almost 80 percent belonged to the top three castes: Brahmin, Kayastha, and Baidya.[7] Since there is no significant Khatriya *varna* in Bengal, the Kayastha and Baidya castes are regarded as belonging to the second tier, after the Brahmins. After Brahmins, they are also the group with the largest landholding and access to professional careers. It may be because of this relative homogeneity that, in the course of my research, there did not appear to be much caste dynamic in the socialization of subgroups within the West Bengali Hindu community. Professional Calcuttan patterns of cross-upper-caste socialization are replicated among Bengali Americans.

The West Bengali community in the United States has not acquired demographic complexity primarily because of (1) the self-selecting nature of immigration laws that are skewed toward professionals; (2) the relatively recent influx of Bengalis; and (3) the sheer paucity of numbers. We are talking about a community that, by optimistic standards, is estimated to number about 30,000 and is widely dispersed in the United States.

Caste operates at the local level; thus, geographic dispersal and class mobility undermine caste loyalties. Class patterns will develop over time as new generations emerge and the family-reunification criteria of the immigration law are used more widely than the specialty-occupation criteria that are the norm today. Nevertheless, I doubt whether there ever will be a caste dynamic within the community because of the immense divide in terms of opportunity between the higher castes mentioned and the lower castes. Aggressive affirmative-action policies in India may marginally increase the number of lower-caste (but higher-class) migrants in the future, but with low total numbers and spatial dispersal, I do not see the possibility of the revival of caste identities (other than as a private matter of domestic ritual). Thus, what I say here merely qualifies the homogeneity of the community. That is why I will have more to say about generational hierarchy than about class or caste dynamic.

Food production and consumption are "maps of social ambitions as well as economic reach" (Chandra Mukerji 1990: 658). Food enables us to find our place in the world, not only in a locale, but also in a social hierarchy. In "Metabolising Judaism," Maurie Sacks (1995: 13) writes:

> Foodways delineate sub-groups within Judaism: stuffed grape leaves are Jewish food—for Sephardim (Jews of Spanish decent). Most American Jews are Ashkenazic (Eastern European) extraction, and therefore do not recognize Mediterranean foods as "Jewish food" right up there with *cholent* (bean casserole traditionally served on the Sabbath) and *gefilte fish* (chopped fish balls).

Similarly, markers of Bengali "culture" (language, literature, and food, to name just a few) are part of a highly nuanced pecking order.

Authenticity takes time and money to reproduce in an alien world. The more difficult the effort, the better kind of Bengali you are, and it matters what kind one is. For instance, almost every Bengali-American suburban home has at least one "ethnic" plant in which it takes great pride, often competing with other households to grow the "most Bengali" of flowers, such as gainda, or African marigold (*Tagetes erecta*), and rajanigandha (*Polianthes tuberosa*) (cf. Chaudhuri 1951: 20–21). Flower pots with such "ethnic" plants become emblems of the effort households invest in replicating Bengaliness. Such small acts of planting an ethnic shrub or large acts of flying to India with the family every year are a source both of existential pleasure and competition. In the process, Bengalis do subtly police the boundaries of their community.

We can see that kind of pressure in the heightened Bengaliness of feasts to which other Bengalis are invited. As mentioned earlier, on these occasions even second-generation Bengali Americans, to their great consternation, are pressured to eat Bengali food. The more exotically Bengali the fish and the more time-consuming the preparation of a particular dish, the more talked about it is and the more requests there are for recipes. That is a clear sign of some status in the community.

We can also see such pressure for status in terms of Bengali-language education of children. Such conspicuous leisure and training (à la Veblen) give Bengalis the requisite cultural markers to fit into status hierarchies. In this perspective, the highest status is attained by those Bengali Americans who are both materially and "culturally" successful. Material success is identified by the usual markers of a comfortable suburban house with ample land for landscaping, a profession (preferably only for the husband), comfortable cars (such as a Lexus), and Ivy League education for the children. These are mostly understood as "American" things. Cultural capital is flaunted through the display of Bengali "culture" primarily to other Bengalis on certain social occasions by way of food, clothing, music, and language. So the taste for things Bengali has become more important as those things become less "useful" in the narrow materialist sense, and that importance increases with migration, which has destabilized social ranking.

My argument here complicates Herbert Gans's (1979) assertions that "symbolic ethnicity"—which, he claims, has become the norm since the 1970s—is a low-cost assertion of identity. It is low cost in two ways: It does not provoke resistance from the mainstream, and it does not take much effort to replicate, in contrast to belonging to ethnic organizations. Both contentions are true for Bengali Americans, but with two exceptions. The cost of and effort involved in flying to India every year are quite substantial. But even more noteworthy, internal ranking in terms of authenticity is psychologically very important, not residual, as Gans implies. The very "use" of such display is in the negotiation of social rank. Competition for Bengali authenticity provides the dynamic behind a system of restratification in an apparently homogenized community where cultural capital becomes more important precisely because material capital is available to all (that is, to all those who matter).

Competition for authenticity is also a disciplinary tool. Surveillance of taste reins in the food practices of disparate households through the power of rumors and stories about the "excessive Americanization" of certain households. Instances of Americanization are clearly identified in the realm of food consumption where households are criticized, for instance, for abandoning the consumption of fish because, as one community elder put it: "Can you believe it? Mrs. Banerjee does not cook fish anymore because she says it smells up the house!" Such markers of excess also flow into judgments about parents' allowing their children to drink alcohol or date. In effect, the policing of cultural practices seeks to stabilize expressive forms around the locus of a clearly imagined Bengaliness that cannot be transgressed.

Further, this policing penetrates deeper where different members of the household are kept in line by crystallizing gender and generational divisions of labor. For instance, it is implied that to be a good Bengali, a woman must cook at least one hot ethnic meal every day. Households that eat out "too often" have to suffer the suspicion that they may have lost their authenticity because their women do not cook. However, eating out can be considered a "good thing" because it is seen as cultivating a certain sophistication of the palate, as long as it is judged not to happen "too often." This is a delicate balancing act between cosmopolitanism and excessive Americanization.

Some of the most important bones of contention between parents and their children center on things parents think children ought to do as Bengalis, such as attend Bengali-language classes on weekends and "respect elders," which can mean a whole range of behaviors, from being obsequious to not dating or drinking and eating Bengali food. In attempting to enforce these norms, parents have to become more authoritarian, because children who neither are haunted by nostalgia nor aspire for difference from their peers see learning Bengali and eating Bengali food in the American context as less useful.

Bengali–American children, in turn, interpret such authoritarianism as a quintessentially Bengali style of parenting. Actors across the generational and gender divide create the image of the authoritarian father (and the subservient mother) as *the* Bengali pattern, ending up in an Orientalist choreography. Here, "Orientals" reinvigorate the very Orientalism they labor against. Thus, the heightened policing of everyday practice creates organizing myths about what a Bengali is, which children strenuously seek to break, resulting in gossip and paranoia among parents who, in turn, desperately seek to avoid such rumors by tightening the screws on their children's behavior, which inevitably generates greater rebellion. This dynamic operates among *all* parents, notwithstanding their ethnic identification, but insecurities about ethnic authenticity add to that dread among Bengali Americans.

The other side of the claim to "authenticity" is a putatively clear demarcation from the American. In Chapter 4, I quoted a number of respondents who quite explicitly mocked "the American" for everything from his crude taste and terrible sociability to his crumbling family. The dominant culture looks quite inferior, and Bengalis are attuned to that perspective. That is why model minorities take their modeling seriously, not only as a standard for other minorities, which is how it has been understood, but also as something to be emulated by the dominant majority. A self-assured sense exists that "we" have culture while the poor American (understood by my respondents as affluent, white suburbanites) is quite clueless. Of course, the caricature of the American is necessary to protect the sacred character of Bengalihood. Emile Durkheim noted in *The Elementary Forms of Religious Life* (1965) that moral authority demands that moral ideas are surrounded by a mysterious barrier, which keeps violators at arm's length. Authenticity performs that role of creating a barrier between the moral community and others. Those hoping to replicate the authentic, such as many first-generation Bengali Americans, appear to respect the barrier with enthusiasm.

Food enables insiders to distinguish between their own culture and that of others and, by extension, between the home and the world. Cuisine also ranks us in a social hierarchy. It enables us to distinguish between those with taste and those without. Rituals associated with food mark our time in life—birth and death, tonsure and marriage. Our people ("us") and other people ("them"), home and away, class and caste, youth and old age—all are relational categories. Food is one way to mark our place within these antinomies. We make claims on the world in terms of place, rank, and age, and food gives us our location. Finding a home 10,000 miles away from home is disorienting, but through food we hope not to lose the East.

Now that I have told you my story about "rice and water" and the violations of geography by history, I cannot but draw your attention to the meta-theoretical bridges I have used. Like a *sutradhar* (the narrator; literally, "one who holds the threads"), I have sought to gather the threads of empirical detail to bear on the problems of modernity, which lie at the heart of what is at stake here.

First and foremost, I have drunk deeply at the well of the world-systems perspective, especially the teachings of Immanuel Wallerstein and Giovanni Arrighi, and I have heeded their call to break through the limits of the nation-state as a unit of analysis. Nevertheless, I have moved away from large-scale, long-term change that is at the heart of their analysis. Instead, my work has focused on medium- to short-term (20–40 years) change with particular regard to the existential conflict of a small number of actors. In addition, I pay much more attention to social process than structure. Nevertheless, I have heeded Wallerstein's call to locate changes in particular places within global dynamics—no place is an island entire to itself anymore. A few Bengali households in Chicago are very much part of a geopolitical and geocultural system. What impinges on their lives, what they do to make their lives livable, and what meanings they make of this are contingent on larger and longer processes of change.

Nevertheless, in the process of drifting away from world-systems analysis, I have also moved away from its two main sources: Karl Marx and Max Weber. I have moved away from production and the economic realm (Marx's favorites) to consumption and the cultural sphere. Yet in another sense my work takes Marx's method to its limit. To understand the realm of circulation and consumption, Marx urged us to enter the hidden abode of production and analyze the social relations underpinning it. I have stumbled through another trapdoor behind the façade of commodity production, into the realm of reproduction of human labor—the home. That is where exchange value intersects use value and more than one-half of all production takes place. This is the realm of noncommodified production, unpaid labor, and noncontractual relationships. It is the realm not of political economy but of the gift economy. It is the glue that holds the rest together.

That is exactly the perspective that can explain why most of my respondents refused to view household relations as either exploitative or disempowering. They refused to see power within the households as an extension of the money economy, with its class actors and rules of exploitation. In the money economy, the one who accumulates the most exercises power. Within the household, that principle works, too, but only up to a point. The other half of the dialectic of power within the household is drawn from the nature of the gift economy. The one who *gives* the most of her labor acquires power. These two sides of household relations are held in tension in almost every home. The dialectic reaches tipping points when either the money economy or the gift economy overwhelms the other. That is when households fall apart, descend into abuse, or both. The larger theoretical point was made long ago by Durkheim that short-term contractual relations can never be the basis of any society, modern or otherwise. In this I have also moved away from Marx toward Durkheim, who held that, contrary to Marx's claim, the economic and the political do not exhaust the modern condition. There is the issue of what Durkheim called the "science of moral life," or what in our times is called the culture of modernity.

My relationship to Weber is more complex. According to Weber, sociology is concerned with the formulation of general principles and generic-type concepts. History, in contrast, "is directed towards the causal analysis and explanation of particular, culturally significant, actions, structures, and personalities" (Weber 1968: 19). He nevertheless holds that both methods are defensible as social science. For Weber, it is the job of historians to explain the causes of, say, the Bolshevik Revolution, while the job of the sociologist is to explain the conditions that lead to such revolutionary situations, such as demographic expansion or dramatic downward mobility. My own trajectory has been the obverse of Weber's, who moved from historical analysis to sociological generalizations. I have shifted from general concerns about capitalism and socialism to particular concerns about particular peoples.

Yet like Weber, I seek interpretative understanding. According to him, one of the main steps in the analysis of social phenomena is the "rendering intelligible" of the subjective basis on which such phenomena rests. In outlining his conception of "interpretative sociology," Weber underlines the importance of the subjective for sociological analysis. This book seeks both subjective and causal explanations of the problem of what to eat in the context of diasporic dispersal.

It is through Weber that I get to Charles Baudelaire's notion of *modernité*, primarily its subjective side, as something transitory, fugitive, and contingent—a nervous disorder born of endless mobility; a neurosis that can be cured only by the pastoral assumptions of backyard gardening and home cooking; a landscape that is presented in the discontinuous dabs of an impressionist canvas; a countryside seen through metropolitan eyes, eyes that need a verdant quietude, and the stillness of the hearth, tired as they are by the assault of color, glass, light, and variety.

Furthermore, my analysis of the Bengali-American community stands closer to Weber's notion of status as a principle of social stratification than to Marx's theory of class. Status is defined by consumption patterns rather than by peoples' places in the process of production. Unlike class, status groups are communities held together by notions of proper lifestyles, with honor and esteem accorded or denied to members. Here we have Weber's notion of a social category that is dependent on the definition people give to these relationships. Ideas matter and are sometimes independent variables, in contrast to the *relatively* more reductionist assumptions of Marx.

There are traces of Durkheim here, too, in the attention paid to rituals of commensality. The coming together of the family for dinner, on weekends, and for the week of the Durga Puja points to moments of collective effervescence so essential to imagining the community. For instance, during the three-day "gala" that is the North American Bengali Conference, the Bengali-American individual is conveyed into a world that is seen as utterly different from the everyday utilitarian world that makes him an American. That is what makes it sacred; that is what makes a Bengali dinner sacred, too, which in turn makes these moments superior to the profane everyday world. Such moments are not just sentimental celebration of a homogenous community. They also harbor competitive claims about authenticity, which are performed with Goffmanesque attention to detail in constructing the expatriate Bengali self.

Just as Durkheim stressed the social over the individual in his lifelong critique of the Utilitarians, Weber critiqued any reification of the social against the German idealists who turned "society" into something with its own acting will. Against them, he never tired of pointing out that society

is never more than the multitudinous interactions of individuals in particular milieu. This tension between Durkheim's and Weber's perspectives
reflects the very real strain between communities and their constitutive
members. And it was Simmel who most clearly adumbrated on the endless
dialectic between group identity and individuality. I have sought to balance
the two polarities—of collective identity and idiosyncratic exception—in
describing the process of the making of Bengali-American consciousness.
The eternal dialectic between group identification and individual differentiation remains unresolved in Simmel's work—and, I think, in the modern
individual. In the case of my respondents, food is used both to affirm a sense
of community and to assert individuality against that community.

The tapestry I have woven also draws on the work of Walter Benjamin
in trying to see the world in a fragment (Benjamin 1969; Buck-Morss
1991; Frisby 1986). For Simmel, the world is revealed in a fragment that
nevertheless carries echoes of the basic geometry of social organization.
For Benjamin, the fragments are arranged in a mosaic. That is the obverse
of the method of Marx and Weber (and Wallerstein), each of whom placed
the fragment in the totality—for instance, the commodity in capitalism and
disenchantment in rationalization. Benjamin (and Simmel) also reject
abstract conceptualization as the starting point of analysis and instead begin
the journey from the immediacy of lived experience. I have tried to do
the same.

This book is a snapshot of a few places—some backyard gardens and a
few kitchens—echoing what the Friedrichstrasse in Berlin was to Simmel
and the arcades of Paris were to Benjamin. Places become important when
the wandering bricoleur is the theorist. Benjamin made that point most
eloquently when he wrote the following about Siegfried Kracauer:

> A rag-picker early in the dawn, who with his stick spikes the snatches
> of speeches and scraps of conversation in order to throw them into
> his cart, sullenly and obstinately, a little tipsy, but not without now
> and then scornfully letting one or other of these discarded cotton rags
> ... flutter in the morning breeze. A rag-picker, early—in the dawn
> of the day of revolution. (as quoted in Frisby 1986: 109)

I seek to emulate the rag-picker buffeted by larger processes he does not
fully comprehend.

Long before Foucault (1986), Simmel and Benjamin problematized the relationship between place and the modern condition. This work pursues that connection. You buy a home and build a garden. In the garden you plant some chilies. With the chili you cook up a world—a world of your dreams; a dream of home, circumscribed by the nightmare of homelessness; a nightmare dreamed up by those who leave, those who try to slip away from the hearth and its constraining domesticities.

Gardening in the backyard is the presumptive cure for the travails of modernity. If, as Simmel contends, the modern is metropolitan, the suburbia is imagined as bucolic, a fragment of the countryside. It embodies in a sentimental form what is lost forever—the relationship between agriculture and culture. Gardening is a heroic attempt of mythic proportions to put the genie back in the bottle—to undo 6,000 years of association between city and civilization.

Culture is the human spirit objectified in things. Such objectification has seen its greatest elaboration with the money economy. It is the realm where everything can be turned into a quantity—some amount of money. This is also what undergirds Marx's notion of alienation—that is, alienation from the products of our labor. Nevertheless, there remains in us an element that seeks incommensurable and unquantifiable qualities that Weber identified as "meaning" and Marx as "species-characteristics." Simmel identifies that as subjective culture, some goal beyond endless movement and quantification.

Authentic food of one's own is about quality, that eternal shadow of an unrelentingly quantifying civilization that we call modernity. If money is about empty quantity, authentic home-cooking is brimming with quality. It is incomparable. It is priceless. At least, that is the claim. It subverts the spectral equality of all things that money can buy. It is also the antidote to mass production. None of the things consumed by us are produced *for* us. In contrast, the household kitchen and the kitchen garden are a few of the places in the modern world where things are tended just for us with care about our idiosyncrasies, taste, and propensities. The point is not that such things are distinctive—everybody grows about the same tomatoes in their backyards—but that things are specifically targeted for us. The producer knows who the consumer will be. It is that intersubjectivity between producers and consumers, the negotiations and the attention to the individual that is impossible to replicate in a mass society. That is what gives to the household economy a feel of authenticity, a sense that there is some quality, some meaning, some subjective relationship to culture, and a lot of messy emotions.

The point of an "authentic" heritage is that "nothing should be new"— it is focused on the past. In contrast, modernity is presumably about the obverse—everything must be new; we look wistfully to the future. If re-visioning the landscape and insisting on an authentic meal are central to the migrant experience, so is the reimagining of time. In fact, the search for the authentic is the reversal of time. The migrant through the sheer act of abandoning the past is made more acutely aware of that betrayal. That is why she hungers to turn the present into the past. That is exactly why the migrant pours so much meaning into the rhythms of eating. That is what gives meaning—breaking up the continuum of time into intersubjectively meaningful units. Meals do that.

It is the impulse to look back that distinguishes what can be characterized as the other side of modernity. It is one among a range of things we evoke with words such as "culture," community, and meaning. It is what is at the root of the longing for religion and behind the nostalgia for nation, tradition, and hierarchy. Authenticity is the elaboration of subjective culture as an essentialist dogma. It is fixed on the past, not the present or the future.

The recognition that antiquity exists *within* modernity is distinctive of Benjamin's perspective. Beneath the arcade and the streets of Paris lies the labyrinth of the catacombs. The past is not only behind us but beneath us; it is on what we stand. Benjamin urges us to find a site on the surface of lived experience and start digging to reveal an archaeology of the modern. That is what I have done in this book. To dig in is to dig up the past. To be modern is not only to pin our hopes on the future but also to hanker for the past. Food is one cheap and portable way of making up a heritage.

Survey Questionnaire

INTRODUCTORY LETTER

June 10, 1996

Dear respondent,

My name is Krishnendu Ray. I teach at the Culinary Institute of America at Hyde Park, New York. I am also a Ph.D. student in sociology at the State University of New York at Binghamton.

This questionnaire is part of my work toward a Ph.D. in sociology. It is being sent to about 1,000 Bengali families in the United States. Your name and address have been selected from various directories of Indians in North America.

My dissertation is titled "Cuisine, Community, and Identity: Immigration and Structures of Everyday Life." It addresses issues of life in America for Bengali residents, especially in the realm of food habits.

Most of what I want to know revolves around the following questions: What do Bengalis eat in America? How is Bengali food and cooking different from what it was in India? How do we adjust to these changes, and how important are they to us?

This questionnaire may take about an hour to complete. The questions can be answered either by the adult male or female in the household. Nonetheless, I would appreciate if it was answered by the primary adult *female* of the household.

I assure you that your privacy will be respected and your anonymity guaranteed in the course of my work. *To ensure privacy I do not ask for your name anywhere in the questionnaire.*

If you find a question difficult to answer or intrusive, please skip it. Feel free to add extensive comments on issues that interest you on additional sheets of paper. I would appreciate return of the completed questionnaire in the stamped, self-addressed envelope enclosed. I offer my sincere gratitude to you.

Sincerely,
Krishnendu Ray

QUESTIONNAIRE

Section 1: General Information

1a. Your personal information

Date of birth: _____

Gender: Female _____   Male _____

Religion: _____

Sect: Shakta _____   Vaishnav _____

Language: _____

Caste: _____

Food habit: Vegetarian _____   Nonveg. _____

Year of migration to U.S.A.: _____

Current visa status: F1 _____   J1 _____   H1 _____

                           Other (specify): _____

Green card: Yes _____   No _____

Citizenship: Yes _____   No _____

1b. Spouse's personal information

Date of birth: _____

Gender: Female _____   Male _____

Religion: _____

Sect: Shakta _____   Vaishnav _____

Language: _____

Caste: _____

Food habit: Vegetarian _____   Nonveg. _____

Year of migration to U.S.A.: _____

Current visa status: F1 _____   J1 _____   H1 _____

                           Other (specify): _____

Green card: Yes _____   No _____

Citizenship: Yes _____   No _____

2. Family structure

How many people live and eat in your house? _____

Please specify below their age and gender and how they are related to you:

Age	Gender	Relationship	Earning/ non-earning
_____	F ___ M ___	_____	_____
_____	F ___ M ___	_____	_____
_____	F ___ M ___	_____	_____
_____	F ___ M ___	_____	_____
_____	F ___ M ___	_____	_____

Do any members of your immediate family live away from you for most of the year? _____

Who are they? _____

3a. Your formal education

Highest degree acquired by you (please circle the relevant degree): Less than High School / High School / B.A. / B.S. / B.Com. / B.E. / M.E. / M.S. / M.A. / M.B.B.S. / M.D. / M.Phil. / Ph.D.

Highest degree acquired by *you* in India *before* emigration:

Degree _____

Name of institution in India _____

Any additional degree acquired in the U.S.A. by *you*:

Degree _____

Name of institution in the U.S.A. _____

3b. Spouse's formal education

Highest degree acquired (please circle the relevant degree): Less than High School / High School / B.A. / B.S. / B.Com. / B.E. / M.E. / M.S. / M.A. / M.B.B.S. / M.D. / M.Phil. / Ph.D.

Highest degree acquired by *your spouse* in India *before* emigration:

Degree _____

Name of institution in India _____

Any additional degree acquired in U.S.A. by *your spouse*:

Degree _____

Name of institution in U.S.A. _____

4. Current occupation

What is your current occupation? _____

What is your spouse's current occupation? _____

What are your children's current occupations?

Child's age	Gender	Year in school/ college	College name	Specify occupation
_____	F ___ M ___	_____	_____	_____
_____	F ___ M ___	_____	_____	_____
_____	F ___ M ___	_____	_____	_____
_____	F ___ M ___	_____	_____	_____

5. Earnings

Give an *estimate* of the combined annual earning of your household for last year $ _____

What is your monthly mortgage payment or rent? $ _____

6. Place of origin

What is the *exact place* you originally come from in India?

_____

Name the place of your last residence in India before migration

_____

What is the *exact place* your spouse originally comes from in India?

_____

Name the last place of residence for your spouse in India before migration _____

7. Language use

How often do *you* speak in an Indian language to your *spouse*?

10% ___   30% ___   50% ___   70% ___   100% ___

Specify the language _____

How often do *you* speak in an Indian language to your *children*?

    10% ___   30% ___   50% ___   70% ___   100% ___

    Specify the language _____

How often do your *children* speak to *you* in an Indian language?

    10% ___   30% ___   50% ___   70% ___   100% ___

    Specify the language _____

Estimate how often your *children* speak to *each other* in an
Indian language?

    10% ___   30% ___   50% ___   70% ___   100% ___

    Specify the language _____

Do your children attend any Indian language school?

    Yes ___   No ___

    Specify the language _____

How good is your *children's* knowledge of an Indian language?
They can:

    Speak ___   Understand ___   Read ___   Write ___

    Specify the language _____

How good is *your* knowledge of an Indian language?   You can:

    Speak ___   Understand ___   Read ___   Write ___

    Specify the language _____

How good is your *spouse's* knowledge of an Indian language?
S/he can:

    Speak ___   Understand ___   Read ___   Write ___

    Specify the language _____

How good is *your* knowledge of English?   You can:

    Speak ___   Understand ___   Read ___   Write ___

How good is your *spouse's* knowledge of English?   S/he can:

    Speak ___   Understand ___   Read ___   Write ___

8. Religious practices

   How often does your family visit a temple/gurudwara/mosque/
   church? _____

How often do you pray at home? _____

How often does your husband pray? _____

How often do your children pray? _____

Do you have an alcove or a closet for a *murti,* holy book or a sign
in your house where you pray? _____

Section 2: Food

1. Who does the cooking in your house? _____

   How often does your husband cook? _____

2. What was today's breakfast in your house? _____

   What is a typical breakfast in your house?_____

   Weekday _____

   Weekend _____

   Does breakfast differ for members of the family? _____

   What are the differences? _____

   At what time do *you* eat breakfast? _____

   At what time do others eat breakfast? _____

   What do you drink at breakfast? (Check all appropriate answers)
   Coffee ____   Tea ____   Juice ____   Milk ____   Soda ____
   Others (specify): _____

   What does your *husband* drink at breakfast? (Check all appropriate
   answers)   Coffee ____   Tea ____   Juice ____   Milk ____
   Soda ____   Others (specify): _____

   What do the *children* drink at breakfast? (Check all appropriate
   answers)   Coffee ____   Tea ____   Juice ____   Milk ____
   Soda ____   Others (specify): _____

   How do you drink your tea and coffee? (Check all appropriate
   answers)   Black ____   With lemon ____
   With sugar only ____   With cream only ____
   With sugar and cream ____

What are the main utensils used for breakfast? _____

What was breakfast in India? _____

How much has your breakfast changed from what it used to be
   in India? (Check the correct answer)
   A lot ____   A little ____   Not at all ____

How would you explain the changes, if any? _____

   _____

3. What was yesterday's lunch in your home? _____

   What is a typical lunch in your house?

   Weekday _____

   Weekend _____

   Does lunch differ for members of the family ? _____

   What are the differences? _____

   At what time do *you* eat lunch? _____

   At what time do others eat lunch? _____

   Where do you eat lunch? (at home, at work, at school, etc.)

   _____

   Where do others eat lunch? _____

   What are the main utensils used for lunch?   Spoon ____
      Fork ____   Knife ____   Fingers of the right hand ____
      Other (specify) _____

   What was lunch in India? _____

   How much has lunch changed from what it used to be in India?
   (Check the correct answer)
   A lot ____   A little ____   Not at all ____

   How would you explain the changes, if any? _____

   _____

4. What was yesterday's dinner in your home? _____

   What is a typical dinner in your house?

   Weekday _____

   Weekend _____

Does dinner differ for members of the family? _____

    What are the differences? _____

At what time do *you* eat dinner? _____

At what time do others eat dinner? _____

Where do you eat dinner? (at home, at work, at school, etc.)

_____

Where do others eat dinner? _____

What are the main utensils used for dinner by you?   Spoon ____
    Fork ____   Knife ____   Fingers of the right hand ____
    Other (specify) _____

What are the main utensils used by the children?   Spoon ____
    Fork ____   Knife ____   Fingers of the right hand ____
    Other (specify) _____

What do you generally drink with your dinner? _____

What do the children drink with their dinner? _____

What was dinner in India? _____

How much has dinner changed from what it used to be in India?
    (Check the correct answer)
    A lot ____   A little ____   Not at all ____

How would you explain the changes, if any? _____

_____

5. Could you write down last week's menu for your family?

    Monday
        Breakfast _____
        Lunch _____
        Dinner _____

    Tuesday
        Breakfast _____
        Lunch _____
        Dinner _____

Wednesday

Breakfast _____

Lunch _____

Dinner _____

Thursday

Breakfast _____

Lunch _____

Dinner _____

Friday

Breakfast _____

Lunch _____

Dinner _____

Saturday

Breakfast _____

Lunch _____

Dinner _____

Sunday

Breakfast _____

Lunch _____

Dinner _____

Is the menu same for adults and children? _____

If the menu is different, what are the differences? _____

_____

6. Whose tastes and dietary needs are the most important in planning a menu? (Rank from 1 to 3, with 1 as most important and 3 as least important; if equal, mark each as 1)
   Husband ____   Wife ____   Children ____

7. Do *you* take snacks?   Yes ____   No ____
   How often in a day? _____
   What is it usually? _____

Do your children take snacks?   Yes ___   No ___

   How often in a day? _____

   What is it usually? _____

8. How often do you eat rice in a week? _____

    What is your monthly rice bill? $ _____

9. How often do you eat fish in a week? _____

    Do you prefer whole fish, fillet, or steak? _____

    What is your weekly fish bill? $ _____

10. What are the non-Indian foods your children like? _____

_____

11. Do you like certain American foods?   Yes ___   No ___

    What are they? _____

12. Does your family eat beef in any form?   Yes ___   No ___

    How often? _____

    Do your family members eat beef at home?   Yes ___   No ___

    Do your family members eat beef only outside the home?
       Yes ___   No ___

    Do you serve beef only in certain forms, such as ground rather
       than steak?   Yes ___   No ___

    What are the forms of beef you and/or your family members
       prefer? _____

    If you eat steak, is there any particular way you like it?
       Rare ___   Medium ___   Well-done ___

    Who eats beef and who does not in your family?

       Eats beef _____

       Does not eat beef _____

    Did anyone in your family eat beef in India?   Yes ___   No ___

       Who? _____

13. Do you think it is alright for a Hindu Indian to eat beef?
    Yes ___   No ___

    Please explain. _____

14. Does anyone in your family eat pork?   Yes ___   No ___
    Who? _____

    How often? _____

15. How often is alcohol consumed by you? _____
    By your spouse? _____
    By your children? _____
    Is any alcohol consumed at home?   Yes ___   No ___
    Does anybody in your family go out to bars?   Yes ___   No ___
    Who (husband, wife, adult children, etc.)? _____
    How often? _____

16. Do you serve any alcohol to your American friends and associates?
    Yes ___   No ___

17. Who shops for groceries (you, husband, adult children)? _____
    _____

    How often is it necessary to do the groceries (every day, once
    every few days, once a week, etc.)? _____

    What is your average weekly grocery bill? $_____

    How often do you shop at a specialist Indian/Asian grocery
    store? _____

    About how much do you spend *per month* at such a store?
    $_____

    What are the kinds of things you purchase at an Asian grocery
    store? _____

18. How many hours a day do you spend in doing groceries, cooking,
    and cleaning in the kitchen? _____

    Does anyone help you in the kitchen?   Yes ___   No ___

Who helps? _____

What are the things they do? _____

19. How many refrigerators/freezers do you have? _____

20. What are the Bengali spices you have the greatest difficulty finding
    in the U.S.A.? _____
    What are the Bengali vegetables you have the greatest difficulty
    finding in the U.S.A.? _____
    What is the Bengali fish you have the greatest difficulty finding
    in the U.S.A.? _____

21. What are the main processes involved in your cooking?
    (Check as many as you want)   Sauteing ____   Frying ____
    Boiling ____   Baking ____   Broiling ____   Poaching ____
    Steaming ____   Grilling ____   Microwaving ____
    Other (specify) _____

22. Do you cook with wine?   Yes ____   No ____

23. Is your cooking any different from your mother's cooking?
    Yes ____   No ____
    How is it different? _____
    Why is it different? _____

24. Do you think your cooking differs from that of your relatives in
    India currently?   Yes ____   No ____
    How so? _____
    Why is it different? _____

25. Has your cooking changed since you moved to the U.S.A.?
    Yes ____   No ____
    What are the changes? _____
    Why has it? _____

26. What do you think are the main differences between Indian
    cooking and American cooking? _____

27. What are the typical foods that come to your mind when you think about American food? _____

28. What are the typical foods that come to your mind when you think about Bengali food? _____

29. Do you think your children's taste differs from yours? What are the differences? _____

30. How often does your family eat out? _____
    How often does your husband eat out? _____
    About how much does your family spend in eating out per week?
    $_____

31. How often do you buy takeout food for the family? _____
    About how much does you family spend *per week* on takeout food?
    $_____

32. Is salad alone good enough as a meal for you?   Yes ____   No ____
    What kind of dressing do you usually have on your salad?
    _____

33. What do you think is more healthy: Indian food or American food?
    _____
    Why? _____

34. What do you think is more tasty: Indian food or American food?
    _____
    Why? _____

35. What do you think is more convenient: Indian food or American food? _____
    Why? _____

36. What looks better: Indian food or American food? _____
    Why? _____

37. What smells better: Indian food or American food? _____
    Why? _____

38. What are the non-Indian cuisines you enjoy (e.g., Chinese, Thai,
    Vietnamese, Japanese, French, Italian, etc.; name as many as you
    want)? _____

39. Can a family be considered Bengali if it does *not* eat Bengali food
    regularly?   Yes ____   No ____
    Explain. _____

40. What is the most important meal of the day for you?
    _____

    Explain. _____

41. What are the things a Bengali family should do in America to
    remain Bengali? _____

42. What do you think people mean when they say, "Her children are
    too American"? _____

43. Should the children be culturally American or Bengali?
    _____

44. What differences do you see between an American and a Bengali
    family in the U.S.A.? _____

45. Name the South Indian foods you are familiar with. _____
    _____

46. Name the North Indian foods you are familiar with. _____
    _____

47. Name the foods from western India that you are familiar with.
    _____

48. What are the major differences in the food from West Bengal and
    Bangladesh? _____

49. Name the foods from Orissa you are familiar with. _____

_____

50. Name the foods from Bihar you are familiar with. _____

_____

51. Name the foods from Assam you are familiar with. _____

_____

52. What are the major differences between Hindu and Muslim food?

_____

53. Do Indians have any national foods? What are they? _____

_____

54. Among all the senses used in the consumption of food—taste, smell, sight, touch—what is the most important for you?

_____

55. Rank the following in terms of their importance to your *ethnic identity* (rank from 1 to 10, with 1 as the most important and 10 as the least important)
Religion ____ Food ____ Choosing marriage partners ____
Clothing ____ Manners ____
Joining Bengali associations ____ Language use ____
Visiting India ____ Respect for elders ____
Other (specify) _____

56. I would appreciate if you could tell me one anecdote that relates to your experience with food in America. _____

_____

_____

_____

_____

_____

_____

_____

APPENDIX 2

Tables

TABLE 1. Foods Consumed Most Widely in Calcutta in 1970 $(N = 2,386)$						
RANK	FOOD	NO.[a]		RANK	FOOD	NO.[a]
1	Salt	2,380		16	Pumpkin	1,442
2	Potato	2,347		17	*Potol* (pointed gourd)	1,347
3	Sugar	2,343		18	Loaf bread (raised)	1,324
4	Turmeric	2,311		19	Onion (small)	1,250
5	Mustard oil	2,262		20	Okra	1,177
6	Rice (parboiled)	2,232		21	Cow's milk (loose)	1,136
7	Chili (dry)	2,178		22	Puffed rice	1,062
8	Cumin seed	2,080		23	Crackers	1,062
9	Green chili	1,954		24	Garlic	1,031
10	Green gram (dal)	1,876		25	Tea (dust)	965
11	Lentil (dal)	1,842		26	Other leafy vegetables	915
12	Wheat flour (*atta*)	1,770		27	Lime	915
13	Coriander seed	1,624		28	*Vanaspati* (hydro-	887
14	Ginger	1,607			genated oil)	
15	Eggplant	1,518		29	Betel nut	886

(continued)

TABLE 1. (*Continued*)

RANK	FOOD	NO.[a]	RANK	FOOD	NO.[a]
30	Tea (leaf)	884	58	Bittergourd (small)	425
31	Bittergourd (regular)	857	59	Plantain (large)	413
32	Ridgegourd	852	60	Banana (large)	396
33	Mustard seed	845	61	Duck egg (large)	392
34	Betel leaf	836	62	Cucumber	377
35	Red gram (dal)	807	63	Betel leaf (finished)	374
36	*Rohu* (fish)	789	64	Fenugreek seed	362
37	Jaggery	773	65	Sweets (*chaña*)	349
38	Onion (large)	734	66	Cardamom	335
39	Green papaya	702	67	Wheat flour (*maida*)	330
40	Ghee	691	68	Rice (boiled/flaked)	330
41	Black pepper	683	69	Cow's milk (bottled)	311
42	Guava	609	70	Plantain (small)	298
43	Colocasia	586	71	Yogurt	289
44	Bengal gram (dal)	581	72	Mixed spices (clove,	289
45	Goat meat	578		cinnamon, cardamom)	
46	Wheat (cracked)	565	73	*Tengra* (fish)	285
47	*Hilsa* (fish)	556	74	Cinnamon	281
48	Apple	543	75	Black gram (dal)	272
49	Butter	542	76	Ashgourd	271
50	Pink beans	531	77	Lentil flour	269
51	*Mayalu* (tuber)	524	78	Biscuit (malted)	263
52	Baby shrimp	495	79	*Horlicks* (powdered	257
53	Dried pea (dal)	490		malted drink mix)	
54	Prepared tea	488	80	Hog plum	255
55	Banana (medium)	470	81	Dried coconut	252
56	*Suji* (cream of wheat)	436	82	*Pappad* (lentil wafer)	249
57	Tilapia (fish)	434	83	Clove	247

Source: USAID (1972: 108).

[a] Number of consuming households.

TABLE 2. Daily Food Budgets of Affluent and Poor Households in Calcutta in 1970 (in percentage share of the daily budget)

	POOREST HOUSEHOLDS	AFFLUENT HOUSEHOLDS	AVERAGE HOUSEHOLD
Cereals	46	17	27
Fish, meat, eggs	8	20	16
Vegetables	9	10	11
Milk	4	13	10
Edible oils	6	7	7
Pulses	5	2	4
Fruit	1	6	4
Sugars	5	3	4

Source: USAID (1972: 16).

TABLE 3. Major Foods Consumed by Rich and Poor per Capita in Calcutta in 1970

	LOW EXPENDITURE	HIGH EXPENDITURE	ALL
Cereal	336.6 (45)	352.0 (31)	342.9 (38)
Pulses and legumes	33.2 (4)	43.2 (4)	37.2 (4)
Liquid milk	52.6 (7)	108.7 (16)	106.3 (12)
Fish, meat, eggs	30.2 (4)	63.5 (6)	44.1 (5)
Edible oils	16.3 (2)	30.3 (3)	22.2 (2)
Vegetables	169.5 (23)	268.2 (24)	210.9 (23)
Fruit	16.4 (2)	61.8 (5)	35.6 (4)
Sugar, etc.	26.2 (3)	39.1 (3)	31.6 (3)
Other	71.9 (10)	87.5 (8)	78.4 (9)
TOTAL	752.3 (100)	1,126.3 (100)	909.2 (100)

Source: USAID (1972: 4).

Note: Consumption is expressed in grams per day, with percentages in parentheses. Low expenditures are less than 300 rupees per month (i.e., less than US$38 in 1970 dollars); high expenditures are more than 300 rupees per month. In 1970, the exchange rate was 8 rupees to the U.S. dollar; in mid-2004, the rate was 44 rupees to the U.S. dollar.

TABLE 4. Calcutta Households Serving Various Dishes by Eating Hour and Meal Type in 1970 (all households; in percentages)

	6 A.M. TO 10 A.M.			10 A.M. TO 2 P.M.		2 P.M. TO 6 P.M.		6 P.M. TO 6 A.M.		ANY HOUR, ALL TYPES
	P	S	ALL	P	ALL	S	ALL	P	ALL	
Rice	33	1	34	85	85	—	—	31	31	94
Rooti	4	48	53	12	14	30	32	77	80	92
Dal	29	1	30	76	76	—	—	46	46	85
Vegetables	33	10	46	88	88	10	17	80	80	88
Fish	14	—	14	36	36	—	—	18	18	40
Meat	—	—	—	7	7	—	—	8	8	11
Tea	—	92	92	—	—	77	77	—	—	94
Crackers	—	22	22	—	—	21	21	—	—	38
Puffed rice	—	11	11	—	—	14	14	—	—	23
Sliced bread	—	31	31	—	—	11	11	—	—	38
Banana	—	5	5	—	—	5	5	2	3	13
Milk	1	19	20	—	—	8	9	22	24	40

Source: USAID (1972: table A29, apps., 23).

Note: P = principal meal; S = supplemental meal. Number of sample households = 2,386. I have omitted columns specifying "both" (i.e., principal and supplemental) that showed insignificant numbers (0–6%).

TABLE 5. The Core–Fringe–Legume Pattern

CORE	FRINGE	LEGUME	EXAMPLE
Maize	Tomatoes Avocados Meat	Beans	Mexico
Wheat/Maize	Olives Eggplants Meat	Lentils	Italy
Rice	Fish Greens	Soy	Japan
Wheat	Greens Chicken Pork	Soy	North China
Rice	Greens Chicken Pork	Soy	South China
Wheat	Greens Potatoes Vegetables	Legumes	North India
Rice/wheat	Greens Potatoes Fish	Legumes	West Bengal

Source: Adapted from Mintz 2001.

TABLE 6. A "Typical" Middle-Class Daily Menu in Calcutta in 1970

Breakfast	Buttered toast and tea (with milk and sugar) *or* *Rooti* and stir-fry of potatoes and onions, with green chilies and *panch phoron*[a] *or* Puffed rice in milk with sugar and sliced bananas
Lunch	Steamed rice *Masur* dal[a] Stir-fry of potatoes and onions Small whole fish in a light sauce[a]
Snack	Tea with milk and sugar and *pokora*[a] (afternoon)
Dinner	Steamed rice Dal Panfried eggplant[a] Fish steaks in rich mustard sauce[a]

[a] A recipe is provided in Appendix 4.

TABLE 7. Distribution of Calcutta Vegetarian and Nonvegetarian Households by Religion and Caste (in percentages)

RELIGION AND CASTE	VEGETARIAN	NONVEGETARIAN	ALL
Hinduism			
Brahmin	2.60	16.76	19.36
Kayastha	0.50	25.35	25.86
Baidya	0.17	3.23	3.39
Others	4.40	33.49	37.89
Islam	0.08	10.22	10.31
Christianity	0.0	1.22	1.22
Sikhism	0.08	0.25	0.34
Jainism	0.75	0.21	0.96
Buddhism	0.0	0.13	0.13
Other	0.21	0.34	0.54
All religions	8.80	91.20	100.00
Number of households	210	2,176	2,386

Source: USAID (1972: table A18, apps., 10).

TABLE 8. Consumption of Certain Foods for Breakfast in Bengali Households in Calcutta and in Bengali-American Households in the United States on a "Typical Weekday" (in percentages)

	UPPER-MIDDLE-CLASS HOUSEHOLDS IN CALCUTTA	UPPER-CLASS HOUSEHOLDS IN CALCUTTA	BENGALI-AMERICAN HOUSEHOLDS IN THE UNITED STATES[a]
Toast and cereal	—	—	35
Toast only	35	56	16
Cereal only	15	11	47
Fruit and juices	9	22	49
Eggs	—	16	11
Milk	26	39	89
Tea and coffee	—	—	13
Tea only	92	90	61
Coffee only	—	—	15
Number of households	572	519	126

Source: The Calcutta figures are from USAID (1972: table A27, apps., 19–20); the U.S. figures are from my survey.

Note: The Calcutta figures are exclusively for upper-class and upper-middle-class households to make the comparison with Bengali-American families more meaningful. Most West Bengali migrants in the United States come from upper-middle-class and upper-class families. Expenditure in the upper-middle-class households in Calcutta was 60–100 rupees per capita per month. For upper-class Calcutta households, monthly expenditure was more than 100 rupees per capita.

[a] The data for Bengali Americans are compiled from self-reported lists of "typical weekday breakfasts." The unit of analysis is the household rather than the individual for reasons of comparability between the Calcuttan and U.S. data. For example, if the wife reported drinking tea and the husband coffee, this is reflected in the figures for "Tea and coffee."

TABLE 9. Consumption of Certain Foods for Lunch in Bengali Households in Calcutta and for Dinner in Bengali-American Households in the United States on a "Typical Weekday" (in percentages)

	UPPER-MIDDLE-CLASS HOUSEHOLDS IN CALCUTTA	UPPER-CLASS HOUSEHOLDS IN CALCUTTA	BENGALI-AMERICAN HOUSEHOLDS IN THE UNITED STATES
Rice	85	84	91
Rooti	18	13	12
Dal	74	73	70
Vegetables (sauteed/curried)	96	99	83
Fish	41	47	63
Meat curry	8	10	66
Hamburger	—	—	26
Pasta	—	—	26
Salads	—	—	13
Number of households	572	519	126

Source: The Calcutta figures are from USAID (1972: table A27, apps., 19–20); the U.S. figures are from my survey.

Note: The Calcutta figures are exclusively for upper-class and upper-middle-class households to make the comparison with Bengali-American families more meaningful. Most West Bengali migrants in the United States come from upper-middle-class and upper-class families. Expenditure in the upper-middle-class households in Calcutta was 60–100 rupees per capita per month. For upper-class Calcutta households, monthly expenditure was more than 100 rupees per capita.

TABLE 10. Time Spent on Food Work by Bengali Americans

TIME SPENT ON FOOD WORK	PERCENTAGE OF BENGALI AMERICANS (N = 110)
0.5–1 hour per day	13
1.5–2 hours per day	38
2.5–3 hours per day	32
3.5–4 hours per day	12
4.5–5 hours per day	3
8 hours per weekend	2

Note: These figures are calculated from estimates of time spent on household work by respondents, which typically produce slightly higher estimates than do time diaries. On different methods of measuring household work and their reliability, see Marini and Shelton (1993).

TABLE 11. Mean Hours per Week Spent on Housework in the United States in 1987

	WOMEN	MEN
Meal preparation	9.8	3.3
Meal clean-up	6.2	2.4
Indoor cleaning	8.5	2.2
Clothing care	4.1	0.9
Outdoor chores, repairs	2.3	5.1
Bills, etc.	1.8	1.6

Source: National survey of families and households conducted in 1987 (Marini and Shelton 1993: 375).

APPENDIX 3

Seven-Day Menu for a Bengali-American Family in the Greater Chicago Area

This family of five lived in a $200,000 house (all values are in 1995 dollars) on the outskirts of Chicago. The father was employed as a chemical engineer at a multinational oil corporation, making about $100,000 per annum. The mother, who did all of the cooking, was employed as a secretary in a doctor's office and as a travel agent working on commission four days a week. She was making about $20,000 per annum. The household had three children—ages 22, 19, and 8. The menus were for days the children were off from school during the summer break.

SATURDAY

Family invited to a birthday party at a friend's house.
Dinner menu for the twenty-five people invited to the party:

7:00 P.M. **Appetizers:** Turkey *pokora* with finely chopped garlic, onion, ginger, and fresh coriander; carbonated drinks and beer.
10:00 P.M. **Dinner:** Rice, potato and cabbage, potato and *chāna,* dal, fish in mustard sauce, goat-meat curry, pineapple chutney, sweets (canned

rossogolla). Alternative menu for children: chicken barbecue, cake, ice cream. Children eat before adults.

SUNDAY

9:00 A.M. **Breakfast:** Omelet and toast; cereal; tea for the adults. Family eats together in a loose sense.

1:00 P.M. **Lunch at a friend's house:** *Singara, pokora, chira bhaja.* Finger food eaten at the same time but not a sit-down meal.

4:00 P.M. **Snack on return home:** Adults: Puffed rice mixed with mustard oil, finely chopped onions, cucumber, green chilies, and savory deep-fried lentil mixture; tea. Children: Ham-and-cheese sandwich.

9:00 P.M. **Dinner:** Lamb curry, rice, Bengali-style salad (onions, cucumber, and tomatoes with lime and salt). Family eats together.

MONDAY

Son's nineteenth birthday.

7:30 A.M. **Breakfast:** Cereal; tea for the adults. Eaten individually.

2:00 P.M. **Lunch:** Ham-and-cheese sandwiches for children made by mother on return from work; husband eats at work.

7:00 P.M. **Dinner:** Rice; shrimp with onion and ginger; dal with fresh coriander garnish; potato, broccoli, and other vegetables in mustard sauce; strawberry shortcake; grape juice. Family eats together.

TUESDAY

7:30 A.M. **Breakfast:** Cereal; tea for the adults. Eaten individually.

— **Lunch:** Adults eat individually at work. Children at home make their own sandwiches.

7:00 P.M. **Dinner:** Bengali-style mashed potato (with raw onions, mustard oil, and *bodi* [lentil croutons]); potato, broccoli stems, and spinach in mustard sauce; braised trout for children and trout *jhol* (with *panch phoron* and fresh coriander) for adults; rice; and Bengali salad. Children eat together served by mother; father eats earlier than mother.

WEDNESDAY

7:30 A.M. **Breakfast:** Milk and bananas or milk and toast; tea for the adults. Eaten individually.

2:00 P.M. **Lunch:** Macaroni and cheese with ground beef cooked Indian-style for children on mother's return from work. Father eats at work; mother picks at tidbits.

7:30 P.M. **Dinner:** Previous day's leftover trout *jhol* and rice, leftover ground-beef curry (reheated), Bengali-style salad. Children eat together; father eats earlier than mother.

THURSDAY

7:30 A.M. **Breakfast:** Cereal; tea or instant coffee for the adults. Eaten individually.

2:00 P.M. **Lunch:** Leftovers and baked potato for children and mother; father eats at work.

7:00 P.M. **Dinner:** Roast chicken legs, rice, American-style salad with French dressing, sauteed bittermelon, grapes, apple juice. Family eats together.

FRIDAY

7:30 A.M. **Breakfast:** Cereal, tea or instant coffee for adults.

— **Lunch:** Children make their own sandwiches at home; father and mother eat at work.

6:30 P.M. **Dinner:** Whole family goes to Red Lobster for dinner.

APPENDIX 4

Recipes

STIR-FRY OF POTATOES AND ONIONS

Serves 4

INGREDIENTS

4 medium to large potatoes, sliced thin

1 medium onion, sliced thin

2 green chilies, whole

2 tablespoons vegetable oil

1/2 teaspoon *panch phoron* (equal proportion of black
mustard seed, fenugreek, onion seed, fennel seed,
and cumin seed)

1/4 teaspoon (a pinch) ground turmeric

Salt to taste

METHODS

1. Heat the oil over medium heat.
2. When oil is hot, add *panch phoron* and stir until spices start crackling.
3. Add green chili.
4. Add sliced onion and stir-fry until translucent.
5. Add thinly sliced potatoes, turmeric, and salt.
6. Stir-fry until done.

Masur Dal (Red Lentils)

Serves 4

INGREDIENTS

3 cups (750 ml) water

1 cup (250 ml) red lentils

1/4 teaspoon turmeric

1/2 teaspoon salt (or to taste)

1 teaspoon sugar

2 tablespoons vegetable oil (mustard oil preferred)

2 whole dried red chilies

1 tablespoon cumin seed

METHODS

1. Bring water to a boil in a deep saucepan over medium heat.
2. Add lentils and turmeric; simmer covered until lentils are tender (15 to 30 minutes, depending on how you prefer them).
3. Add salt and sugar.
4. Heat oil in a skillet over medium-low heat.
5. Add red chilies and cumin seeds; fry for 2–3 minutes until chilies turn dark (be careful not to burn the chilies).
6. Pour into simmering lentils and stir in.
7. Cover and turn off the heat.

SMALL WHOLE FISH IN A LIGHT SAUCE

Serves 4–6

INGREDIENTS

1/2 teaspoon turmeric

1/2 teaspoon salt (to taste)

2 lbs. fish (any small whole fish gutted and scaled with
head on or as you prefer; steaks of halibut and cod;
or fillet of red snapper, walleyed pike, or yellow
perch)

2 tablespoons mustard oil (any vegetable oil will do)

2 bay leaves

1 whole dried red chili

1/4 teaspoon *panch phoron*

1 whole green chili

1/4 cup (60 ml) water

METHODS

1. In a large bowl, combine turmeric and 1/4 teaspoon of salt. Add fish and turn gently to coat each surface of every piece. Set aside.
2. Heat 2 tablespoons of oil in a deep, heavy skillet over medium heat.
3. Fry fish until opaque (about 1 minute, turning once).
4. Remove fish with a slotted spatula and set aside.
5. If skillet is dry, add the remaining 1/2 tablespoon of oil.
6. Heat over medium-low heat.
7. Fry bay leaves and red chili until chili darkens (stop before chili turns black).
8. Add *panch phoron* and stir until the spices start crackling.
9. Add green chili, remaining salt, and water and bring to a simmer (do not boil!).
10. Lower heat to maintain simmer.
11. Add fried fish and simmer covered until done (2–4 minutes).

POKORA
(VEGETABLES DEEP-FRIED IN CHICKPEA BATTER)

Serves 4–8

INGREDIENTS

1 large potato, sliced in cross-sectional discs

1 small cauliflower (or 1/2 large cauliflower), broken into
florets (about 2 inches each)

1 medium onion, sliced and disaggregated into rings

1 cup *besan* (chickpea flour)

1/2 cup water

Salt to taste

1 chopped green chili (optional)

2 cups oil

METHODS

1. Make batter by adding water and salt to the chickpea flour in a large
   bowl.
2. Add chopped chili (optional) and mix in.
3. Heat oil in a wok, fryer, or deep skillet over medium-high heat.
4. Dip vegetables in batter and deep-fry.
5. Remove with slotted spatula and drain on paper towels.
6. Serve piping hot.

PANFRIED EGGPLANT

Serves 4

INGREDIENTS

1 medium eggplant, sliced cross-sectionally into
   1–2 inch discs

1/2 cup oil

Salt to taste, sprinkled on each side of eggplant discs

METHODS

1. Heat oil in wok or deep skillet over medium-high heat.
2. Fry eggplant slices until dark on each side.
3. Serve a slice or two to each person.

FISH STEAKS IN RICH MUSTARD SAUCE

Serves 4

INGREDIENTS

1/2 teaspoon turmeric

1/2 teaspoon salt (or to taste)

1–2 lbs. fish steaks of black cod, halibut, sturgeon, or
   salmon

2 tablespoons mustard oil

1 bay leaf

2 teaspoons ground black mustard in 1 tablespoon water
   (let stand for 30 minutes)

1 whole green chili

3/4 cup (175 ml) water

METHODS

1. Combine turmeric and 1/4 teaspoon salt in a large bowl.
2. Add fish, turning gently to coat each side. Set aside.
3. Heat 2 tablespoons oil in skillet over medium heat.
4. Fry fish until opaque (about 1 minute), turning once. Remove with a slotted spatula and set aside.
5. If skillet is dry, add 2 tablespoons of oil and fry bay leaf for a few seconds over low heat. Add mustard paste and remaining salt. Add green chilies.
6. Simmer. Add fish and cover. Simmer 3–4 minutes, turning the fish once.
7. Remove from heat and serve.

Notes

CHAPTER 2

1. Calcutta was recently renamed Kolkata, but I will continue to use the old spelling for consistency with other sources.
2. The area sown with rice is about 5.9 million hectares, and wheat occupies 0.37 million hectares. West Bengal produced 13.31 million metric tons of rice and 0.78 million metric tons of wheat in 1998–99 (DAC 2000).
3. Although dal is common today, the oldest extant Bengali literature—the *Charyapadas,* which dates to the eleventh century—makes no reference to it. The first mention of dal and its cooking techniques is found in sixteenth-century Vaishnavite literature (Banerji 1997: 22).
4. About 39,000 metric tons of oilseeds are produced in Bengal, with mustard contributing almost one-half of the tonnage (DAC 2000).
5. India is the largest producer of tea in the world, producing about 1 million metric tons per year. A little less than one-half of that is produced in Bengal.
6. The 1970 study identified forty-one different kinds of freshwater fish available in major Calcutta markets, underlining the importance of the deltaic location and the many inland waterways to the diet of Bengalis. Almost 1 million metric tons of fish were caught in West Bengal in 1998–99, about 80 percent of that from inland waters (DAC 2000). West Bengal has the highest fish catch of all the states in India.
7. In 1970, the exchange rate was 8 rupees to the U.S. dollar. In mid-2004, the rate was 44 rupees to the U.S. dollar.

8. The menu is "typical" insofar as it is culled from the survey, interviews about the pre-immigration standard, and my own memory.

9. Indian food awaits what scholars such as Emma Tarlo (1996) and Linda Lynton (1995) have done for Indian clothing. Judith Walsh and Dipesh Chakrabarty are doing exciting work in identifying, analyzing, and translating texts from a genre of domestic-science books written in Bengali during the last half of the nineteenth century. See Walsh (1995, esp. 1997) and Chakrabarty (2000). As a sociologist with inadequate skills of historical analysis and archival work I am particularly indebted to the work of K. T. Achaya, Dipesh Chakrabarty, David Kopf, Tapan Raychaudhuri, Sumit Sarkar, and Tanika Sarkar in making visible to me the world of nineteenth-century Bengali *bhadrasamaj*.

10. The great difficulty of the second step and its associated insecurities are elaborated on by Ashis Nandy (1983: xi), who writes: "This colonialism colonizes minds in addition to bodies and it releases forces within the colonized societies to alter their cultural priorities once and for all. In the process, it helps generalize the concept of the modern West from a geographical and temporal entity to a psychological category. The West is now everywhere, within the West and outside; in structures and in minds."

CHAPTER 3

1. It is important to remember that the percentages I will use throughout this chapter represent not individuals but aggregates for households, which typically have three or four members. Thus, the percentages accentuate the differences between households while smothering the difference within them. In fact, the percentages make generational differences disappear, but I was constrained to use this approach because the pre-immigration data from Calcutta were for households rather than individuals.

2. Schivelbusch (1993) shows how coffee was turned from an unknown drink into a ubiquitous one after its adoption by the bourgeoisie in the eighteenth century. It came to be seen as a sober, anti-erotic drink associated with work, in opposition to beer's disrepute as a "blue" drink and chocolate's languorous association with the Catholic ancien régime.

3. I use the term "housewife" because almost all of the female homemaker respondents identified themselves that way.

4. Talking about her sister, Sara Smolinsky, the narrator in *Bread Givers,* says: "Mashah found out that Jacob liked American cooking, like *salad* and spinach and other vegetables" (Yezierska 1925: 55). Then, when she gets a job and has some money, she celebrates: "For the first time in my life, I knew the luxury of traveling in a Pullman. I even had my dinner in the dining car. How grand it felt to lean back in my chair, a person among people, and order anything I wanted from the menu. No more herring and pickle over dry bread, I ordered chops and spinach and *salad*" (Yezierska 1925: 237; emphasis added).

5. Of course, there is creative mixing "back home." Recipes from the community of Iraqi Jews in Calcutta provide intriguing lessons in syncretism. Mavis Hyman's extraordinary *Indian-Jewish Cooking* (1992) identifies *khichuri,* a stew of rice and legumes, as a popular dish among the Jewish community in Calcutta; she suggests that, although it is popular among local Indians, it may in fact have been brought from Baghdad during the Moghul Empire. Similarly, Hyman says about a recipe for Chicken Dopyasa: "Dopyasa is chicken or lamb curry in a rich onion sauce. The Indian way to prepare

it is to add yogurt or cream to the sauce but this is omitted from the repertoire of the Jewish community" (Hyman 1992: 109).

6. Most Bengali Americans have moved from *rooti* (homemade wheat flat bread) and sauteed vegetables to toast or cereals. Bengali Americans' adoption of industrialized breakfast cereal may be explained, first, by the power of persuasion of the American breakfast-cereal industry; and second, by its convenience for women who do the cooking. A little time saved in making breakfast compensates for the cooking and cleaning that continued late into the previous night (especially because Bengali Americans tend to eat dinner an hour or two later than Anglo-American families). Third, pressures from children in an advertisement-driven consumer society play a part in this transition. Households with children eat more cereal than others. Finally, as noted earlier, middle-class Bengali women in the United States have to make do without the part-time maids and full-time servants who made *rooti* for most middle-class Calcuttan families. The "servant problem" adds to the quest for early-morning convenience.

7. Nirad Chaudhuri (1951: 218) writes: "[Brahmoism] was an application of Christianity to Hinduism as Sikhism was the application of Islam. The Hindu revivalist movement which sprang into existence as a counter-blast to Brahmoism approached morality from the specifically Hindu standpoint, and was not prepared to acknowledge any debt to Western Christianity, but there is no room for doubt that its conscience too was quickened by the example of Brahmoism and by the Christian leaven."

CHAPTER 4

1. Even if the Bangladeshi population is included, that number rises to only 100,000. There are about 2 million South Asians in the United States in all.

CHAPTER 5

1. This figure holds even for Cajun culture, where masculine public cooking is highly valorized. C. Paige Gutierrez cites those exact numbers in *Cajun Foodways* (1992: 69).

2. Ghosh (1995: 22) writes: "As demonstrated by the numerous correspondences between the objects, actions, words, and ideas that constitute the rituals conducted by women and priests, acts by the married kinswomen of the bride and groom must be understood as parallel to those of the priest. The turmeric smearing ritual performed by women on the morning of the wedding, for example, is complemented by the ritual smearing of vermilion sindoor powder on the bride's hair by the groom during the evening ceremony, led by the priest."

3. For a comparative perspective on the formation of the self, see Roland 1988. Drawing on the differences between U.S. and Japanese notions of self, Yoshinori Kamo (1994) shows how a different notion of "fair share" of household labor is developed.

CHAPTER 6

1. For two very different versions of the McDonaldization of the world, see Ritzer 1996 and Watson 1997. For the great flowering of ethnic restaurants in cities, see, for instance, the food section of any major metropolitan newspaper, such as the *New York Times, Wall Street Journal, Chicago Tribune, San Francisco Chronicle*, or *Los Angeles Times.*

2. Bankim, with all his contempt for the Bengali who could not speak his native tongue fluently and his love of the Sanskritic tradition, was by his own confession much more at ease with English than with Bengali or Sanskrit, as noted by his friend Sirischandra Majumdar (cited in Raychaudhuri 1988: 126).

3. Bengal's most venerated writers, such as Rabindranath Tagore and Bankimchandra Chattopadhyay, are addressed by their first names by Bengalis. Thus, I have switched back and forth between "Rabindranath" and the standard "Tagore."

4. "ABCD" is a slightly derisive term used by expatriates for "American-born" members of the second generation and alleged to be culturally "confused." *Desi* literally means "native" or "of the land."

5. There have been intermittent attempts to produce a vernacular paper for West Bengali Americans, but it has largely failed due to a paucity of interest and personnel. The West Bengali-American community around New York City (including New Jersey) has been one of the more energetic communities in producing Bengali-language material, but none has had much reach or longevity. Commemorative booklets produced for annual conferences and Durga Pujas have been more successful than community-wide vernacular newspapers. Bengali newspapers in the United States are primarily targeted at the Bangladeshi audience.

6. See, for example, http://www.virtualbangladesh.com/recipes, http://www.Indian-Recipe.com, and http://www.dreamindia.com/rasoi/rasoi.htm (all accessed June 11, 2004).

7. Almost one-half of the respondents refused to reveal their caste. Nevertheless, last names are a giveaway about caste, and the *Directory of Bengalis in North America* confirms that ratio.

Glossary of Commonly Used
Indian Words

Adda: Masculinized version of gossip

Ahimsa: Nonviolence; non-killing

Ajwain: Spice with a close affinity to thyme (*Trachyspermum copticum*)

Alur dam: Steamed potato curry lightly flavored with asafetida

Aman: Monsoon planting of rice (one of three plantings), harvested in late autumn; the most important crop in Bengal

Anna: Food (sometimes specifically rice or cereal)

Anna-prasanna: The weaning ritual (child's first taking of rice; colloquially called *mukhe-bhat,* or "rice in the mouth")

Arvi: Colocasia (*Colocasia indica*)

Ashtami: Eighth day of the ten-day Durga Puja cycle

Ata: Cheremoy (*Annona cherimola*)

Atta: Wheat flour

Aus: May planting of rice; harvested in August

Aryavarta: Hindu heartland

Baidya: Caste group

Baishak: Spring month in mid-April

Baniya: Non-Bengali trading caste

Barsha: Monsoon (one of six Bengali seasons)

Basanta: Spring (one of six Bengali seasons)

Bhadralok: Gentleman

Bhadrasamaj: Gentlefolk; respectable society
Bhaja: Sauteed/stir-fried
Bhape: Curry (literally, steamed)
Bhat: Steamed rice
Bhelpuri: Savory street food
Biriyani: Rice pilaf with meats and vegetables
Bonti: Special cutting blade
Bou-bhat: Marriage banquet (literally, "wife rice")
Brahmin: Caste group
Chana: Chickpea (*Cicer arietinum*)
Chāna: Farmer cheese
Chapati: Wheat flat bread
Chhachra: Stewed vegetable and fish entrails
Chhattu: Roasted chickpea flour
Checki: Stewed vegetable curry
Chira: Flattened parboiled rice
Chochori: Stewed vegetable curry
Chop: A battered, deep-fried potato/vegetable/meat pancake
Daga: A particular cut of fish (akin to steak)
Dal: Legumes
    Arhar: Pigeon pea (*Cajunus cajun*)
    Chana: Bengal gram (*Cicer arietinum*)
    Masur: Lentil (*Lens culinaris*)
    Mung: Green gram (*Vigna radiata*)
Dalna: Curry
Desi: Expatriate (literally, native)
Dharma: Religion/law/social order
Dhobi: Launderer
Dhooti-punjabi: Wrapped, unstitched garment worn by men under a long shirt
Dom: Curry (pressured steam technique)
Dudh-bhat: Milk rice
Garam/gorom masala: A fresh ground spice mix (often with cardamom, cinnamon, and clove)
Ghee: Clarified butter
Ghonto: Stewed curry
Grishma: Summer (one of six Bengali seasons)
Gulab jamun: Dessert of fried cheese in syrup
Haat: Temporary market
Habishanno: Ritual meal of rice, ghee, and beans
Hemanta: Late Autumn (one of six Bengali seasons)
Ilish: *Hilsa,* fish (*Tenualosa ilisha*)
Jhaal: Curry (with fresh ground brown mustard; literally, "hot")
Jhol: Curry (often with *panch phoron*)
Kalia: Curry (with garam masala)

Kalo jeera: Nigella; onion seed (*Nigella arvensis*)

Kalonji: Nigella (*Nigella sativa*)

Kapura: Testicles

Kasundi: Pickled table mustard

Kayastha: Caste group

Khashi: Castrated male goat

Kheer: Rice pudding in reduced milk

Khesari: Legume (*Lathyrus sativus*)

Khichuri: Stewed rice, dal, and vegetables

Khoa: Milk solids used to make sweets

Kofta: Vegetable balls in a curried sauce (akin to meatballs)

Korma: Curry (with cream)

Kulin brahmin: Caste group

Kurta: Shirt

Kutumba: In-laws

Ladikini: Dessert of cheese in syrup

Lalshak: Greens

Lau: Bottle gourd (*Lagenaria siceraria*)

Loochi: Thin discs of rolled-out wheat dough, deep-fried in ghee

Malpua: Pre-Aryan dessert of sweetened pancakes

Maskalai: Legume

Mataji: Mother Goddess

Mela: Festive gathering

Methi: Fenugreek (*Trigonella foenum-graecum*)

Mishti doi: Sweet yogurt

Mofussil: Provincial

Moghlai porotha: Pan-fried, stuffed flat bread named after the Mughals

Moira: Traditional Bengali sweetmeat maker

Moori: Puffed rice

Murtis: Images of God

Navami: Ninth day of the ten-day Durga Puja cycle

Panch phoron: Distinctive Bengali whole-five-spice mix of mustard, nigella, fennel, fenugreek and cumin

Paneer: Farmer cheese (*chāna*)

Papor/pappad: Sun-dried legume crisps (eaten roasted or fried; often sold as Pappadum in the United States)

Paratha: Pan-fried wheat-dough flat bread

Parva: Festive/holy day

Paurooti: Sliced raised bread

Payas: Rice pudding

Peti: Cut of fish (the fatty "stomach" parts)

Phalahar: Fruit-based diet

Pindas: Balls of rice, barley flour, or *khoa* that symbolize the essence of the dead relative

Pithaparban: Festival of pancakes

Pokora: Vegetable tempura/croquettes

Potol: Pointed gourd (*Trichosanthes dioica*)

Probashi: Expatriate Bengalis

Puja: Festive/holy occasion

Puja pandal: Temporary tent for worshipping

Pullao-mangsa: Pilaf and meat curry

Puri: Deep-fried bread (associated with festive occasions)

Raita: Diced vegetables in yogurt

Randhuni: Mustard seed

Rasamalai: A dessert of flattened *chāna* patties in thickened milk

Rohu: Fish (*Labeo rohita*)

Rooti/roti: Wheat flat bread

Rosogolla: A dessert (cooked balls of *chāna* in syrup)

Salwar-kameez: North Indian variant of drawstring trousers and long shirt worn by women

Samosa/singara: Vegetable turnover

Sandesh: A dessert made of sweetened *chāna*

Sehri: Holy Muslim occasion

Shakta: Hindu sect; worshippers of goddess Shakti

Sharat: Early autumn (one of six Bengali seasons)

Sheet: Winter (one of six Bengali seasons)

Shradha/shradhdha: Mortuary rites

Stri achara: Women's rites associated with the marriage ceremony

Tandoori: Roasts (breads or meats); from the tandoor, a distinctive oven probably of Afghan origin

Tok: Curry (literally, "sour")

Tulsi: Sacred basil (*Ocimum tenuiflorum*)

Uccha/karela: Bitter gourd/melon (*Momordica charantia*)

Vada: Savory South Indian legume doughnuts

Vaishnav/baishnab: Hindu sect; worshipers of Vishnu/Krishna

Vanaspati: Hydrogenated vegetable oil

Varna: Caste

References

WORKS CITED

Achaya, K. T. 1994. *Indian Food: A Historical Companion*. Delhi: Oxford University Press.

Anderson, Benedict. 1991. *Imagined Communities: Reflections on the Origins and Spread of Nationalism*. London: Verso.

Appadurai, Arjun. 1996. *Modernity at Large: Cultural Dimensions of Globalization*. Minneapolis: University of Minnesota Press.

Archer, W. G. 1985. *Songs for the Bride: Wedding Rites of Rural India*. New York: Columbia University Press.

Ashkenazi, Michael, and Jeanne Jacob. 2000. *The Essence of Japanese Cuisine: An Essay on Food and Culture*. Philadelphia: University of Pennsylvania Press.

Atkinson, J., and T. L. Huston. 1984. "Sex Role Orientation and Division of Labor in Early Marriage." *Journal of Personality and Social Psychology* 46: 330–45.

Auboyer, Jeannine. 1965. *Daily Life in Ancient India*. Bombay: Asia Publishing House.

Avakian, Arlene Voski. 1992. *Lion Woman's Legacy: An Armenian American Memoir*. New York: Feminist Press.

———. 1997. *Through the Kitchen Window*. Boston: Beacon Press.

Baldwin, James. 1956. *Giovanni's Room: A Novel*. New York: Delta Trade Paperbacks.

Bandyopadhya, D. 2000. "Land Reform in West Bengal." *Economic and Political Weekly* 35, nos. 20–21 (May 27): 1795–97.

Banerji, Chitrita. 1997. *Bengali Cooking: Seasons and Festivals*. London: Serif.

Barnard, Nicholas, and Robin Beeche. 1995. *Arts and Crafts of India*. London: Conran Octopus.

Baudelaire, Charles-Pierre. 1964. *The Painter of Modern Life and Other Essays,* trans. and ed. J. Mayne. London: Phaidon.

Baxter, Janeen, and Mark Western. 1988. "Satisfaction with Housework: Examining the Paradox." *Sociology* 32, no. 1 (February): 101–21.

Benjamin, Walter. 1969. *Illuminations,* ed. Hannah Arendt, trans. Harry Zohn. New York: Schocken Books.

Berk, Sarah Fenstermaker. 1985. *The Gender Factory: The Apportionment of Work in American Households.* New York: Plenum.

Berman, Marshall. 1988. *All That Is Solid Melts into Air.* New York: Penguin.

Bianco, Carlo. 1974. *The Two Rosetos.* Bloomington: Indiana University Press.

Boner, Alice. 1990. *Principles of Composition in Hindu Sculpture.* London: South Asia Books.

Bourdieu, Pierre. 1977. *Outline of a Theory of Practice,* trans. R. Nice. Cambridge: Cambridge University Press.

———. 1984. *Distinction: A Social Critique of the Judgement of Taste,* trans. R. Nice. Cambridge, Mass.: Harvard University Press.

———. 2001. *Masculine Domination.* Stanford, Calif.: Stanford University Press.

Braudel, Fernand. 1981. *Civilization and Capitalism: 15th–18th Century, Volume 1: The Structures of Everyday Life: The Limits of the Possible.* New York: Harper and Row.

Breckenridge, Carol A., ed. 1995. *Consuming Modernity: Public Culture in a South Asian World.* Minneapolis: University of Minnesota Press.

Bryant, W. Keith. 1996. "A Comparison of the Household Work of Married Females: The Mid-1920s and the Late 1960s." *Family and Consumer Sciences Research Journal* 24, no. 4 (June): 358–84.

Buck-Morss, Susan. 1991. *The Dialectics of Seeing: Walter Benjamin and the Arcades Project.* Cambridge, Mass.: MIT Press.

Chakrabarty, Dipesh. 1997. "The Difference—Deferral of (a) Colonial Modernity: Public Debates on Domesticity in British Bengal." Pp. 373–405 in *Tensions of Empire: Colonial Cultures in a Bourgeois World,* ed. Frederick Cooper and Ann Laura Stoler. Berkeley: University of California Press. (Orig. pub. 1993.)

———. 2000. *Provincializing Europe: Postcolonial Thought and Historical Difference.* Princeton, N.J.: Princeton University Press.

Charles, Nickie. 1995. "Food and Family Ideology." Pp. 100–115 in *The Politics of Domestic Consumption Critical Readings,* ed. Stevi Jackson and Shaun Moores. London: Prentice-Hall/Harvester Wheatsheaf.

Charles, Nickie, and Marion Kerr. 1986. "Food for Feminist Thought." *Sociological Review* 34, no. 3: 537–72.

———. 1988. *Women, Food and Families.* Manchester: Manchester University Press.

Chatterjee, Partha. 1993. *The Nation and Its Fragments: Colonial and Postcolonial Histories.* Princeton, N.J.: Princeton University Press.

Chattopadhyay, Bankimchandra. 1965. *Bankim racanabali* (Collected works of Bankim), vol. 2. Calcutta: Sahitya Samsad.

Chaudhuri, Nirad C. 1951. *The Autobiography of an Unknown Indian.* London: Macmillan.

Clarke, C. G., C. Peach, and S. Vertovec, eds. 1990. *South Asians Overseas: Migration and Ethnicity.* Cambridge: Cambridge University Press.

Coggeshall, John M. 1993. "Sauerkraut and Souvlakia: Ethnic Festivals as Performances of Identity." Pp. 35–48 in *Celebrations of Identity: Multiple Voices in American Ritual Performance,* ed. Pamela R. Frese. Westport, Conn.: Bergin and Garvey.

Coltrane, Scott, and M. Ishii-Kuntz. 1992. "Men's Housework: A Life Course Perspective." *Journal of Marriage and the Family* 54: 43–57.

Covello, Leonard. 1944. "The Social Background of the Italo-American School Child: A Study of the Southern Italian Family Mores and Their Effect on the School Situation in Italy and America." Ph.D. diss., New York University.

Coverman, S. 1985. "Explaining Husband's Participation in Domestic Labor." *Sociological Quarterly* 26: 81–97.

DAC (Department of Agriculture and Cooperation). 2000. [Agricultural Statistics for West Bengal.] Government of India Website. Available at http://www.nic.in/agricoop/stat (accessed February 1, 2000); http://agricoop.nic.in/stats.htm.

Das, S. K. 1995. *The Artist in Chains: The Life of Bankimchandra Chatterji.* Calcutta: Papyrus.

Davis, Mike. 2001. *Late Victorian Holocausts. El Niño Famines and the Making of the Third World.* New York: Verso.

Defoe, Daniel. 2003. *The Political History of the Devil.* London: AMS Press. (Orig. pub. 1726.)

De Quattrociocchi, Niccola. 1950. *Love and Dishes.* Indianapolis: Bobbs-Merrill.

Desai, Anita. 2000. *Fasting, Feasting.* Boston: Houghton Mifflin.

Devasahayam, Theresa W. 1997. "Power and Pleasure around the Hearth: The Construction of Gendered Identity in Middle-Class South Indian Homes in Urban Malaysia." Paper presented at the South Asian Women's Conference, Los Angeles, September 19–22.

DeVault, Marjorie L. 1990. "Conflict over Housework: The Problem That (Still) Has No Name." Pp. 182–202 in *Research in Social Movements, Conflicts and Change: A Research Annual,* vol. 12, ed. L. Krisberg. Greenwich, Conn.: JAI.

———. 1991. *Feeding the Family: The Social Organization of Caring as Gendered Work.* Chicago: University of Chicago Press.

Di Leonardo, Micaela. 1992. "The Female World of Cards and Holidays: Women, Families, and the Work of Kinship." Pp. 246–61 in *Rethinking the Family,* ed. Barrie Thorne and Marily Yalom. Boston: Northeastern University Press.

Diner, Hasia R. 2001. *Hungering for America: Italian, Irish, and Jewish Foodways in the Age of Migration.* Cambridge, Mass.: Harvard University Press.

Divakaruni, Chitra. 1994. "A Distinct Flavor." *Amerasia Journal* 20, no. 3: 35–36.

Dostoevsky, Fyodor. 1990. *Notes from Underground.* New York: Vintage. (Orig. pub. 1864.)

Douglas, Mary. 1975. "Deciphering a Meal." Pp. 249–75 in *Implicit Meanings: Essays in Anthropology.* London: Routledge and Kegan Paul. (Orig. pub. 1972.)

———. 1977. "Introduction." Pp. 1–7 in *The Anthropologists' Cookbook,* ed. J. Kuper. London: Routledge and Kegan Paul.

———. 1990. "Foreword." Pp. vii–xviii in Marcel Mauss, *The Gift.* New York: W. W. Norton. (Orig. pub. 1950.)

Dumont, Louis. 1960. "World Renunciation in Indian Religions." *Contributions to Indian Sociology* 4: 33–62.

Durkheim, Emile. 1965. *The Elementary Forms of Religious Life.* New York: Free Press.

Dutt, Ashok K. 1988. "Daily Shopping in Calcutta." *The Town Planning Review* 59, no. 4 (October): 207–16.

Dutta, Krishna, and Andrew Robinson. 1996. *Rabindranath Tagore: The Myriad-Minded Man.* New York: St. Martin's Press.

Dutta, Krishna, and Andrew Robinson, trans. 1997. *Rabindranath Tagore: An Anthology.* London: Picador.

Ekström, M. 1991. "Class and Gender in the Kitchen." Pp. 145–58 in *Palatable Worlds: Sociocultural Food Studies,* ed. E. L. Fürst, R. Prättälä, M. Ekström, L. Holm, and U. Kjaernes. Oslo: Solum Forlag.

Embree, Ainslie T., ed. 1988. *Sources of Indian Tradition, Volume 1: From the Begining to 1800.* New York: Columbia University Press.

Featherstone, Mike, Scott Lasch, and Roland Robertson, eds. 1995. *Global Modernities.* London: Sage.

Foucault, Michel. 1986. "Of Other Spaces." *Diacritics* 16, no. 1 (spring): 22–27.

Frese, Pamela R., ed. 1993. *Celebrations of Identity: Multiple Voices in American Ritual Performance.* Westport, Conn.: Bergin and Garvey.

Frisby, David. 1986. *Fragments of Modernity: Theories of Modernity in the Work of Simmel, Kracauer and Benjamin.* Cambridge, Mass.: MIT Press.

Fussell, Betty. 1983. *Masters of American Cookery.* New York: Times Books.

Gabaccia, Donna R. 1998. *We Are What We Eat: Ethnic Food and the Making of Americans.* Cambridge, Mass.: Harvard University Press.

Gambino, Richard. 1974. *Blood of My Blood.* Garden City, N.Y.: Doubleday.

Gans, Herbert. 1968. "The Participant-Observer as a Human Being: Observations on the Personal Aspects of Field Work." Pp. 300–317 in *Institutions and the Person,* ed. Howard Becker et al. Chicago: Aldine.

———. 1979. "Symbolic Ethnicity: The Future of Ethnic Groups and Cultures in America." *Ethnic and Racial Studies* 2 (January): 1–18. (Also in Herbert Gans et al., eds. *On the Making of Americans: Five Essays in Honor of David Riesman.* Philadelphia: University of Pennsylvania Press.)

Geertz, Clifford. 1983. *Local Knowledge.* New York: Basic Books.

Gellner, Ernest. 1983. *Nations and Nationalism.* Oxford: Basil Blackwell.

Ghosh, B. 1961. *Bidrohi Derozio* (The rebel Derozio). Calcutta: Book Sahitya.

Ghosh, Pika. 1995. "Household Ritual and Women's Domains." Pp. 21–25 in *Cooking for the Gods: The Art of Home Ritual in Bengal,* ed. Michael W. Meister. Newark, N.J.: Newark Museum.

Ghurye, G. S. 1979. *Vedic India.* Bombay: Popular Prakashan.

Giddens, Anthony. 1990. *The Consequences of Modernity.* Stanford, Calif.: Stanford University Press.

Gioia, Dominique, ed. 1999. *The Measure of Her Powers: An M. F. K. Fisher Reader.* Washington, D.C.: Counterpoint.

Goffman, Erving. 1959. *The Presentation of Self in Everyday Life.* New York: Doubleday.

Goode, Judith G., Karen Curtis, and Janet Theophano. 1984a. "Meal Formats, Meal Cycles, and Menu Negotiation in the Maintenance of an Italian-American Community." Pp. 143–217 in *Food in the Social Order: Studies of Food and Festivities in Three American Communities,* ed. Mary Douglas. New York: Russell Sage Foundation.

———. 1984b. "A Framework for the Analysis of Continuity and Change in Shared Sociocultural Rules for Food Use: The Italian-American Pattern." Pp. 66–88 in *Ethnic and Regional Foodways in the United States: The Performance of Group Identity,* ed. Linda Keller Brown and Kay Mussell. Knoxville: University of Tennessee Press.

Gupta, R. P. 1984. "The Marinated Centuries." *Times of India,* June 3.

Gutierrez, C. Paige. 1992. *Cajun Foodways.* Jackson: University Press of Mississippi.

Hall, Stuart. 1997. "The Local and the Global: Globalization and Ethnicity." Pp. 41–68 in *Culture, Globalization and the World-System,* ed. Anthony D. King. Minneapolis: University of Minnesota Press.

Hall, Stuart, David Held, Don Hubert, and Kenneth Thompson, eds. 1996. *Modernity: An Introduction to Modern Societies.* Oxford: Basil Blackwell.

Handlin, Oscar. 1951. *The Uprooted: The Epic Story of the Great Migrations That Made the American People.* New York: Atlantic Monthly Press.

Harris, Marvin. 1974. *Cows, Pigs, Wars, and Witches: The Riddles of Culture.* New York: Vintage Books.

Harriss, John. 1993. "What Is Happening in Rural West Bengal? Agrarian Reform, Growth and Re-distribution." *Economic and Political Weekly* 27, no. 27 (June 12): 1237–47.

Heath, Rebecca Piirto. 1997. "Life on Easy Street." *American Demographics,* April, 36–37.

Hebdige, Dick. 1987. *Cut'n Mix: Culture, Identity and Caribbean Music.* London: Methuen.

Heesterman, J. C. 1964. "Brahman, Ritual and Renouncer." *Weiner Zeitschrift für die Kunde Sud- und Ost Asiens* 8: 1–31.

Hemingway, Ernest. 1996. *A Moveable Feast.* New York: Simon and Schuster. (Orig. pub. 1964.)

Hollander, John. 1991. "It All Depends." *Social Research* 58, no. 1 (spring): 31–49.

Huntington, Samuel P. 1996. *The Clash of Civilizations and the Remaking of World Order.* New York: Simon and Schuster.

Hyman, Mavis. 1992. *Indian-Jewish Cooking.* London: Hyman Publishers.

Ignatiev, Noel. 1996. *How the Irish Became White.* New York: Routledge.

Inden, Ronald B., and Ralph W. Nicholas. 1977. *Kinship in Bengali Culture.* Chicago: University of Chicago Press.

Iyengar, P. T. S. 1912. *Life in Ancient India.* Madras: Srinivasa Varadachari.

Jha, D. N. 2002. *The Myth of the Holy Cow.* London: Verso.

Kamo, Yoshinori. 1994. "Division of Household Work in the United States and Japan." *Journal of Family Issues* 15, no. 3 (September): 348–78.

Kaplan, Karen. 1996. *Questions of Travel: Postmodern Discourses of Displacement.* Durham, N.C.: Duke University Press.

Katone-Apte, Judit, and Mahadev L. Apte. 1980. "The Role of Food and Food Habits in the Acculturation of Indians in the United States." Pp. 342–62 in *The New Ethnics: Asian Indians in the United States,* ed. Parmatima Saran and Edwin Eames. Boulder, Colo.: Praeger.

Kennedy, J. Gerald. 1993. *Imagining Paris: Exile, Writing, and American Identity.* New Haven, Conn.: Yale University Press.

Khare, Ravindra S. 1976a. *Culture and Reality: Essays on the Hindu System of Managing Foods.* Simla: Indian Institute of Advanced Studies.

———. 1976b. *The Hindu Hearth and Home.* New Delhi: Vikas.

Khateb, George. 1991. "Introduction to the Section 'Exile, Alienation and Estrangement.'" *Social Research* 58, no. 1 (spring): 135–38.

King, Anthony J., ed. 1997. *Culture, Globalization and the World-System.* Minneapolis: University of Minnesota Press.

Kirchner, Bharati. 1992. *Healthy Cuisine of India: Recipes from the Bengal Region.* Chicago: Contemporary Books.

Kopf, David. 1969. *British Orientalism and the Bengal Renaissance.* Berkeley: University of California Press.

———. 1979. *The Brahmo Samaj and the Shaping of the Modern Indian Mind.* Princeton, N.J.: Princeton University Press.

Kosambi, D. D. 1975. *An Introduction to the Study of Indian History.* Bombay: Popular Prakashan.

Kundera, Milan. 2002. *Ignorance.* New York: HarperCollins.

Lahiri, Jhumpa. 1999. *Interpreter of Maladies.* New York: Houghton Mifflin.

Lamont, Michele. 1994. *Money, Morals and Manners: The Culture of the French and American Upper-Middle Class.* Chicago: University of Chicago Press.

Laslett, Barbara. 1991. "Biography as Historical Sociology: The Case of William Fielding Ogburn." *Theory and Society* 20, no. 4: 511–38.

Leonard, Karen Isaksen. 1993. "Ethnic Celebrations in Rural California: Punjabi-Mexicans and Others." Pp. 145–60 in *Celebrations of Identity: Multiple Voices in American Ritual Performance,* ed. Pamela R. Frese. Westport, Conn.: Bergin and Garvey.

———. 1997. "Finding One's Own Place: Asian Landscape Re-visioned in Rural California." Pp. 118–36 in *Culture, Power, Place: Explorations in Critical Anthropology,* ed. Akhil Gupta and James Ferguson. Durham, N.C.: Duke University Press.

Levenstein, Harvey. 1988. *Revolution at the Table: The Transformation of the American Diet.* New York: Oxford University Press.

———. 1994. *Paradox of Plenty: A Social History of Eating in Modern America.* New York: Oxford University Press.

Lévi-Strauss, Claude. 1978. *The Origin of Table Manners.* London: Jonathan Cape.

Lindenbaum, Shirley. 1986. "Rice and Wheat: The Meaning of Food in Bangladesh." Pp. 253–75 in *Food, Society, and Culture: Aspects in South Asian Food Systems,* ed. Ravindra S. Khare and M. S. A. Rao. Durham, N.C.: Carolina Academic Press.

Lockwood, Yvonne R., and William G. Lockwood. 1991. "Pasties in Michigan's Upper Peninsula. Foodways, Interethnic Relations, and Regionalism." Pp. 3–20 in *Creative Ethnicity: Symbols and Strategies of Contemporary Ethnic Life,* ed. Stephen Stern and John A. Cicala. Logan: Utah State University Press.

Louie, David Wong. 2000. *The Barbarians Are Coming.* New York: G. P. Putnam.

Lynton, Linda. 1995. *The Sari: Styles, Patterns, History, Techniques.* New York: Harry N. Abrams.

Maira, Sunaina. 2002. *Desis in the House: Indian American Youth Culture in New York City.* Philadelphia: Temple University Press.

Majumdar, R. C. 1943. *History of Bengal, Volume 1: Hindu Period.* Dacca: University of Dacca Press.

Malamoud, Charles. 1996. *Cooking the World: Ritual and Thought in Ancient India,* trans. David White. Delhi: Oxford University Press.

Malpezzi, Frances M., and William M. Clements. 1992. *Italian-American Folklore.* Little Rock, Ark.: August House.

Mangione, Jerre. 1978. *An Ethnic at Large: A Memoir of America in the Thirties and Forties.* New York: G. P. Putnam.

Marini, Margaret Mooney, and Beth Anne Shelton. 1993. "Measuring Household Work: Recent Experience in the United States." *Social Science Research* 22, no. 4 (December): 361–82.

Márquez, Gabriel García. 1970. *One Hundred Years of Solitude,* trans. Gregory Rabassa. New York: Harper and Row.

Masuoka, Jitsuichi. 1945. "Changing Food Habits: The Japanese in Hawaii." *American Sociological Review* 10, no. 6 (December): 759–65.

McIntosh, Alex, and Mary Zey. 1989. "Women as Gatekeepers of Food Consumption: A Sociological Critique." *Food and Foodways* 3, no. 4: 317–32.

Mills, C. Wright. 1959. *The Sociological Imagination.* Oxford: Oxford University Press.

Milosz, Czeslaw. 2001. *New and Collected Poems (1931–2001).* New York: HarperCollins.

Mintz, Sidney. 2001. "Food Patterns in Agrarian Societies: The Core–Fringe–Legume Hypothesis." *Gastronomica* 1, no. 3 (summer): 40–52.

Mogelonsky, Marcia. 1996. "America's Hottest Markets." *American Demographics,* January, 20–31.

Morton, William. 1987. *A Collection of Proverbs.* Calcutta: Aparna Book Distributors.

Mukerji, Chandra. 1990. "Reading and Writing with Nature." *Theory and Society* 19: 651–79.

Mukherjee, Bharati. 2003. "Who or What Is an American?" *India Abroad,* January 24, A8.

Naipaul, V. S. 1961. *A House for Mr. Biswas.* Harmondsworth: Penguin.

———. 1988. *The Enigma of Arrival.* New York: Vintage Books.

———. 1992a. *An Area of Darkness.* Harmondsworth: Penguin.

Nandy, Ashis. 1983. *The Intimate Enemy: Loss and Recovery of Self under Colonialism.* New York: Oxford University Press.

Narayan, R. K. 1988. *A Writer's Nightmare: Selected Essays 1958–1988.* New Delhi: Penguin.

Norman Brown, W. 1957. "The Sanctity of the Cow in Hinduism." *Madras University Journal* 28: 29–49.

NRA (National Restaurant Association). 2000. *Ethnic Cuisines II.* Washington, D.C.: National Restaurant Association.

Oblate Sisters of the Sacred Heart of Jesus. 1990. *La Cucina dell'Amore: The Kitchen of Love.* Youngstown, Ohio: Ralph R. Zerbonia.

Park, Robert E. 1914. "Racial Assimilation in Secondary Groups." *American Journal of Sociology* 19, no. 5 (March): 606–23.

Parry, Jonathan. 1985. "Death and Digestion: The Symbolism of Food and Eating in North Indian Mortuary Rites." *Man* 20, no. 4: 612–30.

Patterson, Orlando. 1991. "Slavery, Alienation, and the Female Discovery of Personal Freedom." *Social Research* 58, no. 1 (spring): 159–87.

Paz, Octavio. 1997. *In Light of India.* New York: Harcourt Brace.

Pellegrini, Angelo. 1971. "An Italian Odyssey: From Famine to Feast." Pages 27–47 in *American Cooking: The Melting Pot,* ed. James P. Shenton, Dale Brown, Angelo M. Pellegrini, Israel Shenker, Peter Wood, and the Editors of Time–Life Books. New York: Time–Life Books.

Pleck, J. H. 1985. *Working Wives/Working Husbands.* Beverly Hills, Calif.: Sage.

Polanyi, Karl. 1980. *The Great Transformation.* Boston: Beacon Press.

Proust, Marcel. 1970. *Remembrance of Things Past, Volume 1: Swann's Way,* trans. C. K. Scott Moncrieff. New York: Vintage.

Ravage, Marcus. 1917. *An American in the Making.* New York: Harper and Brothers.

Ray, Gopalchandra. 1979. *Anya ek Bankimchandra* (Another Bankimchandra). Calcutta.

Raychaudhuri, Hashi and Tapan. 1981. "Not by Curry Alone: An Introductory Essay on Indian Cuisines for a Western Audience." Pp. 45–56 in *Proceedings of the Oxford Symposium on National and Regional Styles of Cookery,* ed. Alan Davidson. London: Prospect Books.

Raychaudhuri, Tapan. 1988. *Europe Reconsidered: Perceptions of the West in Nineteenth Century Bengal.* Oxford: Oxford University Press.

Revel, Jean-François. 1982. *Culture and Cuisine,* trans. Helen R. Lane. New York: Doubleday. (Originally published as *Un festin en paroles.* Paris: J. J. Pauvett, 1979.)

Richards, Audrey. 1939. *Land, Labour and Diet in Northern Rhodesia.* London: Oxford University Press.

Rieu, E. V., trans. 1946. *The Odyssey* (Homer). Harmondsworth: Penguin.

Ritzer, George. 1996. *The McDonaldization of Society.* Thousand Oaks, Calif.: Pine Forge Press.

Rocher, Rosanne, ed. 1978. *India and Indology: Selected Articles of W. Norman Brown.* Delhi: Motilal Banarasi Das.

Roediger, David R. 1999. *The Wages of Whiteness: Race and the Making of the American Working Class.* London: Verso.

Roland, Alan. 1988. *In Search of Self in India and Japan: Towards a Cross-Cultural Psychology.* Princeton, N.J.: Princeton University Press.

Roy, Nilanjana S. 1999. "Niblings at the Edges." *Biblio* 4, nos. 7–8 (July–August): 20.

Roy, Sandip. 2003. "Post-Wedding Blues." *India Abroad,* July 25, M4.

Rozin, Elisabeth. 1992. *Ethnic Cuisine: How to Create the Authentic Flavors of Thirty International Cuisines.* New York: Penguin.

Rushdie, Salman. 1980. *Midnight's Children.* Harmondsworth: Penguin.

———. 1991a. *Haroun and the Sea of Stories.* London: Granta Books.

———. 1991b. *Imaginary Homelands.* Harmondsworth: Penguin.

———. 1995. *East, West: Stories.* New York: Vintage.

———. 1999. *The Ground Beneath Her Feet.* New York: Henry Holt.

Rykwert, Joseph. 1991. "House and Home." *Social Research* 58, no. 1 (spring): 51–62.

Sachau, E. C. 1910. *Alberuni's India.* London: Kegan Paul, Trench, Truber.

Sacks, Maurie. 1995. "Metabolising Judaism." *Digest* 15: 12–13.

Sarkar, Sumit. 1998. *Writing Social History.* New Delhi: Oxford University Press.

Saussure, Ferdinand de. 1983. *Course in General Linguistics,* trans. Roy Harris. London: Duckworth.

Schivelbusch, Wolfgang. 1993. *Tastes of Paradise: A Social History of Spices, Stimulants, and Intoxicants,* trans. David Jacobson. New York: Pantheon.

Shapiro, Laura. 1995. *Perfection Salad: Women and Cooking at the Turn of the Century.* Boston: North Point Press.

———. 1997. "Household Appliances: How Appliances Have Changed Housework." *Newsweek* 130, no. 24-A, 36–39.

Simmel, Georg. 1950. *The Sociology of Georg Simmel,* ed. and trans. Kurt H. Wolff. New York: Free Press.

———. 1991. *Theory, Culture and Society* 8, no. 3 (August [special issue devoted to Georg Simmel]). (Orig. pub. 1908.)

Simoons, Frederick J. 1994. *Eat Not This Flesh: Food Avoidances from Prehistory to the Present,* 2nd ed. Madison: University of Wisconsin Press.

Smith, Timothy. 1978. "Religion and Ethnicity in America." *American Historical Review* 83 (December): 1155–85.

Suleri, Sara. 1989. *Meatless Days.* Chicago: University of Chicago Press.

Sutton, David E. 2001. *Remembrance of Repasts: An Anthropology of Food and Memory.* Oxford: Berg.

Tagore, Rabindranath. 1961. *Rabindra-Rachanabali* (Collected works of Rabindranath Tagore). Calcutta: Government of West Bengal.

Tarlo, Emma. 1996. *Clothing Matters: Dress and Identity in India.* Chicago: University of Chicago Press.

Thapar, Romila. 1978. "Renunciation: The Making of a Counter-Culture?" Pp. 63–104 in *Ancient Indian Social History: Some Interpretations.* New Delhi: Orient Longman.

Theophano, Janet, and Karen Curtis. 1991. "Sisters, Mothers and Daughters: Food Exchange and Reciprocity in an Italian-American Community." Pp. 147–71 in *Diet and Domestic Life in Society,* ed. Anne Sharman, Janet Theophano, Karen Curtis, and Ellen Messer. Philadelphia: Temple University Press.

Theroux, Paul. 1998. *Sir Vidia's Shadow: A Friendship across Five Continents.* Boston: Houghton Mifflin.

Thompson, Linda, and Alexis J. Walker. 1989. "Gender in Families." *Journal of Marriage and the Family* 51: 845–71.

Turner, Bryan. 1987. "A Note on Nostalgia." *Theory, Culture, and Society* 4, no. 1: 147–56.

Turner, Victor W., ed. 1986. "Dewey, Dilthey, and Drama: An Essay in the Anthropology of Experience." Pp. 33–44 in *The Anthropology of Experience,* ed. Victor W. Turner and Edward M. Bruner. Urbana: University of Illinois Press.

USAID (United States Agency for International Development). 1972. *A Study of Food Habits in Calcutta.* Calcutta: Hindustan Thompson Associates.

U.S. Government, Census Bureau. 1997. *Money Income in the United States: 1996. Current Population Reports, P60-197.* Washington, D.C.: U.S. Government Printing Office.

U.S. Government, Census Bureau. 1998. "Section 14: Income, Expenditures, and Wealth." Pp. 446–84 in *Statistical Abstract of the United States: 1998.* http://www.census.gov/prod/3/98pubs/98statab/sasec14.pdf (accessed June 11, 2004).

Vertovec, Steven. 1995. "Hindus in Trinidad and Britain: Ethnic Religion, Reification, and the Politics of Public Space." Pp. 132–56 in *Nation and Migration: The Politics of Space in the South Asian Diaspora,* ed. Peter van der Veer. Philadelphia: University of Pennsylvania Press.

Walsh, Judith. 1995. "The Virtuous Wife and the Well-Ordered Home: The Re-conceptualization of Bengali Women and their Worlds." Pp. 331–63 in *Mind, Body and Society: Life and Mentality in Colonial Bengal,* ed. Rajat Kanta Ray. Calcutta: Oxford University Press.

———. 1997. "What Women Learned When Men Gave Them Advice: Rewriting Patriarchy in Late-Nineteenth-Century Bengal." *Journal of Asian Studies* 56, no. 3 (August): 641–77.

Warde, Alan, and Kevin Hetherington. 1994. "English Households and Routine Food Practices: A Research Note." *Sociological Review* 42, no. 4: 758–78.

Waters, Alice. 1999. "Food for Tomorrow's Table." Lecture, French Culinary Institute, New York, May 13.

Watson, James L., ed. 1997. *Golden Arches East: McDonald's in East Asia.* Stanford, Calif.: Stanford University Press.

Weber, Max. 1968. *Economy and Society,* 2 vols. Berkeley: University of California Press.

Williams, Phyllis. 1938. *South Italian Folkways in Europe and America.* New Haven, Conn.: Yale University Press.

Witt, Doris. 1999. *Black Hunger: Food and the Politics of U.S. Identity.* New York: Oxford University Press.

Yezierska, Anzia. 1925. *Bread Givers.* New York: Persea Books.

OTHER WORKS CONSULTED

Abu-Lughod, Janet. 1997. "Going Beyond Global Babble." Pp. 131–37 in *Culture, Globalization and the World-System,* ed. Anthony D. King. Minneapolis: University of Minnesota Press.

Adler, Patricia, and Peter Adler. 1987. *Membership Roles in Field Research.* Beverly Hills, Calif.: Sage.

Aguilar-San Juan, Karin, ed. 1996. *The State of Asian America: Activism and Resistance in the 1990s.* Boston: South End Press.

Alba, Richard D. 1990. *Ethnic Identity: The Transformation of White America.* New Haven, Conn.: Yale University Press.

Angell, Dorothy, and Enayetur Rahim. 1998. "Bangladeshis in the United States: Community Dynamics and Cultural Community." Pp. 39–79 in *Contributions to Bengal Studies:*

An Interdisciplinary and International Approach, ed. Enayetur Rahim and Henry Schwarz. Dhaka: Pustaka.

Antrim, Donald. 2000. *The Verificationist.* New York: Alfred A. Knopf.

Appadurai, Arjun. 1988. "How to Make a National Cuisine." *Society for the Comparative Study of Society and History* 30, no. 1 (January): 3–24.

Archdeacon, Thomas J. 1983. *Becoming Americans: An Ethnic History.* New York: Free Press.

Archer, W. G. 1953. *Bazar Paintings of Calcutta.* London: Her Majesty's Stationery Office.

Arnott, Margarett L., ed. 1976. *Gastronomy: The Anthropology of Food and Food Habits.* The Hague: Mouton.

Asian Women United of California, ed. 1989. *Making Waves: An Anthology of Writings by and about Asian American Women.* Boston: Beacon Press.

Bakhtin, M. M. 1984. *The Dialogic Imagination: Four Essays.* Minneapolis: University of Minnesota Press.

Banerjee, Sumanta. 1989. *The Parlour and the Streets: Elite and Popular Culture in Nineteenth-Century Calcutta.* Calcutta: Seagull Books.

Banerjee, Swapna. 1996. "Exploring the World of Domestic Manuals: Bengali Middle-Class Women and Servants in Colonial Calcutta." *Sagar: South Asian Graduate Research Journal* 3, no. 1, http://link.lanic.utexas.edu/asnic/pages/sagar/SAGAR3.r.html (accessed June 11, 2004).

Banerji, Chitrita. 2002. "Dining on Faith." *Gourmet,* February, 72–76, 126.

Barkan, Elliot. R. 1995. "Race, Religion, and Nationality in American Society: A Model of Ethnicity—From Contact to Assimilation." *Journal of American Ethnic History* 14, no. 2 (winter): 38–75.

Barth, Frederick. 1969. *Ethnic Groups and Boundaries.* Boston: Little, Brown.

Barthes, Roland. 1979. "Towards a Psychosociology of Contemporary Food Consumption." Pp. 166–73 in *Food and Drink in History: Selections from the Annales, Volume 5: Economies, Societies, Civilisations,* ed. Robert Forster and Orest Ranum. Baltimore: Johns Hopkins University Press.

Basu, A. K. 1970. "Agriculture of West Bengal." Pp. 85–95 in *West Bengal: A Publication of the Geographical Institute, Presidency College, Calcutta,* ed. A. B. Chatterjee, Avijit Dasgupta, and Pradip K. Mukhopadhyay. Calcutta: Firma K. L. Mukhopadhyay.

Basu, Monindra Mohan, ed. 1934. *Chandidas Padavali.* Calcutta: Calcutta University Press.

Baudelaire, Charles-Pierre. 1997. *Baudelaire in English,* ed. Carol Clark and Robert Sykes. Harmondsworth: Penguin Books.

Baxandall, Rosalyn, and Elizabeth Ewen. 2000. *Picture Windows: How the Suburbs Happened.* New York: Basic Books.

Beardsworth, Alan, and Teresa Keil. 1997. *Sociology on the Menu: An Invitation to the Study of Food and Society.* New York: Routledge.

Bell, Daniel. 1975. "Ethnicity and Social Change." Pp. 141–74 in *Ethnicity: Theory and Experience,* ed. Nathan Glazer and Daniel Patrick Moynihan. Cambridge, Mass.: Harvard University Press.

Benet, S. M., and Natalie F. Joffe. 1943. *Some Central European Food Patterns and Their Relationship to Wartime Problems of Food and Nutrition.* Washington, D.C.: National Research Council on Food Habits.

Bentley, Amy. 1998. *Eating for Victory: Food Rationing and the Politics of Domesticity.* Chicago: University of Chicago Press.

Berk, R. A., and S. F. Berk. 1979. *Labor and Leisure at Home.* Beverly Hills, Calif.: Sage.

Bhabha, Homi. 1997. "Of Mimicry and Man: The Ambivalence of Colonial Discourse." Pp. 152–60 in *Tensions of Empire: Colonial Cultures in a Bourgeois World,* ed. Frederick Cooper and Ann Laura Stoler. Berkeley: University of California Press.

Bhardwaj, Sunder Mohan. 1973. *Hindu Places of Pilgrimage in India: A Study in Cultural Geography.* Berkeley: University of California Press.

Bird, G. W., G. A. Bird, and M. Scruggs. 1984. "Determinants of Family Task Sharing: A Study of Husbands and Wives." *Journal of Marriage and Family* 46: 345–55.

Blair, S. L., and D. T. Lichter. 1988. "Measuring the Division of Household Labor: Resources, Power, and Ideology." *Journal of Family Issues* 9: 177–200.

Bourdieu, Pierre. 1965. "The Sentiment of Honour in Kabyle Society." Pp. 191–241 in *Honour and Shame: The Values of Mediterranean Society,* ed. J. G. Peristiany. London: Weidenfeld and Nicholson.

———. 1990. *In Other Words: Essays toward a Reflexive Sociology,* trans. M. Adamson. Cambridge: Polity.

———. 1993. "Concluding Remarks: For a Sociogenetic Understanding of Intellectual Works." Pp. 263–75 in *Bourdieu: Critical Perspectives,* ed. Craig Calhoun, Edward LiPuma and Moishe Postone. Chicago: University of Chicago Press.

Braunstein, Susan L., and Jenna Weisman Joselit, eds. 1990. *Getting Comfortable in New York: The American Jewish Home, 1880–1950.* New York: Jewish Museum.

Breytenbach, Breyten. 1991. "The Long March from Hearth to Heart." *Social Research* 58, no. 1 (spring): 68–83.

Brown, Linda Keller, and Kay Mussell, eds. 1984. *Ethnic and Regional Foodways in the United States: The Performance of Group Identity.* Knoxville: University of Tennessee Press.

Bumiller, Elisabeth. 1999. "At 34, Worldly-Wise and on His Way Up." *New York Times,* September 24, Metro section, 2.

Burawoy, Michael, Joshua Gamson, and Alice Burton. 1991. *Ethnography Unbound: Power and Resistance in the Modern Metropolis.* Berkeley: University of California Press.

Burke, Peter. 1978. *Popular Culture in Early Modern Europe.* London: Temple Smith.

Cain, G. 1984. *Women and Work: Trends in Time Spent in Housework.* Discussion paper no. 747–84, Institute for Research on Poverty, University of Wisconsin, Madison.

Camp, Charles. 1979. "Food in American Culture: A Bibliographic Essay." *Journal of American Culture* 2: 559–70.

Carson, Gerald. 1957. *Cornflake Crusade.* New York: Rinehart.

Chai, Karen J. 1998. "Competing for the Second Generation: English-Language Ministry at a Korean Protestant Church." Pp. 295–332 in *Gatherings in Diaspora: Religious Communities and the New Immigration,* ed. R. Stephen Warner and Judith G. Wittner. Philadelphia: Temple University Press.

Chang, K. C., ed. 1977. *Food in Chinese Culture.* New Haven, Conn.: Yale University Press.

Charles, Nickie. 1995. "Food and Family Ideology." Pp. 100–115 in *The Politics of Domestic Consumption: Critical Readings,* ed. Stevi Jackson and Shaun Moores. London: Prentice-Hall/Harvester Wheatsheaf.

Chatterjee, A. B., Avijit Dasgupta, and Pradip K. Mukhopadhyay, eds. 1970. *West Bengal: A Publication of the Geographical Institute, Presidency College, Calcutta.* Calcutta: Firma K. L. Mukhopadhyay.

Chatterjee, Lata. 1970. "The Climate of West Bengal: A Genetic Approach." Pp. 38–49 in *West Bengal: A Publication of the Geographical Institute, Presidency College, Calcutta,* ed. A. B. Chatterjee, Avijit Dasgupta, and Pradip K. Mukhopadhyay. Calcutta: Firma K. L. Mukhopadhyay.

Chatterjee, Partha. 1992. "A Religion of Urban Domesticity: Sri Ramakrishna and the Calcutta Middle Class." Pp. 40–68 in *Subaltern Studies VII: Writings on South Asian History and Society,* ed. Partha Chatterjee and Gyanendra Pandey. Delhi: Oxford University Press.

Chattopadhyay, Saratchandra. 1986. *Sarat Sahitya Samagra* (Selected Works), ed. Sukumar Sen. Calcutta: Ananda Publishers.

Chaudhuri, Amit. 1998. *Freedom Song.* New York: Vintage.

Chodorow, Nancy. 1978. *The Reproduction of Mothering.* Berkeley: University of California Press.

Cohen, Abner. 1974. *Urban Ethnicity.* London: Tavistock.

———. 1980. "Drama and Politics in the Development of a London Carnival." *Man* 15: 65–87.

———. 1981. *The Politics of Elite Culture.* Berkeley: University of California Press.

Collins, Randall. 1994. *Four Sociological Traditions.* Oxford: Oxford University Press.

Coltrane, Scott. 1989. "Household Labor and the Routine Production of Gender." *Social Problems* 36: 473–90.

Cooley, Charles Horton. 1930. *Sociological Theory and Social Research.* New York: Holt, Rinehart and Winston.

———. 1962. *Social Organization.* New York: Schocken Books.

———. 1964. *Human Nature and the Social Order.* New York: Schocken Books.

Corwin, Lauren Anita. 1989. "Female Roles: Change over Time in Middle-Class Calcutta." Pp. 181–189 in *Shaping Bengali Worlds: Public and Private,* ed. Tony K. Stewart. East Lansing: Michigan State University.

Coser, Lewis. 1965. *Georg Simmel.* Englewood Cliffs, N.J.: Free Press.

———. 1977. *Masters of Sociological Thought.* New York: Harcourt Brace Jovanovich.

Counihan, Carole, and Penny Van Esterik, eds. 1997. *Food and Culture: A Reader.* New York: Routledge.

Coverman, S. 1983. "Gender, Domestic Labor Time, and Wage Inequality." *American Sociological Review* 48: 623–37.

Cowan, Ruth Schwartz. 1983. *More Work for Mother: The Ironies of Household Technology from the Open Hearth to the Microwave.* New York: Basic Books.

Cummings, Richard Osborn. 1940. *The American and His Food.* Chicago: University of Chicago Press.

Cussler, Margaret, and Mary L. de Give. 1952. *Twixt the Cup and the Lip: Psychological and Sociocultural Factors Affecting Food Habits.* New York: Twayne.

Daniels, Roger. 1990. *Coming to America: A History of Immigration and Ethnicity in American Life.* New York: HarperCollins.

Das, Arvind N. 2000. "Nonresident Nationalism in the Age of Globalized Ethnicity," *India Abroad,* January 28, 2.

Dasgupta, Shamita Das. 1998. "Gender Roles and Cultural Community in the Asian Indian Immigrant Community in the U.S." *Sex Roles* 38, nos. 11–12 (June): 953–75.

Davidson, Alan, ed. 1981. *Proceedings of the Oxford Symposium on National and Regional Styles of Cookery.* London: Prospect Books.

Davis, Fred. 1994. *Fashion, Culture, Identity.* Chicago: University of Chicago Press.

De Certeau, Michel. 1984. *The Practice of Everyday Life.* Berkeley: University of California Press.

De Certeau, Michel, Luce Giard, and Pierre Mayol. 1998. *The Practice of Everyday Life,* vol. 2. Minneapolis: University of Minnesota Press.

De Give, Mary L., and Margaret T. Cussler. 1944. *Bibliography and Notes on German Food Patterns.* Washington, D.C.: National Research Council Committee on Food Habits.

Del Giudice, Luisa, and Gerald Porter. 2001. *Imagined States: Nationalism, Utopia and Longing in Oral Cultures.* Logan: Utah State University Press.

Desai, Anita. *Diamond Dust.* Boston: Houghton Mifflin.

Douglas, Mary. 1978. "Culture." Pp. 55–81 in *Annual Report 1977–78 of the Russell Sage Foundation.* New York: Russell Sage Foundation.

————. 1991. "The Idea of a Home: A Kind of Space." *Social Research* 58, no. 1 (spring): 287–307.

Douglas, Mary, ed. 1984. *Food in the Social Order: Studies of Food and Festivities in Three American Communities.* New York: Russell Sage Foundation.

Douglas, Mary, and Michael Nicod. 1974. "Taking the Biscuit: The Structure of British Meals." *New Society* 30, no. 637: 744–47.

Dubois, Abbe J. A. 1906. *Hindu Manners, Customs, and Ceremonies.* Oxford: Clarendon Press.

Dumont, Louis. 1980. *Homo Hierarchicus: The Caste System and Its Implications.* Chicago: University of Chicago Press. (Orig. pub. 1966.)

Durkheim, Emile. 1950. *The Rules of Sociological Method.* New York: Free Press.

————. 1951. *Suicide.* New York: Free Press.

————. 1964. *The Division of Labor in Society.* New York: The Free Press.

Economic and Political Weekly Research Foundation. 1994. "Social Indicators of Development for India." *Economic and Political Weekly,* May 14, 1227–40.

Elias, Norbert. 1978. *The History of Manners: The Civilizing Process, Volume 1,* trans. Edmund Jephcott. New York: Pantheon Books. (Orig. pub. 1939.)

————. 1970. *What Is Sociology?* London: Hutchinson.

Erikson, Erik H., ed. 1950. *Childhood and Society.* New York: Norton.

Farley, John. 1783. *The London Art of Cookery.* London: J. Fielding, J. Scatcherd, J. Whitaker.

Farquhar, Judith. 2002. *Appetites: Food and Sex in Post-Socialist China.* Durham, N.C.: Duke University Press.

Featherstone, Mike. 1996. "Localism, Globalism and Cultural Identity." Pp. 46–77 in *Global/Local: Cultural Production and the Transnational Imaginary,* ed. Rob Wilson and Wimal Dissanayake. Durham, N.C.: Duke University Press.

Fenton, John. 1988. *Transplanting Religious Traditions: Asian Indians in America.* New York: Praeger.

Fischler, Claude. 1980. "Food Habits, Social Change and the Nature/Culture Dilemma." *Social Science Information* 19, no. 6: 937–53.

Fishman, Joshua, ed. 1966. *Language Loyalty in the United States.* The Hague: Mouton.

Fliegel, Frederick. 1961. *Food Habits and National Background.* Agricultural Experimental Station Bulletin no. 684, Pennsylvania State University, University Park, October.

Foner, Nancy, ed. 1987. *New Immigrants in New York.* New York: Columbia University Press.

Forster, Robert, and Orest Ranum, eds. 1979. *Food and Drink in History: Selections from the Annales, Volume 5: Economies, Societies, Civilisations.* Baltimore: Johns Hopkins University Press.

Freeman, Michael. 1977. "Sung." Pp. 141–76 in *Food in Chinese Culture,* ed. K. C. Chang. New Haven, Conn.: Yale University Press.

Frese, Pamela R. 1992. "Artifacts of Gendered Space: American Yard Decoration." *Visual Anthropology* 5: 17–42.

Fürst, E. L., R. Prättälä, M. Ekström, L. Holm, and U. Kjaernes. 1991. *Palatable Worlds: Sociocultural Food Studies.* Oslo: Solum Forlag.

Gamarnikow, Eva, E. Morgan, J. Purvis, and D. Taylorson, eds. 1983. *The Public and the Private.* London: Heinemann.

Ganguly, Keya. 2001. *States of Exception: Everyday Life and Postcolonial Identity*. Minneapolis: University of Minnesota Press.

Gans, Herbert. 1956. "American Jewery: Present and Future." *Commentary* 21, no. 5 (May): 422–30.

———. 1962. *The Urban Villagers: Group and Class in the Life of Italian-Americans*. New York: Free Press of Glencoe.

———. 1967. *The Levittowners: Ways of Life and Politics in a Suburban Community*. New York: Pantheon.

———. 1992. "Comment: Ethnic Invention and Acculturation, a Bumpy-Line Approach." *Journal of American Ethnic History* 12, no. 1 (fall): 42.

Geerken, M., and W. R. Gove. 1983. *At Home and at Work: The Family's Allocation of Labor*. Beverly Hills, Calif.: Sage.

George, Sheba. 1998. "Caroling with the Keralites: The Negotiation of Gendered Space in an Indian Immigrant Church." Pp. 265–94 in *Gatherings in Diaspora: Religious Communities and the New Immigration*, ed. R. Stephen Warner and Judith G. Wittner. Philadelphia: Temple University Press.

Germann, Jennie. 1997. "Fast Food: Singapore's Addition to Tradition." *Digest* 17: 31–37.

Giddens, Anthony. 1971. *Capitalism and Modern Social Theory*. Cambridge: Cambridge University Press.

———. 1976. *New Rules of Sociological Method: A Positive Critique of Interpretive Sociologies*. New York: Basic Books.

Gillespie, Angus K. 1979. "Towards a Method for the Study of Food in American Culture." *Journal of American Culture* 2: 393–406.

Gizelis, Gregory. 1970–71. "Foodways Acculturation in the Greek Community of Philadelphia." *Pennsylvania Folklife* (winter): 9–15.

Gizzardini, G., and Natalie F. Joffe. 1942. *Italian Food Patterns and Their Relationship to Wartime Problems of Food and Nutrition*. Washington, D.C.: National Research Council Committee on Food Habits.

Glants, Musya, and Joyce Toomre, eds. 1997. *Food in Russian History and Culture*. Bloomington: Indiana University Press.

Glazer, Nathan. 1983. "Universalisation of Ethnicity." Pp. 233–53 in *Ethnic Dilemmas, 1964–1982*. Cambridge, Mass.: Harvard University Press. (Orig. pub. 1976.)

Glazer, Nathan, and Daniel Patrick Moynihan. 1963. *Beyond the Melting Pot: The Negroes, Puerto Ricans, Jews, Italians and Irish of New York City*. Cambridge, Mass.: MIT Press.

Glazer, Nathan, and Daniel Patrick Moynihan, eds. 1975. *Ethnicity: Theory and Experience*. Cambridge, Mass.: Harvard University Press.

Gleason, Philip. 1980. "American Identity and Americanization." Pp. 31–58 in *Harvard Encyclopedia of American Ethnic Groups*, ed. Stephen Thernstrom. Cambridge, Mass.: Harvard University Press.

———. 1983. "Identifying Identity: A Semantic History." *Journal of American History* 69, no. 4 (March): 910–31.

———. 1992. *Speaking of Diversity: Language and Ethnicity in Twentieth-Century America*. Baltimore: Johns Hopkins University Press.

Gode, P. K. 1969. *Studies in Indian Cultural History*. Poona: Bhadarkar Oriental Research Institute.

Goffman, Erving. 1967. *Interaction Ritual: Essays in Face-to-Face Behavior*. Chicago: Aldine.

Goody, Jack. 1982. *Cooking, Cuisine and Class*. Cambridge: Cambridge University Press.

Gordon, Milton. 1964. *Assimilation in American Life.* New York: Oxford University Press.

Gottlieb, David, and Peter H. Rossi. 1961. *A Bibliography and Bibliographic Review of Food and Food Habits Research.* Washington, D.C.: Quartermaster Food and Container Institute for the Armed Forces.

Gupta, Akhil, and James Ferguson, eds. 1997. *Culture, Power, Place: Explorations in Critical Anthropology.* Durham, N.C.: Duke University Press.

Gvion-Rosenberg, Liora. 1991. "Telling the Story of Ethnicity: American Cookbooks, 1850–1990." Ph.D. diss., State University of New York at Stony Brook. UMI Dissertation Service no. 9219312.

Hall, Dennis. 1996. "A Garden of One's Own: The Ritual Consolations of the Backyard Garden." *American Studies* 19, no. 3 (fall): 9–13.

Handlin, Oscar. 1941. *Boston's Immigrants, 1790–1865: A Study in Acculturation.* Cambridge, Mass.: Harvard University Press.

Hansen, Marcus Lee. 1987. *The Problem of the Third Generation Immigrant.* Rock Island, Ill.: Swenson Swedish Immigration Research Center, Augustana College Library. (Orig. pub. 1937.)

Herberg, Will. 1955. *Protestant–Catholic–Jew: An Essay in American Religious Sociology.* Garden City, N.Y.: Doubleday.

Higham, John. 1975. *Send These to Me: Jews and Other Immigrants in Urban America.* New York: Atheneum.

Hobsbawm, Eric, and Terence Ranger, eds. 1983. *The Invention of Tradition.* Cambridge: Cambridge University Press.

Hochschild, Arlie Russell. 1997. *The Time Bind: When Work Becomes Home and Home Becomes Work.* New York: Henry Holt.

Howe, Irving. 1976. *World of Our Fathers.* New York: Harcourt Brace Jovanovich.

Humphrey, Theodore C., and Lin T. Humphrey, eds. 1991. *"We Gather Together": Food and Festival in American Life.* Logan: Utah State University.

Hutchinson, John, and Anthony D. Smith, eds. 1996. *Ethnicity.* New York: Oxford University Press.

Ishi-Kuntz, Masako, and Scott Coltrane. 1992. "Predicting the Sharing of Household Labor: Are Parenting and Housework Distinct?" *Sociological Perspectives* 35, no. 4: 629–47.

Jackson, Stevi, and Shaun Moores, eds. 1995. *The Politics of Domestic Consumption: Critical Readings.* London: Prentice-Hall/Harvester Wheatsheaf.

Jing, Jun, ed. 2000. *Feeding China's Little Emperors: Food, Children, and Social Change.* Stanford, Calif.: Stanford University Press.

Joffe, Natalie F., and T. T. Walker. 1944. *Some Food Patterns of Negroes in the United States of America and Their Relationship to Wartime Problems of Food and Nutrition.* Washington, D.C.: National Research Council Committee on Food Habits.

Jones, Michael Owen, Bruce Giuliano, and Roberta Krell, eds. 1983. *Foodways and Eating Habits: Directions for Food Research.* Los Angeles: California Folklore Society.

Kacapyr, Elia. 1996. "Are You Middle Class?" *American Demographics,* October, 30–35.

Kapadia, Ashish. 2000. "Pressures of Being Young Indian-American." *India Abroad,* January 28, 4.

Katone-Apte, Judit. 1976. "Dietary Aspects of Acculturation: Meals, Feasts and Fasts in a Minority Community in South Asia." Pp. 315–326 in *Gastronomy: The Anthropology of Food and Food Habits,* ed. Margaret L. Arnott. The Hague: Mouton.

Kaviraj, Sudipta. 1989. "Bankimchandra and the Making of Nationalist Consciousness." Centre for Studies in Social Sciences Occasional Papers 108–10, Calcutta.

Kazal, Russell A. 1995. "Revisiting Assimilation: The Rise, Fall, and Reappraisal of a Concept in American Ethnic History." *American Historical Review* 100, no. 2 (April): 437–71.

Kennedy, Melville T. 1993. *The Chaitanya Movement: A Study of Vaishnavism in Bengal.* New Delhi: Munshirain Manoharlal Publishers. (Orig. pub. 1925.)

Khandelwal, Madhulika S. 2002. *Becoming American, Being Indian: An Immigrant Community in New York City.* Ithaca, N.Y.: Cornell University Press.

Khare, Ravindra S., and M. S. A. Rao, eds. 1986. *Food, Society, and Culture Aspects in South Asian Food Systems.* Durham, N.C.: Carolina Academic Press.

Kirschenblatt-Gimblett, Barbara. 1990. "Kitchen Judaism." Pp. 75–105 in *Getting Comfortable in New York: The American Jewish Home, 1880–1950,* ed. Susan L. Braunstein and Jenna Weisman Joselit. New York: Jewish Museum.

Kolpan, Steven, Brian H. Smith, and Michael A. Weiss. 1996. *Exploring Wine: The Culinary Institute of America's Complete Guide to Wines of the World.* New York: Van Nostrand Reinhold.

Kulke, Herinann, and Dietmar Rothermund. 1996. *A History of India.* London: Routledge.

Kuper, J., ed. 1977. *The Anthropologists' Cookbook.* London: Routledge and Kegan Paul.

Kurien, Prema. 1998. "Becoming American by Becoming Hindu: Indian Americans Take Their Place at the Multicultural Table." Pp. 37–70 in *Gatherings in Diaspora: Religious Communities and the New Immigration,* ed. R. Stephen Warner and Judith G. Wittner. Philadelphia: Temple University Press.

Lazarsfeld, P. F. 1934. "The Psychological Aspect of Market Research." *Harvard Business Review* 13: 54–71.

Lee, Dorothy. 1957. "Cultural Factors in Dietary Choice." *American Journal of Clinical Nutrition* 5: 166–70.

Leonard, Karen Isaksen. 1992. *Making Ethnic Choices: California's Punjabi Mexican Americans.* Philadelphia: Temple University Press.

Lessinger, Johanna. 1995. *From the Ganges to the Hudson: Indian Immigrants in New York City.* Boston: Allyn and Bacon.

Lévi-Strauss, Claude. 1965. "The Culinary Triangle." *Partisan Review* 33: 586–95.

———. 1967. *Structural Anthropology.* Garden City, N.Y.: Doubleday.

———. 1969. *The Raw and the Cooked.* London: Jonathan Cape.

———. 1979. *Myth and Meaning.* New York: Schocken Books.

———. 1991. *Conversations with Claude Lévi-Strauss.* Chicago: University of Chicago Press.

Lipovetsky, Gilles. 1994. *The Empire of Fashion: Dressing Modern Democracy,* trans. Catherine Porter. Princeton, N.J.: Princeton University Press.

Lynd, Robert S., and Helen Merrell Lynd. 1929. *Middletown: A Study in Modern American Culture.* New York: Harcourt, Brace and World.

Maira, Sunaina, and Rajini Srikanth, eds. 1996. *Contours of the Heart: South Asians Map North America.* New York: Asian American Writers' Workshop.

Maret, E., and B. Finley. 1984. "The Distribution of Household Labor among Women in Dual-Earner families." *Journal of Marriage and Family* 46: 357–64.

Marini, Margaret Mooney. 1993. "Measuring Household Work: Recent Experience in the United States." *Social Science Research* 22, no. 4 (December): 361–82.

Mars, Leonard. 1997. "Food and Disharmony: Commensality among Jews." *Food and Foodways* 7, no. 3: 189–202.

Marzio, Peter. 1976. *A Nation of Nations: The People Who Came to America as Seen through Objects and Documents Exhibited at the Smithsonian Institution.* New York: Harper and Row.

McIntosh, William Alex. 1996. *Sociologies of Food and Nutrition*. New York: Plenum Press.

McMohan, Anthony. 1999. *Taking Care of Men: Sexual Politics in the Public Mind*. Cambridge: Cambridge University Press.

Mead, Margaret. 1950. "Cultural Contexts of Nutritional Patterns." Pp. 103–11 in *Centennial: Collected Papers Presented at the Centennial Celebration*. Washington, D.C.: American Association for the Advancement of Science.

———. 1964a. *Food Habits Research: Problems of the 1960s*. Publication no. 1225, National Research Council, National Academy of Sciences, Washington, D.C.

———. 1964b. *Manual for the Study of Food Habits*. Bulletin no. 111, National Research Council, Washington, D.C.

———. 1964c. *The Problem of Changing Food Habits*. Bulletin no. 108, National Research Council, Washington, D.C.

———. 1970. "The Changing Significance of Food." *American Science* 58: 176–81.

Mennell, Stephen. 1985. *All Manners of Food: Eating and Taste in England and France from the Middle Ages to the Present*. Oxford: Basil Blackwell.

Mennell, Stephen, Anne Murcott, and Anneke H. van Otterloo. 1992. *The Sociology of Food: Eating, Diet, and Culture*. Newbury Park, Calif.: Sage.

Michell, George. 1988. *The Hindu Temple: An Introduction to Its Meaning and Forms*. Chicago: University of Chicago Press.

Miller, Daniel. 1987. *Material Culture and Mass Consumption*. Oxford: Basil Blackwell.

Mintz, Sidney. 1985. *Sweetness and Power: The Place of Sugar in Modern History*. Harmondsworth: Viking Penguin.

Mintz, Sidney, and Daniela Schlettwein-Gsell. 2001. "Food Patterns in Agrarian Societies: The Core-Fringe-Legume Hypothesis." *Gastronomica* 1, no. 3 (summer): 40–52.

Model, S. 1981. "Housework by Husbands: Determinants and Implications." *Journal of Family Issues* 2: 225–37.

Mogelonsky, Marcia. 1995. "Asian-Indian Americans." *American Demographics*, August, 32–39.

Moore, Harriet Bruce. 1957. "The Meaning of Food." *American Journal of Clinical Nutrition* 5: 77–82.

Morawska, Ewa. 1994. "In Defense of the Assimilation Model." *Journal of American Ethnic History* 13 (winter): 76–87.

Mukhopadhyay, Bhudev. 1905. *Bibidha prabandha, volume 2: Hindu samaje khawa dawa* (Hindu food habits and ritual restrictions). Calcutta.

Murcott, Anne, ed. 1983. "'It Is a Pleasure to Cook for Him': Food, Mealtimes and Gender in Some South Wales Households." Pp. 110–19 in *The Public and the Private*, ed. Eva Gamarnikow, David H. J. Morgan, June Purvis, and Daphne Taylorson. London: Heinemann.

———. 1983. *The Sociology of Food and Eating*. Aldershot: Gower.

Murcott, Anne, and Anneke H. van Otterloo. 1992. *The Sociology of Food: Eating, Diet and Culture*. London: Sage.

Murshid, Ghulam. 1983. *Reluctant Debutante: Response of Bengali Women to Modernization*. Rajshahi, Bangladesh: Sahitya Samsad, Rajshahi University Press.

Myerhoff, Barbara. 1978. *Number Our Days*. New York: Simon and Schuster.

Naipaul, V. S. 1982. *Among the Believers: An Islamic Journey*. New York: Random House.

———. 1992. *India: A Million Mutinies Now*. Harmondsworth: Penguin.

———. 1992. *The Mimic Men*. Harmondsworth: Penguin.

———. 1999. *Beyond Belief: Islamic Excursions among the Converted Peoples*. New York: Vintage.

Narayan, Uma. 1995. "Eating Cultures: Incorporation, Identity and Indian Food." *Social Identities* 1, no. 1: 63–86.

Nasrin, Taslima. 1995. *The Game in Reverse: Poems.* New York: George Braziller.

Nedelmann, Brigitta. 1991. "Individualization, Exaggeration and Paralysation: Simmel's Three Problems of Culture." *Theory, Culture and Society* 8, no. 3 (August [special issue devoted to Georg Simmel]): 169–93.

Novak, Michael. 1971. *The Rise of the Unmeltable Ethnics.* New York: Macmillan.

NRA (National Restaurant Association). 1995. *Ethnic Cuisines: A Profile.* Washington, D.C.: National Restaurant Association.

Ohnuki-Tierney, Emiko. 1993. *Rice as Self: Japanese Identities through Time.* Princeton, N.J.: Princeton University Press.

Ory, Pascal. 1997. "Gastronomy." Pp. 442–67 in *Realms of Memory: The Construction of the French Past,* ed. Pierre Nora. New York: Columbia University Press.

Ortner, Sherry B. 1984. "Theory in Anthropology since the Sixties." *Comparative Studies in Society and History* 26, no. 1: 126–66.

Pandey, B. N. 1982. *A Book of India.* New Delhi: Rupa.

Park, Robert E. 1950. *Race and Culture.* New York: Free Press.

———. 1952. *Human Communities.* New York: Free Press.

Park, Robert E., and Ernest W. Burgess. 1921. *Introduction to the Science of Sociology.* Chicago: University of Chicago Press.

Paul, Asit, ed. 1983. *Woodcut Prints of Nineteenth-Century Calcutta.* Calcutta: Seagull Books.

Pearson, Anne Mackenzie. 1996. *"Because It Gives Me Peace of Mind": Ritual Fasts in the Religious Lives of Hindu Women.* Albany: State University of New York Press.

Perrot, Philippe. 1994. *Fashioning the Bourgeoisie: A History of Clothing in the Nineteenth Century,* trans. Richard Bienvenu. Princeton, N.J.: Princeton University Press.

Pillsbury, Richard. 1998. *No Foreign Food: The American Diet in Time and Place.* Boulder, Colo.: Westview Press.

Pirkova-Jakobson, Svatava, and Natalie F. Joffe. 1943. *Some Central European Food Patterns and Their Relationship to Wartime Problems of Food and Nutrition.* Washington, D.C.: National Research Council Committee on Food Habits.

Popper, Karl. 1959. *The Logic of Scientific Discovery.* London: Hutchinson.

———. 1963. *Conjectures and Refutations.* London: Routledge and Kegan Paul.

Pozzetta, George E., ed. 1991. *Ethnicity, Ethnic Identity, and Language Maintenance.* New York: Garland.

Prashad, Vijay. 2000. *The Karma of Brown Folk.* Minneapolis: University of Minnesota Press.

Raheja, Gloria Goodwin. 1988. *The Poison in the Gift: Ritual, Prestation, and the Dominant Caste in a North Indian Village.* Chicago: University of Chicago Press.

Ray, Nihar Ranjan. 1995. *Bangalir Itihash* (A History of Bengal). Calcutta: Dey Publishing.

Rayaprol, Aparna. 1997. *Negotiating Identities: Women in the Indian Diaspora.* Delhi: Oxford University Press.

Robinson, J. P. 1985. "The Validity and Reliability of Diaries versus Alternative Time Use Measures." Pp. 33–61 in *Time, Goods, Well-Being,* ed. F. T. Juster and F. P. Stafford. Ann Arbor: Survey Research Center, Institute for Social Research, University of Michigan.

———. 1988. "Who's Doing the Housework?" *American Demographics,* December, 24–28, 63.

Root, Waverly, and Richard de Rochemont. 1976. *Eating in America.* Hopewell, N.J.: Ecco Press.

Roth, Philip. 2000. *The Human Stain.* Boston: Houghton Mifflin.

Roy, Arundhati. 1997. *The God of Small Things.* New York: HarperCollins.

Roy, Parama. 1998. *Indian Traffic: Identities in Question in Colonial and Postcolonial India.* Berkeley: University of California Press. Also available online at http://ark.cdlib.org/ark:/13030/ft8s20097j/ (accessed June 11, 2004).

Rushdie, Salman. 1988. *The Satanic Verses.* New York: Viking.

Rxroat, C., and C. Shehan. 1987. "The Family Life Cycle and Spouses' Time in Housework." *Journal of Marriage and Family* 49: 737–50.

Said, Edward. 1978. *Orientalism.* London: Routledge.

———. 1998. "Review of *Beyond Belief*." *The Progressive* 62, no. 11 (November): 40–43.

Saran, Parmatma, and Edwin Eames. 1980. *The New Ethnics: Asian Indians in the United States.* Boulder, Colo.: Praeger.

Sarkar, Tanika. 1992. "The Hindu Wife and the Hindu Nation." *Studies in History* 8, no. 2: 213–34.

———. 2001. *Hindu Wife, Hindu Nation: Community, Religion, and Cultural Nationalism.* Bloomington: Indiana University Press.

Schrag, Peter. 1971. *The Decline of the WASP.* New York: Simon and Schuster.

Shiva, Vandana. 2000. *Stolen Harvest: The Hijacking of the Global Food Supply.* Cambridge, Mass.: South End Press.

———. 2002. "The World Is Not an Oil Well. It Is a Planet." *India Abroad,* February, 32.

Shortridge, Barbara, and James R. Shortridge, eds. 1998. *The Taste of American Place.* New York: Rowan and Little.

Sinha, A. K. 1994. "Sweetmeats of Bihar and West Bengal in India: A Study of Diffusion." *Man in India* 74: 383–402.

Smith, W. Robertson. 1889. *Lectures on the Religion of the Semites.* New York: D. Appleton.

Sollors, Werner, ed. 1989. *The Invention of Ethnicity.* New York: Oxford University Press.

———. 1996. *Theories of Ethnicity: A Classical Reader.* New York: New York University Press.

Sombart, Werner. 1969. *Luxury and Capitalism.* Ann Arbor: University of Michigan Press. (Orig. pub. 1913.)

South Asian Descent Collective, ed. 1993. *Our Feet Walk the Sky: Women of the South Asian Diaspora.* San Francisco: Aunt Lute Books.

Spate, O. H. K., and A. T. A. Learmonth. 1967. *India and Pakistan: A General and Regional Geography.* London: Methuen.

Stayman, Douglas M., and Rohit Deshpande. 1989. "Situational Ethnicity and Consumer Behavior." *Journal of Consumer Research* 16, no. 3 (December): 361–73.

Steinberg, Stephen. 1989. *The Ethnic Myth: Race, Ethnicity and Class in America.* Boston: Beacon Press. (Orig. pub. 1981.)

Stern, Stephen, and John Allan Cicala, eds. 1991. *Creative Ethnicity: Symbols and Strategies of Contemporary Ethnic Life.* Logan: Utah State University Press.

Stewart, Tony K., ed. 1989. *Shaping Bengali Worlds: Public and Private.* East Lansing: Michigan State University Press.

Suri, Manil. 2002. *The Death of Vishnu: A Novel.* New York: Perennial.

Sutton-Smith, Brian. 1970. "The Psychology of Childlore: The Triviality Barrier." *Western Folklore* 29: 1–8.

Swamidass, Paul M. 2000. "Need for NRIs [Non-Resident Indians] to Help Combat Sectarian Violence." *India Abroad,* January 28, 2.

Szalai, A., ed. 1972. *The Use of Time.* The Hague: Mouton.

Tagore, Rabindranath. 1991. *Selected Short Stories,* trans. William Radice. Harmondsworth: Penguin.

Tagore, Rabindranath, and Abanindranath Tagore, eds. and comps. 1995. *Chelebhulano Charra* (Nursery rhymes). Calcutta: Ananda.

Takaki, Ronald, ed. 1987. *From Different Shores: Perspectives on Race and Ethnicity in America.* Oxford: Oxford University Press.

Taylor, Charles. 1993. "To Follow a Rule . . ." Pp. 44–60 in *Bourdieu: Critical Perspectives,* ed. Craig Calhoun, Edward LiPuma, and Moishe Postone. Chicago: University of Chicago Press.

Thernstrom, Stephen. 1980. *Harvard Encyclopedia of American Ethnic Groups.* Cambridge, Mass.: Harvard University Press.

Thorne, Barrie, and Marilyn Yalom, eds. 1992. *Rethinking the Family.* Boston: Northeastern University Press.

Todorov, Tzvetan. 1984. *Mikhail Bakhtin: The Dialogical Principle.* Minneapolis: University of Minnesota Press.

Tull, Marc. 1978. "Kosher Brownies for Passover." *New York Folklore* 4, nos. 1–4: 81–88.

Turner, Victor W., ed. 1982. *Celebration: Studies in Festivity and Ritual.* Washington, D.C.: Smithsonian Institution Press.

Tweed, Thomas A., and Stephen Prothero, eds. 1999. *Asian Religions in America: A Documentary History.* New York: Oxford University Press.

U.S. Government, Bureau of Labor Statistics. 1997. *Consumer Expenditure Survey.* Washington, D.C.: U.S. Government Printing Office.

———. 1974. "Time Spent on Housework." *Scientific American,* vol. 231, 116–20.

Varley, H. Paul, and George Elison. 1981. "The Culture of Tea: From Its Origins to Sen no Rikyu." Pp. 187–222 in *Warlords, Artists and Commoners: Japan in the Sixteenth Century,* ed. George Elison and Bardwell L. Smith. Honolulu: University of Hawaii Press.

Vaultier, Roger. 1940. "La gastronomie régionale en France pendant la Revolution." *Grandgousier* 7, no. 4: 79–87.

Veblen, Thorstein. 1899. *The Theory of the Leisure Class.* London: Macmillan.

Vecoli, Rudolph J. 1964. "*Contadini* in Chicago: A Critique of *The Uprooted.*" *Journal of American History* 1, no. 3 (December): 404–17.

Vertovec, Steven. 1989. "Hinduism in Diaspora: The Transformation of Tradition in Trinidad." Pp. 157–86 in *Hinduism Reconsidered,* ed. Gunther Sontheimer and Hermann Kulke. New Delhi: Manohar.

———. 1992. *Hindu Trinidad: Religion, Ethnicity, and SocioEconomic Change.* London: Macmillan.

Vice, Sue. 1998. *Introducing Bakhtin.* Manchester: Manchester University Press.

Walker, K. E., and M. E. Woods. 1976. *Time Use: A Measure of Household Production of Family Goods and Services.* Washington, D.C.: Center for the Family, American Home Economics Association.

Wallerstein, Immanuel M. 1974. *The Modern World-System I: Capitalist Agriculture and the Origins of European World-Economy in the Sixteenth Century.* New York: Academic Press.

———. 1991a. "Culture as the Ideological Battleground of the Modern World-System." Pp. 31–56 in *Global Culture: Nationalism, Globalization and Modernity,* ed. Mike Featherstone. London: Sage.

———. 1991b. *Geopolitics and Geoculture: Essays on the Changing World-System.* Cambridge: Cambridge University Press.

———. 1997. "The National and the Universal: Can There Be Such a Thing as World Culture?" Pp. 91–105 in *Culture, Globalization and the World-System,* ed. Anthony J. King. Minneapolis: University of Minnesota Press.

Warner, R. Stephen. 1993. "Work in Progress toward a New Paradigm for the Sociological Study of Religion in the United States." *American Journal of Sociology* 98 (March): 1044–1193.

Warner, R. Stephen, and Judith G. Wittner, eds. 1998. *Gatherings in Diaspora: Religious Communities and the New Immigration.* Philadelphia: Temple University Press.

Warner, W. Lloyd, and Leo Srole. 1945. *The Social Systems of American Ethnic Groups.* New Haven, Conn.: Yale University Press.

Watson, James L., and Evelyn S. Rawski, eds. 1988. *Death Ritual in Late Imperial and Modern China.* Berkeley: University of California Press.

West, Candace, and Donald Zimmerman. 1987. "Doing Gender." *Gender and Society* 1: 125–51.

Whit, William C. 1995. *Food and Society: A Sociological Approach.* Dix Hills, N.Y.: General Hall.

Whyte, William Foote. 1993. *Street Corner Society: The Social Structure of an Italian Slum.* Chicago: University of Chicago Press. (Orig. pub. 1943.)

Wilson, Rob, and Wimal Dissanayake, eds. 1996. *Global/Local: Cultural Production and the Transnational Imaginary.* Durham, N.C.: Duke University Press.

Wittgensten, Ludwig. 1973. *Philosophical Investigations,* trans. by G. Anscombe. New York: Macmillan.

Yan, Yunxiang. 1997. "McDonald's in Beijing: The Localization of Americana." Pp. 39–76 in *Golden Arches East: McDonald's in East Asia,* ed. James L. Watson. Stanford, Calif.: Stanford University Press.

Yoder, Don. 1971. "Historical Sources for American Foodways Research and Plans for an American Foodways Archives." *Ethnologia Scandanavica* 5: 41–44.

———. 1972. "Folk Cookery." Pp. 325–50 in *Folklore and Folklife,* ed. Richard M. Dorson. Chicago: University of Chicago Press.

Zlotnick, Susan. 1996. "Domesticating Imperialism: Curry and Cookbooks in Victorian England." *Frontiers* 16, nos. 2–3: 51–60.

Index

About the Author

KRISHNENDU RAY is an Associate Professor of Liberal Arts and Management at the Culinary Institute of America.